Praise for
MICHAEL HUYGHUE

"Michael signed me to an NFL contract with the Jacksonville Jaguars during their inaugural 1995 season. He was among the first black executives in charge of football operations in the League. He paved the way for other black executives, and I was proud to see him in that leadership role.

"His book is an inspirational journey of facing the intersection of race and culture in professional sports and specifically the NFL.

"This is a must-read for anyone who ever wanted to be a fly on the wall to see, fully comprehend, and appreciate the many challenges and obstacles that are unique to minorities in the workplace."

**—Desmond Howard, former Heisman Trophy winner
and ESPN college football analyst**

"Michael actually gave me my first job in the NFL front office with the Jacksonville Jaguars. He understood the importance of not only setting such a positive example for other minorities in the league but reaching out to help all along the way."

**—Doug Williams, Super Bowl–winning quarterback
of the Washington Redskins**

"It was clear to me when I got involved in the UFL that if we were going to have any chance of success, it was because of Michael's leadership. He understands the dynamics of organizing a professional football team and has the leadership skills to blend all the personalities and egos of owners, coaches, and players. He is a unique talent and a stand-up guy."

—**Jim Fassel**, **former head coach of the New York Giants**

"Michael is very unique in that he has strong leadership and business skills, yet totally understands football and in particular the coaches' and players' mentality. That unique blend of talent, along with some real smarts, made him a successful leader. He was not only a role model for minorities in the league but for all young front-office people."

—**Jerry Glanville**, **former head coach of the Atlanta Falcons**

"Michael is unique in that he combines brilliant knowledge of the sports industry along with integrity and a sense of identity. Even now he motivates me to want to do more in my life both professionally and off the course."

—**Jim Thorpe**, **PGA and Champions Tour winner**

"Michael helped to guide not only my professional football career but my off-the-field life as well. He was not only my agent and business adviser but a close friend, too."

—**Eric Crouch**, **former Heisman Trophy winner**

BEHIND THE LINE
OF SCRIMMAGE

Inside the
Front Office of the
NFL

MICHAEL
HUYGHUE

CENTER
STREET

NEW YORK NASHVILLE

Copyright © 2018 by Michael Huyghue

Cover design by Edward A. Crawford. Cover photography by Mark J. Rebilas / USA Today Sports and Getty Images. Cover copyright © 2018 by Hachette Book Group, Inc.

Center Street
Hachette Book Group
1290 Avenue of the Americas, New York, NY 10104
centerstreet.com
twitter.com/centerstreet

First Edition: August 2018

Center Street is a division of Hachette Book Group, Inc. The Center Street name and logo are trademarks of Hachette Book Group, Inc.

The publisher is not responsible for websites (or their content) that are not owned by the publisher.

The Hachette Speakers Bureau provides a wide range of authors for speaking events. To find out more, go to www.HachetteSpeakersBureau.com or call (866) 376-6591.

Credits for endpapers begin on page 321.

Library of Congress Control Number: 2018943189

ISBNs: 978-1-4789-2013-7 (hardcover), 978-1-4789-2014-4 (ebook)

Printed in the United States of America

LSC-C

10 9 8 7 6 5 4 3 2 1

*To Kim, my wife, partner, and soul mate,
who steadfastly helped me see the forest through
the trees, keep my feet on the ground, and strive
to be a stalwart and loving father to our three beautiful
children, Kristen, Kathryn, and Tyler.*

Contents

BEHIND THE LINE
OF SCRIMMAGE

CHAPTER 1

Kneeling Down

President Trump was in Huntsville, Alabama, for a campaign-style rally with his base supporters. I watched the news on TV as Trump rambled on, congratulating himself for the self-proclaimed amazing job he had done so far as president in such a short time. "This man is truly delusional!" I yelled out from the living room to my wife, who was, fortunately for me, cooking dinner. She had reached her limit of the broadcast and my "guess what" Trump updates. "Too depressing," Kim would usually say, but this time she called back nonchalantly, "What's he saying now?," still not turning her head toward the television.

Although her tone suggested she really didn't care to know, her natural curiosity and accumulated knowledge belied that suggestion. Kim's stay-at-home wife/mom title is a designation that doesn't fit the Harvard-educated, authentically beautiful independent black woman with whom I'm blessed to have shared my life for twenty-five years.

"Same old bullshit!" I shouted back, reminding myself that she's much smarter than me. Then, somewhat randomly, Trump switched subjects and began a rant on black NFL players who were bending a knee during the national anthem to bring awareness to social injustice in the black community.

"Wouldn't you love to see one of these NFL owners, when somebody disrespects our flag, to say, 'Get that son of a bitch off the field right now. Out. He's fired. He's fired,'" Trump said.

I stood up from my easy chair, my mouth wide open, aghast. I could not believe he'd actually said what he said. I heard a raucous ovation of approval from the crowd.

"Disrespecting *our* flag," I said out loud. "It's the whole nation's flag. The flag doesn't belong to just a portion of the country," I continued, directing my rebuttal toward the television.

"He has now become unhinged," Kim chimed in, overhearing my muttering and affirming her steadfast belief that the man was not mentally competent.

"He has not taken the time nor the interest to drill down on what the NFL players' protest is all about. He just hijacked a racially divisive hot topic and used it to—"

"Enough of this crap," she said. "I took all this time to cook, so let's eat." Kim spared me any more agony by grabbing the television remote from my hand and clicking it off. Okay, fair enough; she's the boss at home.

The NFL players' protest first arose in 2016 when then backup quarterback Colin Kaepernick, of the San Francisco

49ers, began kneeling during the national anthem to protest racial injustice in America. A small number of his black teammates knelt in support of him, as did other black players spottily across the league. Kaepernick is biracial, with a white mother and a black father, though he was adopted by white parents.

Racial makeup and delineation always seem to be important in the race discussion, as if we need to define someone as either partially or fully black. It's irrelevant. Race is not just skin tone or even DNA. It's one's self-identification and embrace of the culture that defines racial makeup. Labels can be misleading. When people ask upon what basis Kaepernick, a biracial player, could lead a cause primarily connected to black people, my answer is that Kaepernick obviously identifies with the black community.

At the start of the 2017 season, no NFL team signed the then twenty-nine-year-old free agent Kaepernick, even though his skills seemed to clearly warrant his making an NFL roster. Just a few years prior, Kaepernick led the San Francisco 49ers to a division title with a regular-season record of 12-4. No team publicly acknowledged that he was being blacklisted, though as a longtime NFL insider, I knew his signing would have rattled and upset the fan base of any team. NFL owners never lose sight of the pulse of their fan base. As Weeb Ewbank, the 1969 Super Bowl–winning coach of the New York Jets, once famously said, "We are in the business of selling tickets." Owners know the lifeblood of their teams is ticket sales.

Television revenues pay the bills, but ticket sales speak to the stature of a team. Owners typically steer clear of highly controversial players.

As we ate, I barely tasted the meal Kim was so proud of. I began to search my nearly thirty years of experience in and around the NFL for an answer to why race in the NFL had become headline news and presidential political football.

Kaepernick pledged more than $1 million of his own money to organizations that work in oppressed communities, including the Black Lives Matter movement, which organizes rallies around the country against police brutality and the killing of young African American men. Kaepernick also made it abundantly clear in his messaging about his protest that he was *not* disrespecting the flag or the men and women of the armed services. To the contrary, he was attempting to use his celebrity to bring attention to and provoke conversation about racial injustices in black communities.

In large measure, Kaepernick was viewed as genuine and sincere, and what predominantly white Americans took issue with was his kneeling during the anthem. It was to them, notwithstanding the apparent legitimacy of his intentions, disrespectful. Kaepernick remained unsigned. Even as several teams experienced injuries at the quarterback position, he was bypassed, and less-qualified players were signed to NFL rosters. There was no way for the black players to view Kaepernick's rejection other than as his being blackballed by the NFL.

Throughout the 2017 NFL season, more black players and indeed even full teams of white and black players began kneeling during the anthem, raising fists, and locking arms. I felt that all too familiar sense of the system working against us as I watched Trump identify this prolonged player protest as an "unpatriotic act" and use it shamelessly as an opportunity to whip up base supporters. The president had a keen sense of his audience and knew exactly which buttons to push to trigger an explosion of controversy. What most in his audience didn't know was that Trump himself had a long-standing feud with the NFL.

As owner of the spring league United States Football League's New Jersey Generals in 1984, he sought to compete directly with the NFL by moving the league from the spring to the fall season. As part of the move, Trump and the owners sued the NFL on antitrust grounds, claiming the NFL was an unlawful monopoly. Ultimately Trump and the USFL did win the antitrust case, but the damages awarded were $1; yes, one dollar. Shortly thereafter, the USFL shuttered its business operations. Trump was left without a team and was persona non grata with NFL owners. As I reflected on Trump's rant about black NFL players, I wondered if Trump was perhaps just posturing Trump, resurrecting his grudge against the NFL.

But following his divisive remarks in Alabama, many NFL owners actually denounced Trump's venomous words and pushed back. Robert Kraft, the owner of the Super Bowl Champion New England Patriots and a longtime

Trump supporter and personal friend, even issued the following statement:

> I am deeply disappointed by the tone of the comments made by the President on Friday. I am proud to be associated with so many players who make such tremendous contributions in positively impacting our communities.

A handful of other NFL owners similarly followed suit, including New York Giants owners John Mara and Steve Tisch, San Francisco 49ers CEO Jed York, and Green Bay Packers president Mark Murphy.

The players themselves responded with full-team demonstrations of solidarity, including at NFL games across the pond in London, where Jacksonville Jaguars owner Shad Khan, a man of Pakistani decent and the only minority owner in the NFL, locked arms with his full team on the field.

Commissioner Roger Goodell initially did not succumb to the pressure from Trump; instead, he publicly stated that while the NFL encourages its players to stand for the national anthem, he and the league supported their right to protest.* I knew that Goodell was genuine in his comments because I have known him personally for the last twenty years. I also knew that this issue would cause a great deal of resentment among the league's fan base and had the potential to cause permanent damage to the league's image and brand, something Commissioner Goodell cared about greatly and would not jeopardize.

I have frequently offered my thoughts on issues pertaining to race to Goodell. I first worked with him when I was a young lawyer with the NFL Management Council and he worked in the league office. Over the years, we worked together on such projects as the NFL spring football league (the World League) and other labor-related issues with the players. We got along well even when our relative positions in the league required us to disagree. Once he became commissioner, I continued to offer my advice, even unsolicited, and he was always responsive. I felt compelled to reach out to him on this issue. I had already spoken about the issue to the few black senior executives at the league office, as well as a few of the black general managers. We are a small, close-knit community and find solace in our camaraderie. It was clear to us that if the league did not support the black players, kneeling would be only the first step in their protest.

Players are often viewed as becoming wealthy too quickly, and any strong views they might hold on issues outside of football are dismissed out of hand. But black senior execs and GMs in the NFL know that players in general, and in particular black players, don't twist their wealth with privilege. They may be wealthy, but they also recognize that they do not enjoy the same social privileges usually associated with wealth. Issues in the communities where many of them grew up still matter to them. Police brutality matters to them. Black lives do matter to them. Respect matters to them.

A few days after Trump's diatribe in Alabama, I sent an e-mail to Goodell letting him know that President Trump's comments had stoked flames that would entrench black players in their cause for justice, despite any bad publicity their protests might generate. I knew Commissioner Goodell had understood the severity of Trump's words when he responded to my e-mail the next day. Goodell thanked me for my note and indicated that the league had been working with several players for months on this initiative. He indicated that any progress would likely be driven by the clubs that were seriously engaged on the matter.

Goodell and I both knew that the issue wasn't going away on its own. Players felt disrespected. This protest was about issues that affected many of the young black men who lived in the neighborhoods where NFL players were born and raised. And it appeared to these players that the league was not standing up in support of them. Black players know how revered they are among the fans for the talents they exhibit on the playing field; but off the field, these same players often feel inconsequential and invisible. They are roundly applauded for their football prowess but nothing more. Their beliefs, concerns, and needs as individuals are largely ignored.

Some black players becoming millionaires through their lucrative NFL contracts does not mean they suddenly forget where they grew up. The damage from long-standing derogatory jokes (e.g., "What do you call a black millionaire?" Answer: "Nigger!") are firmly embedded in their minds. They don't forget or ignore the stark realities that exist for many young African American men who live— and often senselessly die—in those poor communities. To assume that wealthy black NFL players would simply turn their backs or remain silent concerning these highly personal issues is the highest insult and disrespect to them. To them, Trump was saying, "You get paid a lot of money, so keep your mouth shut about America's racism."

My thought was, *Why should NFL players' opinions on race have less value just because they are wealthy?* As the news continued day after day, I related to them. Like me, they do not live in heavily crime-ridden or depressed neighborhoods, but they still care about those neighborhoods, places where some of them grew up. Don't NFL players deserve a voice? Don't *they* matter? I had faced the same you-are-an-exception mind-set in my white counterparts throughout my career. Since I was successful, many thought I didn't have credibility to speak to issues in the inner city. Worse, I was viewed as some assimilated Uncle Tom who could no longer relate to the struggles in the black community. The truth is, like the NFL players who knelt in protest, I couldn't forget or pretend the issues of the black community didn't affect me and my family, regardless of my success or wealth. When I look in the mirror each morning, the first thing I see is a black man. The same black man I've always seen—not a lawyer, NFL executive, or successful entrepreneur—a black man.

I worked for nearly three decades in professional football, as a legal intern with the NFL Players Association (NFLPA) and a lawyer with the NFL Management Council. I also served as a general manager and senior executive with various NFL teams, and in most cases I was the first black person to hold those positions. Later I built my own sports agency practice. The varied positions I have held in professional football afforded me a range of up-close perspectives. I gained keen insight into the mind-sets and thought processes of NFL owners, team executives, union representatives, players, and agents. Rare views from so many vantage points have uniquely qualified me to opine on the subject of what drives and motivates the wide range of individuals who all have a stake in resolving issues of race in the NFL.

I understand fully, for example, why NFL players would willingly risk financial security for a cause they believe in. I know why they would stand up—or, in this case, kneel down—to effect social change. It's because some issues are truly personal for players and are prefaced upon respect. Players know the difference between applause and respect. They see the translucency of respect as soon as they sign their NFL player contracts. By the simple stroke of a pen, these young men become highly sought after by home builders, car dealers, jewelers, financial managers, and other business professionals who previously would have viewed them as inconsequential.

When social norms have told you for most of your life that people who look like you don't matter, it's easy to see the ruse when you are treated differently. Newly minted NFL millionaires see past the autograph requests and on-field cheers and know that their circumstances remain "if not for." If not for the fact that they are professional football players, those who feign color blindness would not waste their time on them. If not for their football prowess and money, these NFL players know they would not be placed on a pedestal by others in society. It's a sham game, and the players see right through it. They enjoy the spoils, but they are not fooled into believing they are viewed equally in society.

Why shouldn't black athletes in the NFL be allowed, even encouraged, to use their platform to shed light on social issues and racial injustices, particularly when these issues are so personal to many black athletes? Who has the right to determine what method of nonviolent protest is acceptable—the president of the United States, the NFL owners, the fans? Kneeling during the anthem is nonviolent protest. We must look at both the validity of the protest and the act of protest.

If police brutality in black communities is a relevant issue, then we must support the players' protest, even if we don't fully agree with such conduct during the national anthem and believe there are better forums in which to demonstrate and protest. Many people have died—black and white—defending the flag, and military families and others who do not condone utilization of the anthem in an act of protest have a fair point. I might not have personally chosen the same venue for a protest, but I can certainly understand and support Kaepernick's choice to provoke a more positive discussion on race and bring recognition to a crisis that is destroying the black community.

Throughout my career in football, I kept a commitment to myself that if I ever felt compromised in my integrity or degraded because of my race, in any positon that I held, I would walk—no matter what the consequences. I learned in law school that the art of negotiating was premised on the ultimate ability to walk away; if you could not honestly negotiate from a final take-it-or-leave-it position, you no longer had true leverage. I believe Kaepernick had simply reached his final position. He most assuredly understood the consequences of his act, yet he held to his principles at a great personal sacrifice on a matter he felt deserved such attention. For that, I respect him.

The history of disruptive disputes between the players and the NFL owners is not new; in fact, such disputes date to the very beginning of the players' formation of a union in 1956 as their collective bargaining representative. At the expiration of almost every collective bargaining agreement, owners and players have faced off in a work stoppage of some sort—either a players' strike or an owners' lockout. I first began working as a lawyer in the NFL in 1987, and I saw firsthand that black players have a history of activism, particularly when related to issues of race, freedom, and social injustice. Becoming millionaires does not detract black NFL players from understanding and supporting the cause for equality. If anything, they are more emboldened and prone to enter the fray once they have a meaningful voice.

Almost one month to the day after I received Goodell's reply to my e-mail, the league entered into an agreement with the NFL Players Coalition, a group of primarily black players led by Philadelphia Eagles safety Malcolm Jenkins. They had been meeting regularly with the NFL to find common ground. The NFL ultimately agreed to contribute almost $90 million over seven years to national and local projects directed at social justice issues in black communities, including the eradication of police brutality.

Although the agreement was not predicated on the NFL players' ending the anthem protest, the players ended the pregame protest shortly thereafter. Overall, players felt that the league had stepped up in its support of the players. And, for the first time, the black players finally perceived the owners as supporting their cause. A culmination in *respect*. It is always about respect with the players, even though most football fans think it's solely about the money. To these young black pros, respect is their holy grail.

Jenkins was quoted as saying, "My whole motivation was to draw awareness to disenfranchised people, communities of color, injustices around the country, our criminal justice system. I feel like [this agreement] has presented a bigger and better platform to continue to raise that awareness." The money the NFL is contributing to black communities will most assuredly have a positive impact on the issues players first began protesting over.

And while Kaepernick became the sacrificial lamb, his voice was chiefly responsible for effecting change. Kaepernick likely knew, when he first knelt down on the playing field during the national anthem, that he might not ever wear another NFL uniform. But he believed enough in the fight for the lives of young black men whose voices have been muted and tuned out that his sacrifice was worth it.

I have seen positive change happen when we as African Americans exercise our collective voices in our "professional worlds." Sometimes, only one voice is required to cry out among many to promote that change. That was a lesson I held on to early in my career, to not be afraid to exercise my voice, to stand up for issues that affect black people, and to provide opportunities for others to follow. That was my moral compass. I wasn't always successful, and indeed, throughout my career I willingly ate a bunch of humble pie, but in the end I felt true to myself. I've also learned that speaking out loud on issues like race and prejudice can be meaningful, can promote discussion, and, most important, can effect change. The NFL kneeling protests are a modern example of change that was prompted fifty years ago by marches in southern streets. Today, each professional sphere has its own fitting actions to promote change.

From behind the white lines of my thirty years spent working in the inner sanctum of the professional sports industry, and climbing the ladder as the "first black" in almost every position, I've seen change, and perhaps been a change agent by breaking down barriers. I've struggled inside and outside the exclusive and restrictive organization that is the NFL, and I believe my story can shed light on concerns about race in the NFL and sports in general.

*Following the 2017 season, the NFL owners, in a May meeting, changed their policy on the national anthem without consulting with the NFLPA. They required players, if on the field, to stand for the anthem. (Teams had the right to keep all players in the locker room during the national anthem.) Any protests during the anthem by players would result in a fine to the team. Team owners were authorized to unilaterally impose new rules, if they wanted, requiring players on their team to stand for the anthem or to subject players on their team to individual fines. The owners caved, and Goodell looked sheepish in his explanation.

CHAPTER 2

Rules of the Game

Football is a game of rules, and I've never really thought of myself as a rule breaker. Still, I started my career as a sports attorney in the NFL by breaking a cardinal rule: in 1987, I left the union that represents the interests of football players to go to work for the organization that represents the interests of team owners.

I was the youngest and only black legal intern on staff at the NFL Players Association, and no one had ever jumped ship to go over to the NFL Management Council. The two organizations were—and still are—often at odds with each other, and there has been an ongoing history of mistrust.

At the time, Gene Upshaw was the first black person to helm the NFLPA, and he was leading a mostly black membership made up of hundreds of pro football players. By contrast, not a single person of color was among the rank and file of NFL team owners, and Norman Jenkins was the only African American on the executive staff of the Management Council, which represented the owners' interests.

Added to the insult I was unwittingly committing was that, when I jumped ship, the NFLPA and the Management Council were in the middle of a contentious contract negotiation, which ultimately led to the infamous 1987 players' strike, replete with "scab" replacement players and picket-line brawls.

Had I been less naive, I likely would have thought longer and harder before making the move that catapulted me into having daily contact with the NFL's moneymen. But at age twenty-five, I was credulous and cocky enough to believe that my departure from the union into enemy territory wouldn't mean much. In my mind, I hadn't been privy to any great secrets. I didn't hold any earth-shattering information about case strategy or contract negotiation techniques. What difference did it make that I was leaving? It was, after all, my career. Working for the Management Council and consequently with NFL team owners would put me in a better position to pursue my long-held dream. I wanted to one day be the NFL commissioner—today Goodell's job, then held by Pete Rozelle. That goal had been driving my choices since high school.

Fresh out of law school, I still believed I could crash that glass ceiling as a black man. I'm getting ahead of my story, but you already know I am not nor was I ever commissioner of the NFL, but that goal still led me to splinter some other racial ceilings in the NFL. I'm not sure exactly why or how I decided at a young age that I wanted to become the commissioner of the NFL. Like most black youth with a talent for sports, my focus was on being an athlete.

I always felt there was more to what I wanted out of life than actually playing the game. The primary reason I went to law school was to follow in the footsteps of attorneys who led the professional sports leagues. Fay Vincent Jr. was commissioner of Major League Baseball about the same time as Paul Tagliabue took the reins at the NFL after the three-decade tenure of the legendary Pete Rozelle. Tagliabue earned a full scholarship to play basketball at Georgetown University prior to earning his law degree from New York University. Vincent was an athlete in college and earned his law degree from Yale University. David Stern, also a lawyer, became commissioner of the National Basketball Association in 1984, having worked his way up through the NBA ranks as their executive vice president and general counsel before being tapped for the job. Even the National Hockey League followed a similar path in promoting senior vice president and general counsel Gary Bettman (a Cornell graduate like me) to be its first commissioner. All four men were attorneys who worked within their leagues primarily in a legal capacity before attaining the position of commissioner.

When I joined the NFLPA as an intern in the summer of 1986, I was excited to be spending several months away from my law books. That my then girlfriend, Kim, also would be working in DC at a law firm that summer was an added bonus. We found an apartment in Alexandria, Virginia, right outside the city. Neither of us had given much thought at that point about whether the relationship would get serious, but we both had friends in the area. We saw only a summer with no books and a chance to determine if we were right for each other. Kim felt I was holding my true-feelings cards very close to the vest, which was likely true. My first love, undoubtedly, and my passion was my career in sports—off the field. I was willing to sacrifice anything to succeed.

I spent that summer shadowing the staff attorneys, helping to write briefs, and ironing out the details of a new mandatory drug-screening program for players. I worked closely with Buck Briggs, an NFLPA attorney who had preceded me at Cornell undergrad by about a decade. Buck recruited me to intern for the organization in 1982 after I met him on the sidelines of a Cornell football game during my sophomore year.

Buck was a bit nerdy and passionate about sports— particularly baseball, which he'd played in school. He collected a ton of memorabilia and had an incredible memory when it came to players' stats and pretty much any other trivia question you could throw at him. He was a staunch Cornell alum who continued announcing the school's games on the radio for years after he graduated, and he regularly made the trip from his home just outside Washington, DC, to Ithaca, New York, to teach a sports law class at the university. He even bought a house right on Cornell's campus to accommodate his frequent visits.

It always amazed me how white people seemed to build such an instant and long-standing bond with their alma maters. To me, and to other black students I knew, these institutions were there solely to serve a purpose, to provide an education and degree and enhance our network. Now, years later, I connect to my college as a vehicle to help other minority students advance. Kim and I provide a full-tuition scholarship each year to one deserving female minority student majoring in science. I also served on the board of trustees at Cornell to address issues of diversity. I believe change is best effected from within. Still, I fully understand why many black people do not feel the hip-hip-hooray connection with their white alma maters.

African Americans typically make up far less than 10 percent of the entire student body at top-rated schools, into which they were not admitted until relatively recently. From the first day we walk through their hallowed halls, blacks are reminded that the schools' history and lineage are devoid of people who resemble us. We are always among the scattered few faces of color in their lecture halls. Many of us scurry to find a semblance of familiarity in recently formed school organizations whose names start with the word *Black*. We, in large measure, face constant glares and hear disparaging words about affirmative action.

Faculties have so few black professors that it is possible to attend all four years and never sit in a class taught by a person of color. School fight songs speak to alliances that do not include us in any meaningful way. And perhaps most important, notwithstanding the heavy financial sacrifices we make to attend these places of higher learning, we often face a greater uncertainty in job placement and

career advancement than our more privileged, less qualified white classmates. In our postcollege careers, despite
having earned diplomas from these elite institutions, we
still need someone white to vouch for us. Attending such
universities is just another necessary step in the process of
advancement, a necessary means to an unpredictable and
likely unequal end.

Working at the NFLPA was like being in a college fra-
ternity. I spent all day hanging with current and former
athletes. We worked in a very laid-back atmosphere. We
wore jeans every day. The only time we ever put on a tie
was when we had an arbitration case. The staff typically
traveled together if we needed to be out of town, and we
even had an office softball team. The NFLPA was like a
flashback to undergrad for me. Being considered a "good
guy" socially was as, if not more, important than anything
else, including productivity.

At the end of the summer, Kim went back to law school,
but since the school didn't have a sports law track, I'd
been able to convince the powers that be at the University of
Michigan to let me continue my internship in lieu of the
fall semester. When Kim left, I moved into the Cheverly,
Maryland, frat, uh, I mean town house that Buck shared
with several other Cornell grads. The daily house routine
during those months was shower, work, barhop, sleep, wake
up, and repeat. The NFLPA was hard work, but once the
day wrapped, there was plenty of time to hang out, and
I took full advantage. Plus, it was becoming clear to me
that being completely immersed in the party culture of

professional sports was nearly as important as being good at your job—and in some cases could get you a lot further.

It was a demanding grind, but I was in my twenties, up for it, and thoroughly enjoying being a bachelor with a high-profile job in the nation's capital. Kim and I had had a great summer, but a few weeks into the fall, the demands of her law classes and my job got the better of both of us, and the calls became fewer and fewer until finally they just stopped altogether. We never officially broke up, though, and I knew that at some point I would want her back in my life. But the challenge of a long-distance relationship and monogamy was more than either of us could commit to. Plus, I'd heard through the grapevine that she was seeing someone else. Fortunately, work kept me too busy to dwell on what might happen if she really liked the guy, and I was cocky enough to believe that he wouldn't be much competition once I got back to school.

At work, I spent a lot of time researching and coming up with recommendations for the mandatory drug-testing program that was part of the collective bargaining agreement the NFLPA and the NFL Management Council were in the middle of negotiating. The NFL owners had been trying to institute random drug screening for a number of years, but the players had resisted, saying it would violate their privacy and leave them open to public criticism. By 1986, however, everyone recognized that some type of mandatory drug-testing program was all but a fait accompli. The only unanswered question was how stringent it would be.

Critics of the excesses within pro football had been

calling for player drug testing since the 1970s, when stories about rampant cocaine use and freebasing by entertainment and sports stars began to saturate the news. Accusations about pro athletes and drug use were hardly new, but the face of football had begun to shift from a majority of white players to largely black players by the late '70s. Disco was a cultural obsession, and illicit activity occurred behind the velvet ropes of nightclubs where the worlds of athletes, entertainers, and drug dealers collided on a regular basis. Around the same time, the smuggling of cocaine into the United States had grown exponentially, and state and federal drug enforcement agencies began to pay attention. More than a few players were caught in the fallout.

The first big shakeup came in 1977 when Don Reese and Randy Crowder, two defensive players from the Miami Dolphins, were each sentenced to a year in prison for selling cocaine to an undercover police officer. Two years later, Dallas Cowboys wide receiver Bob Hayes was sentenced to five years, also for selling cocaine. Several other high-profile drug convictions of football players took place in the early 1980s, and while black players weren't the only ones using drugs, they were typically the ones prosecuted and convicted, while their white counterparts, including Minnesota Vikings quarterbacks John Reaves and Tommy Kramer, avoided arrest by going to rehab. Fast-forward to 1986, and many black players felt they were being unfairly targeted by the NFL's efforts to institute mandatory drug testing. The distrust made them particularly wary of the rules that team owners were seeking.

My job was to outline a plan that was palatable to players: one that wouldn't criminalize those who had drug problems or be unfairly punitive, and would protect their privacy. I'd spent enough time around athletes in high school and college to know that players who used drugs would do whatever it took to mask their use, so I believed a strong drug-testing policy was needed if the league was going to bring about positive change. But I also knew that the players' concerns were valid; the owners weren't above using the threat of exposure to limit a player's salary or benefits.

Tim English, who'd been on staff with the NFLPA for about a decade by the time I came on board in the summer of 1986, was immensely helpful to me in sorting out a policy recommendation. He pointed out that pro athletes were at a greater risk for drug use and abuse if for no other reason than that they happen to fall within the age range of the population most likely to experiment with drugs. Plus, they function in an atmosphere that often has them grappling with physical pain, higher-than-normal career uncertainty, and the weight of huge family responsibilities at a young age. Combine all of that with the fact that pro athletes tend to crave adrenaline rushes, have easy access to drugs, and are surrounded by a plethora of folks who will cover up for them, and you have a high-risk formula for drug addiction.

Tim's insight helped me to keep my eye on outlining a policy that was geared toward reducing drug use and getting players who had problems help instead of penalizing them. I looked to the NBA for guidance. Pro basketball players had been subject to random drug testing since 1983, and it hadn't seemed to have the devastating effect on privacy that NFL players were concerned about. But I also knew that I'd have to come up with recommendations that were slightly more substantial than the NBA's, which was under a spotlight because of the case of Len Bias, a twenty-two-year-old University of Maryland player who died from a cocaine overdose just two days after being drafted by the Boston Celtics. Everyone was waiting to see whether the NBA would tighten its policy for new and existing players in the wake of Bias's death.

In outlining a proposed plan for the NFL, I suggested that we could avoid players' having to submit to random testing at any time by offering instead mandatory testing at specific times during the season. All testing would be done by an independent agency hired by the league, and if a player tested positive, he would be required to go to an approved counseling and rehab program. Team management would be informed only if the player was subject to disciplinary action—reducing the chance that a player's career would be negatively affected. Team management would still have the authority to order a random test if they had reasonable suspicion that a player was using drugs or abusing alcohol.

During my internship at the NFL Players Association, I was asked to draft a policy that allowed NFL players two or three failed drug tests before they would potentially face expulsion from the league. This was counterintuitive to my personal beliefs that professional athletes who act as role models for our kids should hold themselves to a higher standard. I don't want to teach a young person that he can accumulate three strikes before he will be punished for illegal drug use. I want to teach him not to use drugs at all. But later, after I left the union and began handling drug cases for the NFL Management Council, I realized that the drug-use issue was not so clear-cut. I observed many players who were under tremendous pressure, undergoing significant pain, or experiencing severe depression that contributed to their alcohol and substance abuse. Treatment, not punishment, was the proper remedy in those cases. These athletes needed help, and when I was asked to evaluate player behavior or attitudes, my subsequent experiences with athletes who used drugs caused me to look deeper into the why, rather than to automatically judge them.

When I wasn't working on the drug-screening program, I was helping out with player grievances. One of the first cases I worked on with Buck was a dispute that a black injured player had with the San Diego Chargers. The player had been released from his contract, and he was trying to get full payout of his annual salary.

There had been rumblings about the team's physician not being very good, plus, during a visit to the stadium, Buck noticed that the physician's practice was promoted on the venue signage. That made us a bit suspicious. We wondered if the physician had been chosen less for his qualifications and more for his willingness to provide medical service to the team in exchange for marketing opportunities.

Sure enough, we looked into his background and discovered that not only was he allegedly a personal friend of Dean Spanos—son of Chargers owner Alex Spanos—but he also had apparently required several tries before becoming board-certified in orthopedic surgery. This was a huge red flag, since the physician seemed to lack the requisite credentials one would expect for a team physician hand-picked by the club.

The NFLPA hired two independent orthopedic surgeons to take a look at the player's surgical video and postprocedure X-rays. It turned out the player had an ACL injury, but no torn meniscus. In fact, the meniscus was still there and intact, which suggested the physician's documented records were at worst falsified or at best a total mess. When we got to arbitration and deposed him, it was pretty clear that we were dealing with someone who was more interested in the celebrity that came along with being team doctor for the Chargers than with providing appropriate care. He was just over six feet, weighed about 185 pounds, and sported a tan that suggested he was spending more time on the beach or the golf course than with patients. He had a cocky demeanor and was a flashy dresser.

The cockiness disappeared, however, when Buck questioned him under oath. Buck ran a clip of the surgery video. A few minutes in, he stopped the tape, pointed to a piece of cartilage inside the player's exposed knee, and asked, "Doctor, isn't that the meniscus?" The doctor was stumped, and he couldn't explain the discrepancy between his medical records and what was clearly on the tape. Buck paused for a second, fixed a look of confusion on his face, and said, "So...do they grow back?"

The question completely obliterated the doctor's credibility, and it showed how fast and loose the organization was playing with the players' health. The arbitrator ruled in the player's favor. Several years later, I heard that the physician's medical practice imploded. He had to leave the practice when his addiction to pain medications was discovered, and his partners faced a number of malpractice lawsuits filed by a variety of professional sports players.

The irony that an NFL team would let a doctor with a drug problem care for its players while NFL team owners pushed for a random drug-testing policy was pretty standard fare for much of what I would see throughout the NFL and its affiliate organizations during my career there. Disputes like the one I worked on with the Chargers were typical of the cases we handled at the NFLPA. The owners weren't necessarily malicious; many teams lacked the management skills needed to protect their players' careers and welfare. Maybe because there was always new talent on the horizon, the owners saw player care as fungible. NFL owners didn't invest in running the teams as efficiently as they did their other moneymaking businesses.

NFL general managers were often former players who had already seen a good deal of increased accountability on behalf of the owners since their days on the field. Or sometimes they were former scouts or coaches without any real business training. Few were skilled at creating procedures that would make sure teams had the appropriate resources. Players received a lot of random care. When one was released from his contract, it wasn't unusual for the player to receive nothing more than a cursory exam, if the exit physical occurred at all. Serious injuries were frequently discovered when it was too late to do anything about them, or the cost of addressing them became exorbitantly expensive.

I found a wide distinction between the teams that lacked good-quality medical care and the teams, such as the New York Giants, that utilized the best medical care and that incidentally had at that time the only black head trainer in the NFL, Ronnie Barnes. Not surprisingly, the teams that focused on outstanding medical care for their players—teams like the Pittsburgh Steelers and the Washington Redskins— were also the most successful on the playing field.

Gene Upshaw, however, was a standout from most of the other ex-players who'd gone on to work on the business side of the game. As head of the NFLPA, it was his mission to fight for fair benefits and compensation, given the risk players took and the money team owners made on the backs of players. Gene was an offensive guard when he played pro football, so he'd taken and given some serious hits and spent time at the bottom of pileups trying to recover a ball. This made him particularly well attuned to players' injuries and the apparent lack of attention team owners gave those players' welfare.

One reason Gene was so committed to getting free agency for players was to help shift the balance of power. Not only would it give players more earning potential and money to take care of themselves after their careers were over—a crucial concern since the average player is on the field just three to six years—it would also put them in a better position to make demands concerning the quality of care should owners have to compete against other teams to hold on to star players.

Gene was a tall, strapping man who had played an aggressive game—meaning that more often than not, he knocked his opponents flat on their asses. His leadership style was similar, but it also had a subversive element. He wasn't above challenging someone to step outside as a means of settling a dispute—like I saw him do one time when an agent complained that some of NFLPA's maneuvers were cutting into his fees. But, when it came time to negotiate, you always had the sense Gene was holding a card or two in his back pocket, and he was going to play them when you least expected it and at just the right moment.

The circumstances of his estate when he died in 2008 are a good example of this. Gene had negotiated a $15 million deferred compensation agreement with the NFLPA that almost no one—not even his wife—knew about until his death. His penchant for surprises like that intimidated more than a few people and confounded the NFL team owners when it came time for negotiating.

Whatever the owners thought about Gene, he was in some ways a calming force throughout the league, as he would prove some years later when he settled the troubled waters between the players and NFL commissioner Paul Tagliabue. Before taking the helm at the NFL in 1989, Paul was a buttoned-up attorney with the DC-based law firm of Covington & Burling. That demeanor didn't change much after he joined the league. Whenever I encountered Paul, it was clear to me that he was the smartest guy in the room, and he never felt compelled to turn down the volume on his intellectual speak. That didn't sit well with a lot of the players and a good number of the owners. For the owners, Paul's composure brought a level of legitimacy and seriousness to the NFL's public profile—something that had previously been lacking—so they saw value in him leading the organization. The players were less tolerant of his inability to code-switch between corporate and professional sports culture.

Gene, like a lot of successful black folks, was a master at code-switching. He grew up in a working-class family in Texas. His father was an oil refinery laborer, and as a kid, he and his brothers would sometimes pick cotton to earn money. Gene went on to graduate from Texas A&I, become a first-round draft pick for the Raiders, and was elected president of the players union before taking over as executive director. When he lived in Oakland, he also became active in Bay Area politics and attended the Golden Gate University School of Law before having to drop out in 1982 to contend with a two-month-long players' strike. Gene could talk your language whether you were a down-home Texan, a boardroom executive, or a newly minted player who felt uncomfortable in the posh world of professional sports.

Gene also had a jokester streak. He wasn't averse to engaging in the hazing that is so rampant in pro football, even beyond the locker rooms. On my first day at the NFLPA, he called me into his office and handed me the keys to his Charger and a garage ticket. "My car is parked in the building garage, and I want you to go get it and bring it around to me," he said. I didn't think much of it. I just stood there for a second waiting for him to give me money to pay the attendant. Instead, Gene gave me some cryptic instructions. "When you get to the exit gate, give the guy the ticket and drive on out of the garage," he said. I wasn't quite sure what to make of his instructions, nor was I even sure it was possible, but when the top boss asks you—the legal *intern*—to do something on your first day on the job, you can't say no and expect to make a good impression. I took the keys and headed to the garage, figuring I'd just pay the bill myself and figure out a way to expense it.

When I got to the car, I looked at the ticket and saw that Gene had parked it nearly a month earlier on a daily rate. There was no way I could cover the cost. I sat for a minute trying to figure out a plan. Finally, I started the engine and began inching toward the exit. I knew I wasn't going to be able to talk the attendant into letting me out of the garage without paying, but I had to get the car out. There was only one option, so when I got to the booth I handed the guy the ticket, and while he was looking down at it, I hit the gas and peeled out of the garage before he had a chance to get a good look at the car, the license plate, or me.

I halfheartedly joked with Buck about what I'd done when I got back to the office, and the story eventually made its way to Dick Berthelsen, the NFLPA's general counsel.

Dick—furious that Gene had put me in the position of breaking the law and risking my career—went directly to Gene and told him not to ever pull anything like that again. And he didn't. But the incident did give me a starting point for a growing friendship and mentorship with Gene. Once he saw I could take a lick and wasn't afraid to hustle, he took an interest in me. He knew I'd played a lot of different sports in high school, including golf, so he invited me on occasion to join a regular game that he played with former NFL wide receiver Roy Jefferson, who had helped take the Colts, when they were in Baltimore, and the Washington Redskins to the Super Bowl. We played at a club in Maryland, and there was always a good deal of beer drinking and trash-talking.

The months passed quickly, and before I knew it, it was time to head back to law school. I left with an offer for a full-time position on the NFLPA legal staff after graduation. I was excited for the opportunity, but I also felt that I should keep my options open and see what else materialized in the coming months because, as a young attorney, I needed to be in a place that had a few more resources and protocol. The NFLPA wasn't exactly a finely tuned organization, not the best place to train as an attorney. I was in my final few weeks at the NFLPA when a chance meeting with Jack Donlan, head of the NFL Management Council, led to an offer to work for the competition.

Before going back to the University of Michigan for my final semester, I was at the NFLPA office one day in November finishing up some work ahead of the holiday break. Jack was visiting our offices on business and walked into the copy room, looking to use the machine. I happened to be making copies of my résumé, which I planned to send out to a few places. "I'm Michael Huyghue," I said, introducing myself. "I worked with the legal team." "I know who you are," he answered. I was surprised, but I figured Gene or Dick must have mentioned me at some point. I was the only black person on the legal team, so it wasn't likely he'd confuse me with someone else.

"May I make the copy for you?" I offered, but Jack said, "No, I want to make sure none of *those union guys* get their hands on this." We both laughed at that. Then, with little forethought, I handed him one of my résumés. "Just in case you guys are looking to add to the legal team," I said. I truly don't know what prompted me to do it. I was happy at the NFLPA, and they'd already offered me a job come June. The NFL Management Council wasn't even on my list of places to apply—partially because there was a history of distrust between the two organizations. I didn't think Jack or anyone else at the Management Council would take me seriously given that history. But, with him standing right there, what the hell? Not too far back in my mind, I still dreamed of becoming commissioner one day, and that certainly would not happen working for the players union.

Jack took my résumé without comment.

I was surprised when I got a call about a week later from Dennis Curran, who was head of labor relations for the Management Council. Jack had told him to call, and Dennis wanted to meet me at the Hay-Adams Hotel restaurant the following Thursday at exactly 1:00 p.m. "Don't mention this to anyone at the union," Dennis said. It felt very cloak-and-dagger.

I was antsy the next several days, afraid word of the meeting might get back to folks at work. Dennis hadn't let on why he wanted to meet me. That left me with a lot to imagine.

On the day of the meeting, I cut through the hotel lobby and headed toward the restaurant, feeling conspicuous and out of place. It was my first time there, and I'd never been anywhere so staid. The Hay-Adams's marbled floors, dark wood pillars, and Roman arches make it as blue-blooded as it gets. I informed the maître d' that I was meeting Dennis Curran there for lunch. She asked my name.

I glanced around and noticed there was not another black person in the restaurant—even with so many black professionals in Washington, DC. It strikes some white people oddly or even offensively when blacks note the number of other blacks in the room. "Why does that matter?" one white colleague challenged me. My response was to highlight the disparity that exists for black Americans, who often are required to fully assimilate to white culture. Imagine spending your day in a work environment where your coworkers were overwhelmingly of another race, then later dining at a restaurant and perhaps having a nightcap at a local bar under the same conditions. Most white people never experience this and can't begin to appreciate or understand the impact it has on people of color.

While I felt the only-black-in-the-room tinges of doubt,

the hostess glanced down at what I imagined to be a highly exclusive reservations list and said, "Okay; yes, this way, please."

I was shocked that she was expecting me. The experience was very surreal.

She escorted me to a corner booth that was partially blocked by one of those large pillars, handed me a menu, and then left. I sat there for ten minutes, which felt like an eternity, and wondered where Dennis was, hoping I hadn't gotten the time wrong. I looked around every few seconds until I saw him approaching. Dennis sat, and we went through our awkward introductions. I still wasn't sure what was going on. A few seconds later, Jack Donlan arrived. Now I was confused. Dennis hadn't mentioned that Jack, executive director of the NFL Management Council, would be joining us. I stood up quickly. "Hi, Mr. Donlan. How are you?" We shook hands. Sat. Silence while we all browsed the menus.

Jack and Dennis ordered full meals. I ordered a Caesar salad; I knew I wouldn't be able to eat. (When the waiter brought the salad, he had loaded it with cracked pepper and I was so afraid one of the peppercorns would get stuck in my teeth, I didn't even eat the salad.) I was nervous, caught totally off guard, and uncertain what was about to transpire. Maybe this was an informal meeting, but it felt quite formal. The NFLPA and the NFL Management Council were in a collective bargaining negotiation. I became even more anxious that someone at the NFLPA might find out I was meeting with them. I wasn't even sure it was legal for me to be talking with them, and I worried I might be breaching confidentiality rules.

Jack finally broke the silence: "Well, I looked over your résumé. I wanted to get to know you a bit better." He asked about the cases and projects I'd worked on. With great trepidation, I told him about the drug-testing program. I thought maybe he was trying to get information, but I also knew I was the low man on the totem pole at the NFLPA and didn't have any information that they didn't already know. I tried to be somewhat coy in what I shared about the drug program. Dennis never said a word throughout the entire meeting. Then Jack asked, "Could you see yourself working for the Management Council?"

I hadn't fully anticipated that our meeting would be a job interview, and I hadn't prepared an answer. Long seconds passed before I uttered: "Well, I always thought of myself as somebody who wants to represent players." That was the truth. I stopped short of sharing my questionable feelings about the players union as an organization or as a place for a young attorney to cut his teeth. That's why I hadn't immediately committed to the NFLPA's job offer.

"So are you wedded to one side?" Jack asked.

"I think I could represent whatever side the case required me to," I said. "I have an affinity for players because I know them. But could I be aggressive against one if a case required it? Yes, absolutely."

I felt that my answers resonated with Jack, but when I looked at Dennis's face, I sensed that I'd said all the wrong things.

Therefore, I was quite surprised when I got a call a couple of days later with an offer to go to work for the NFL Management Council after graduation. I felt amazing and awful all at the same time. Having such a fantastic opportunity result from an impulsive act gave the situation a fairy-tale aura. And as with every fairy tale, my good fortune had a dark side—having to break the news to my colleagues at the NFLPA. I dreaded it, especially because Buck, who'd lobbied for me to work at the union, had subsequently become a good friend. He might see my decision as a betrayal.

I went in the next day and told Buck about the offer. "Do not repeat this story to anyone around here," he commanded me, furious. "You have to really ask yourself why they want you." He said the Management Council was only interested in either pumping me for the minuscule amount of confidential information I possessed or using my defection to intimidate the NFLPA. As angry as Buck was, I understood he was actually trying to protect me from the wrath of the higher-ups and prevent me from making what he believed to be a bad career decision. I felt that he was saying the Management Council didn't want to hire me based upon my abilities—that they had only ulterior motives. That disheartened me. I'd had the same thought initially, but neither Jack nor Dennis had asked me for the NFLPA's playbook as a condition of my employment.

I felt Buck should have given me credit for being shrewd enough to not let myself be used. I knew the real reason why they wanted to hire me: I was young, smart, and, most important, black. Even though I was not yet out of law school, I knew there was no such thing as color-blind hiring. When you are a black man and you get hired into a majority white organization, you know it is in large measure because they are looking to hire someone of the black race. Rarely do they just stumble upon a black hire. Blacks are hired intentionally. Some delude themselves when they say: "I am a lawyer and a professional who just happens to be black." I would say to them, "That was likely not the order of the criteria on which you were selected. Most likely the company was looking for the most talented black candidate they could find, and you were a 'fit' with their organizational culture. That doesn't detract from your ability or mean you don't deserve the job. Take the job with self-confidence, recognizing the climate of diversity hiring."

I didn't budge on my decision to accept the offer from the NFL Management Council, despite Buck's cajoling. I could tell by the look in his eyes that while we might remain acquaintances, the bond we had shared as close friends was broken. I had stepped outside the boundaries, and there was no turning back. Disappointing Buck was not a good feeling, but I would have felt much worse had I stayed.

Buck told me to let him break the news to Doug, who called me into his office and sat me down with Buck present. "They're just using you," he said. "Taking this job is the last thing you want to do." He even offered me a higher salary and more responsibility to convince me to stay. He'd never given me that much attention before, and

I realized my poaching was more mental warfare between the two organizations than the belief that I held any real trade secrets.

I sat, mostly silent, through Doug's offers and warnings. Finally, I said, "As much as I appreciate that, I think I need to go over to the Management Council."

"We'll block your ability to go there," Doug threatened. He got up from his seat, stood over me, and began accusing me of breaching fair labor rules that prohibited the Management Council from hiring me away. "I will make sure that I submit to the bar that you are not fit to be an attorney—that you took our information and used it as a turncoat and a traitor."

His threats frightened me and likely would have worked had I been a less determined person. "Well, Doug, you do whatever you think is best, but I'm going to work for the Management Council," I responded. I was walking on thin ice, but I'd learned to be firm by watching Gene deal with difficult negotiations. It's live bullets, and shit's going to happen. I wasn't sure if Doug was prepared to hit me or not, but I was prepared to defend myself, even if it meant getting my ass kicked. I could have been making a colossal mistake, but I'd decided I was going to make the move.

When Doug realized I wouldn't change my mind, he told me I needed to clear out my desk on the spot. He didn't want to risk my staying around and having access to information that the Management Council could use to its advantage.

Tim English—who'd been so helpful to me when I was

working on the drug-screening program details—heard about my decision and came by my office to verify the rumor for himself. "We just don't do that. We don't go to work for the other side," he told me, shaking his head. I think I detected more concern for my welfare than anger in his eyes. It wasn't just that they were coming after what I might know, he said. It was that I was going to become a different person working with the team owners. Tim had long since planted his roots on the players' side. For him there was only good and evil, and the owners represented evil. I tried to explain to Tim that I could be fair from either perch. He said I was naive.

I believed that to create policies that were fair to both the players and the management, I needed to understand both sides. I viewed working with the Management Council as a chance to get inside the inner sanctum of NFL franchise owners and learn how the folks holding the purse strings—at the time all white and male with the exceptions of Chicago Bears female owner Virginia Halas McCaskey and the Los Angeles Rams' Georgia Frontiere—strategized and worked. I saw it as an important step toward diversifying the voices that advised that very homogeneous group.

It had long been my personal ambition to one day become NFL commissioner, and working at the Management Council would, I thought, put me in direct contact with the people who select the person who governs the NFL. Looking back on that youthful dream now, I realize I didn't have a clue about the process of selecting the commissioner. There was never a way for me to position myself for the commissioner's job. Like those just-happen-to-be-blacks, at this early stage of my career I was deluding myself. The truth was that I *wanted* to work for the Management Council. Irrespective of what I was telling myself about an allegiance to the NFL players, management was the path I wanted to follow. The rest was just talk.

I left DC in December 1986 in a haze of contained controversy. Negotiations between the NFLPA and the NFL Management Council were becoming less and less productive, and talk about a possible players strike was less speculation and more a probability. The players were demanding more autonomy over their careers, and the owners were doubling down on their refusal to consider free agency. Those brewing troubles weren't yet mine to contend with.

CHAPTER 3

First-Quarter Offensive

When I arrived in the summer of 1987 to start my job with the NFL Management Council, New York City had lost a lot of its sparkle. The effects of a near bankruptcy twelve years earlier were visible everywhere. The subway was graffiti-covered; the parks were dilapidated and host to a prolific drug trade; and glass from broken car windows regularly littered the ground as a testament to stolen dashboard radios.

The New York Giants had beaten the Denver Broncos earlier that year to bring home the Super Bowl trophy. But instead of looking like a city of champions, New York seemed to be on the edge of catastrophe in many ways. The stock market was on a roller-coaster ride that would culminate in its crash in mid-October. Homelessness rates were on the rise, and in response New York City mayor Ed Koch had instituted a controversial initiative to round up and forcibly treat mentally ill people living on the streets.

The boroughs were simmering cauldrons of racial tension in the aftermath of the murders of Michael Stewart, Eleanor Bumpurs, and Michael Griffith—unarmed black residents who in the first two cases were killed by the police and in the latter by a racially charged white mob in Howard Beach, Queens.

But despite the tense, uncertain future hanging over the city, I joined the phalanx of young professionals who trekked there because we saw New York as a beacon guiding us toward the fulfillment of our biggest dreams.

I spent the last semester of law school rekindling my relationship with Kim. The distance had given us each a chance to reevaluate where the relationship was headed. Neither of us wanted to make a commitment. My career was my priority, and she was still trying to determine where I fit into her plans. Unspoken, though, was the fact that a bond had developed, and Kim was the only person I fully trusted. Vulnerability was not my strong suit. I had always felt like the odd man out in my childhood as the youngest of three children; my older siblings seemed to be smarter and garnered more focused attention from my parents. Going it alone was my theme. Making myself vulnerable to Kim was a big first such step in my life.

Kim accepted a job at a law firm in DC, initially thinking we both might begin our careers in Chocolate City. But my gig with the NFL Management Council put a damper on that. We agreed to continue our relationship long-distance. While we both had professional careers and wanted children, I felt she would have to be the one who might potentially have to forgo a career. It would be fine with me if she also wanted to work outside the home—I always acknowledged Kim was much smarter than me—but sacrificing *my* career was not an option. However, just starting her career, Kim wasn't sure that sacrifice was an option for her either.

I moved to New York City right after I graduated from law school. Having successfully crossed the bar exam hurdle and passed both the New York and the New Jersey exams, I was, at last, officially an attorney. Despite having an entire semester to get used to the idea that I was going to work with the NFL's top brass, I was still in a state of disbelief. The Management Council hadn't hired a new attorney in ten years, and I'd landed the job right out of law school. It gained me benevolent envy from some of my classmates, along with a healthy dose of anxiety.

I was making $75,000 right out of law school in 1987, so I was living fairly affluently, even in New York City. I would be the youngest attorney and one of only two black executives at the Management Council. I knew I was part of a diversity plan to add more black attorneys, and if I didn't perform well on the job, they would fire my ass in a New York minute, black or not.

I was in awe of the star power that directed the organization and often showed up at the offices to talk business. The Management Council's job was to represent the team owners in disputes with players and to negotiate their collective bargaining agreement. Jack Donlan, who was leading the organization, had come over in 1981 from National

Airlines. Jack had worked in the airline industry for some time, and he was known as an unsparing contract negotiator who often got the shareholders and top management what they wanted when he went up against the unions. He didn't perfume bullshit, and his often-used expression was "Fuck 'em and make it retroactive." His aggressive style was just what the team owners—which included Hugh Culverhouse of the Tampa Bay Buccaneers, Clint Murchison Jr. of the Dallas Cowboys, and Wellington Mara of the New York Giants—were looking for to clamp down on an intensifying effort by the players to gain free agency. Jack was a hired gun. A tough Irish son of a bitch that the owners knew would protect their asses at any cost.

It's hard to overstate the cultural differences between the NFL Players Association and the NFL Management Council. Both had membership requirements, but where the former felt like hanging out with your frat brothers, the latter felt like you were schmoozing it up with members of a country club—a very exclusive, private country club. I recognized the limitations of my new membership in the Management Council. I was at best the low man on the totem pole. On the surface, I may have been a member, but I certainly didn't have full privileges. As one of only two minorities in the entire office, I couldn't escape the appearance of tokenism and the ways my new colleagues went out of their way not to appear racially offensive. That awkward politeness was oddly disturbing. For instance, when they congratulated me on my academic career: "Wow! Cornell and Michigan Law, very impressive!," it came off as backhanded, even if it was a genuine compliment. I downplayed it, wondering if a young white attorney would have been so applauded.

The Management Council offices were located at 410 Park Avenue at East Fifty-Fourth Street. When I got there in '87, it was one of the few areas in the city that had managed to escape the kind of tarnish that other parts of Manhattan and most of the outer boroughs had accumulated in abundance. Midtown East, then as it is today, was dotted with investment banks and Ivy League clubhouses. If you walked a few blocks north, you found yourself in one of the city's toniest and most exclusive neighborhoods, where penthouse apartments with cloistered rooftop gardens and a single subway line that historically was intended to limit access were located.

In 1989 I moved into a spot on Seventy-Sixth Street and Park Avenue, not far from the office, which I had rented sight unseen because I needed a place quickly. I learned that to rent sight unseen was actually commonplace in New York. I lucked out on the spot because then newly appointed commissioner Paul Tagliabue, then moving from DC to New York, was looking for an apartment near the offices. Tagliabue thought the place was too big for his individual needs and passed on it. Someone from human resources tipped me on the rent-controlled apartment, and I jumped on it.

What I heard about New York City led me to expect a tiny box of a place, especially since it was on the Upper East Side. I was flabbergasted to find a spacious three-bedroom apartment with hardwood floors, servants' quarters, a huge living room with a fireplace, multiple bathrooms, and an eat-in kitchen. It even had a formal dining room with French doors and huge windows that faced Park Avenue. The rent I paid was a mere $600 a month—a price for hovels in the city. It was far too sophisticated for a twenty-five-year-old, but somehow, I'd been given the gift of an urban legend: one of those inexpensive New York City luxury apartments that everyone hears exists but has never found. I didn't have much interaction with my neighbors, who were older, sometimes with kids, and mostly Jewish. I was cordial, but I never made the effort to get to know any of them, and they left me alone—which was sociable enough for me.

I began to believe this was going to be my life, although I knew my good fortunes were only partially the result of hard work, positive thought, and plain old-fashioned luck. Some of it was also because I was a cocky young black man in the front office of the sports world, which had historically locked out black execs the way they locked out players. But good karma was the norm for me, and that helped keep my dream of still becoming commissioner fresh. I probably always knew in the back of my mind that it was a pipe dream, but the swells of good fortune did nothing to eradicate it.

Kim was in DC doing her thing, and I was here doing mine, so I had no one with whom to share this good fortune. Going solo diminished what should have been a pinch-yourself experience. I hardly ever used any part of the apartment other than my individual bedroom.

On a typical day, I walked to the Management Council,

getting there around 7:00 a.m., and settled into my office, the first to arrive. My "office" was a storage closet that they'd partially cleared and moved a desk and chair into. It was a statement that I was low man on the totem pole. I was already keenly aware of my token hiring, and the office was de rigueur for my status. To me, it might well have been the Taj Mahal. They still kept office supplies in the cabinets, and staff stopped in periodically to remove items and restock. Having so many regular walk-ins made me feel popular. I enjoyed these interruptions, always with a smile on my face. My attitude surprised everyone. Perhaps this was a test of how well I could eat humble pie.

In typical rookie form, I inherited a stack of cases that none of the other attorneys wanted. They mostly involved low-level players filing grievances under the collective bargaining agreement against one of the less notable teams for injury compensation. Yet another message of my junior status. But, like the closet office, I was not chagrined. I was happy with any size office I had to myself and was thrilled to have cases of my own, even if they were all loser cases. One of the cases was so bad we didn't even file a defense to the complaint. Any sharp attorney can craft some sort of viable defense to any claim. And we did not forget to file a defense. This case was so bad none of us could come up with a plausible defense. That was the type of case I was initially assigned.

The third day or so I was in my office familiarizing myself with the shitty cases I was assigned when Jack's secretary, Donna Bush, knocked on my door and told me

Jack wanted me to come to the conference room. I knew Jack was meeting there with a group of team owners and general managers who were in town to discuss strategy for ending the growing dispute with the NFLPA. I quickly put on my suit jacket, ran my tongue against the front of my teeth, adjusted my tie, and grabbed my legal pad. I had no idea why I was being called into the conference room, but I was excited, albeit a bit nervous, at the prospect of meeting the power brokers around the table. This would be a chance to impress and start building relationships with the very men who could be essential to my quest to one day become NFL commissioner.

When I tapped on the conference room door, I heard Jack tell me to come in. I stood in the doorway for a second, aware that I suddenly felt uncomfortable because staff members in the outer office were watching me, the new guy, the young black attorney, being afforded the special privilege of entering this inner sanctum of NFL leadership. Sitting around the table was the group that oversaw the council: Hugh Culverhouse, chair of the board; then Dallas Cowboys president and general manager Tex Schramm, the de facto decision maker sitting in for the team's recently deceased owner, Clint Murchison Jr.; Dan Rooney, whose father, Art Rooney Sr., owned the Pittsburgh Steelers; John Mara of the Giants; Joe Robbie, who owned the Miami Dolphins; and Mike Brown, who was being groomed by his father, Paul Brown, to take over the Cincinnati Bengals.

I told myself to breathe and remember the hard work and savvy that had brought me here. I reminded myself that

I was smart enough and confident enough to answer any of their questions. I had nothing to fear and no NFLPA secrets to share. I walked into the room and softly pulled the door closed behind me.

"Fellas, this is our new attorney, Michael Huyghue," Jack told the men assembled around the table. His introduction generated little to no visible response over an awkward period of time.

Before I could break the ice, Mr. Culverhouse, who as chair of the council was Jack's boss, said in a very low baritone southern drawl, "Hello, son."

I looked him square in the eye and firmly shook his hand.

"Listen," he continued, "there is a horse racing today. I'll be damned if it isn't named Joe Robbie, and it doesn't even belong to Joe."

I was a little bewildered. As far as I knew, this was normal conversation among the owners, so I just smiled and stayed silent as the men seated at the table began reaching into their pockets, pulling out large wads of cash and passing it clumsily toward Mr. Culverhouse. He stuffed the bills randomly into an envelope and handed it to me. "We just have to put some money on that horse to win," he said, laughing. "Take this down to OTB and place it on Joe Robbie."

I had no clue what was going on. There had been no introductions, no professional questions, and certainly no invitation to sit down. I grabbed the envelope and said, "Sure thing, Mr. Culverhouse." I turned and left the conference room and I did as I was told.

When I got back to my office, I sat down, opened the

envelope, and counted out almost $10,000 in cash. I was nervous. I had never seen that much cash all at once—not even when I worked as a cashier one summer as a teenager at a drugstore in my hometown of Windsor, Connecticut. It baffled me that they thought I was the right person for this task. I didn't have the courage to tell Mr. Culverhouse that I had never placed a bet at OTB—the offtrack betting offices that were plentiful in the city at that time.

I pulled out the phonebook, looked up the location of the nearest OTB, grabbed the envelope, and headed out. I didn't tell any of the other attorneys what had happened or where I was going. I was embarrassed. I wasn't sure what the confidentiality rules were. I also thought it might be some sort of test.

I remembered when I'd worked at the drugstore and a customer walked up to my cash register and handed me a $10 bill, no explanation. Without thinking, I put the money in the register. At the end of my shift I told my manager what happened and why I had an extra $10 in my drawer. He looked at me and explained that the customer was actually a secret shopper the store occasionally hired to test the honesty of new employees working the cash register. "I am surprised you didn't pocket the money," he said. I had wondered why my boss thought he needed to test my honesty and whether it had anything to do with the color of my skin. Of course, I knew the answer.

As I walked over to the OBT, I asked myself if this was a test to see if I would pocket the money the owners had given me for the bet. It had to be! Why else would they select me for this task? I was a lawyer, not a secretary or a personal assistant—both positions in that era no one would have given a second thought to assigning such a task. Despite my law degree, my new suit from Barneys, and my $600 briefcase from Crouch and Fitzgerald that I carried proudly to the office every day, I found myself anxiously walking several blocks to the nearest OTB to place a bet on a long-shot horse that was the namesake of one of the NFL owners.

I was being hazed because I was the new, young gun, I thought. Gene, who is black, had similarly pranked me when I first started at the NFLPA. This was probably a typical hazing that would have happened to me as the newbie no matter the color of my skin. But there was no ignoring the pervasive stereotype surrounding black men and gambling addictions that owners in that room were aware of when they sent me on the errand. Was that the joke they were playing at my expense? Yes or no, the errand felt insulting.

When I got to the OTB, I stepped around a few homeless people to enter. I was greeted by a gruff and disinterested clerk sitting behind a bulletproof window who took my bet and then the money, which he counted several times. He examined each bill closely to make sure it was real, all while I kept my head on a swivel. Finally satisfied, he handed me a receipt and I left hurriedly.

When I returned to the offices, I was never invited back into the meeting. I waited for someone to ask me for the receipt. No one ever did. At the end of the day, I called

OTB to see how the horse did in the race: he finished second to last.

Only a few days into the job, I was already getting a sense of the distance I'd have to travel to be taken seriously by the owners and the staff at the Management Council. I began to question my dream of reaching the highest levels in NFL management, becoming a contender for NFL commissioner. Did I really even want such a job? How could I start out as the owners' bookie and one day morph into their commissioner? Even someone as potentially head-in-the-sand naive as me knew that was unlikely. Were these the kinds of men who could ever view a black man as an equal? At this point I really didn't want to know the answer.

I remained excited about the work I was doing, though I felt nervous about going up against attorneys I'd previously huddled with in preparation for players' cases against the team owners.

A couple of months into the job, I was assigned to work on a case for the Indianapolis Colts. One of their former players—a guy who, along with a number of others, had been hired to compete only during the training camp season when the rosters are increased to eighty players instead of the final fifty-three men, sustained a knee injury during practice and was ultimately cut before the start of the season. His fate was typical of most street free agent players, who are essentially hired to serve as punching bags for the draft picks and returning veteran players. Free agents take a lot of hits and frequently end up at the bottom of pileups, which the owners basically view as the price they pay for the privilege of suiting up in an NFL uniform. The teams aren't inclined to compensate them generously when they get cut.

Still, street free agents believe they are going to be the rare lightning-in-a-bottle player who makes the team and becomes part of the lineup despite being passed over during the draft of some 270 college players. They not only fail to make the team but can also end up with a potentially lifelong injury. The teams don't offer them much compensation for an injury, and it wasn't unusual for training camp players to go after more. In some cases, however, players would overstate their injuries to bolster their cases.

This particular player was asking the Colts for a season and a half's worth of salary—about twenty-four weeks—as compensation for medial collateral ligament (MCL) and posterior cruciate ligament (PCL) tears in his knee. The club was offering the injured player six to eight weeks' pay. My job was to reach a deal that brought the team as little financial loss as possible. It was a small case that likely would have gotten little attention and time from one of the Management Council's more seasoned attorneys, but I went all in, digging up information about the player's previous injuries that ultimately turned the case in the Colts' favor.

To do research for the case, I took a trip out to the team's facility in Indianapolis. This was in the days before e-mail and scanners made it easy to send over records and video conferencing allowed remote evidentiary interviews. Traveling on the team owners' dimes was in sharp contrast to how we traveled when I worked for the players union. Flights were first-class instead of coach. Hotels were typically the Ritz-Carlton or the Four Seasons rather than the Marriott. We rented Cadillacs instead of Accords. And $300 dinners at the end of a day were routine. I loved it! I was working with and getting to know some of the people who I knew would be instrumental as I moved up the ladder in the league, and I was having fun in the process.

I spent time talking to coaches, physicians, and other members of the Colts staff to gather the evidence I needed to win the case in arbitration. Going through medical records confirmed a suspicion I first had while working with the NFLPA: the teams didn't keep very good records of players' injuries. The player who filed the grievance in this case was piling onto a prior injury he'd sustained in college. While the MCL tear came during preseason NFL games, the PCL tear was an old injury that had never received the care it needed. The team owed the player recuperative compensation for the MCL tear, but not the PCL. I was able to tease that out by talking to doctors and hunting down the player's old medical records—records that the team's coaches and management weren't even aware existed.

After I'd pieced together the bones of the argument I was building, I asked the Colts owner's son and general manager Jim Irsay—a bodybuilder who when he spoke reminded me a bit of Rocky Balboa—if we could sit down for a five-minute discussion of the case. We ended up talking for about thirty minutes. I was surprised that Jim was willing to spend so much time with a rookie attorney on a pretty minor case. I quickly realized that it had less to do with the case and more to do with Jim's feeling that his franchise, along with a few others in the league, wasn't getting the respect and attention it was due from the Management Council attorneys.

Jim and I were both in our twenties when we met. He was in line to take over ownership of the Colts from his father, but a number of the league's team owners and the Management Council's older attorneys didn't put much stock in his abilities. Jim was determined to learn as much as he could about what was going on with his team. Jim and I may have been from two different worlds, but at that moment, we both shared youth and the need to prove our worth in the heady world we were navigating. Like me, Jim was working hard to be taken seriously by the tight-knit group of men who were running the NFL. I could relate better to Jim than to the other owners. He was an owner's son standing in the line of succession, and he needed to prove that he deserved to be in an ownership role, not just given one. As a black man, I shared something in common with Jim: we both wanted and needed to make our own impact and to distinguish ourselves as being deserving of respect.

I told Jim I thought we had a good chance of winning in arbitration and that I believed the roughly $60,000 in compensation the team was offering was likely to prevail over the $185,000 (about $400,000 today) payout that the union was seeking for the player. When we got to the hearing, the arbitrator agreed, and the player received only seven weeks of salary—$60,000—as compensation. On one level I had won a case, and winning always feels good. But I had won against the NFLPA, the lawyers I'd jumped ship on, the ones who originally nurtured me and gave me my first opportunity. I wasn't sure if I should have felt conflicted or not by the victory, but in the end I didn't feel conflicted. I felt good. The win affirmed that I was becoming a competent attorney and that I had made the right decision to leave the union.

I was always looking to prove my worth. A few months into my job, I came up with an idea for better communicating case strategy for arbitration hearings to the owners and senior team management. One of the things I started doing was writing detailed summary memos outlining the case facts and my recommended approach. I was surprised that for an organization with so much on the line financially and so many cases, no one had previously thought to do this. It was a simple action that the teams' management seemed to like, and not long after I'd started doing the memos, a team owner (I never found out who) complimented them to Jim Conway, general counsel for the Management Council. Jim came into my office, stood in front of my desk, and said, "I hear you're writing these summary memos to the owners."

"Yes I am," I said. I could tell immediately that he wasn't happy about it and asked, "Did I get something wrong in one of them? Is there a problem with the information in any of the memos?"

"It's making the other lawyers look bad. I want you to stop writing them," he ordered. It took me a second to comprehend what I was hearing—that he wasn't unhappy with the quality of my work, but that I was raising the bar for the rest of the staff. For a few minutes I reasoned with him about how the memos could save us time educating team management during the course of the case and also be useful in writing the briefs we submit to arbitrators, but Jim wasn't having any of it. He told me I was grandstanding and not being a team player.

It wasn't above me to grandstand. I was, after all, trying to build a reputation that would fast-track me into the system of NFL management, but this was no such attempt. I was doing my job in the way that I believed would produce the best results, and the owners themselves had complimented me. I hadn't considered how the memos might affect the other attorneys. Frankly, I didn't care, because none of them had bothered to share with me what they did in handling their own cases. They piled their worst cases on my desk with the obvious presumption that I would not prevail in many of them. I was determined to prove them wrong. I wanted to be better than they were and show them that I was better. Blacks learn from an early age that you have to perform twice as well as your white counterparts, and that has always been part of my mind-set. It is still commonly echoed in the black community that "if you want to get ahead in life, you have to be twice as good as the white man."

When I realized nothing I had to say to Jim—no matter how logical—was up for discussion, I looked back down at the papers on my desk that I'd been reading before he'd come in and said, "Jim, if you want me to stop writing the memos, you're going to have to tell Jack to come in here and tell me that."

I didn't hear a response. After a few seconds, I looked up and saw Jim was seething at me, a black kid of twenty-something, barely four months into the job, challenging him, telling him what I wasn't going to do. "You're gonna want to pack up your desk," he finally said before he walked out of my little storage-closet-turned-office.

I sat there reminding myself that as a black man, I was particularly vulnerable to being viewed through the "uppity nigger" lens. But I knew that if I backed down on what I felt strongly about, I would set a precedent that would be difficult to reverse. I made a promise to myself not to compromise my integrity. If that meant getting fired, so be it. I suddenly developed a nervous stomach. My thoughts raced. I felt a little sweat along my brow. I decided to finish what I was working on and figure out if my next step was a trip to human resources or Jack's office.

I didn't have a chance to decide. A few minutes later, Jim came back and said Jack wanted to see us. When we got to his office, Jack asked a few questions to sort out the details. Then he rendered a verdict: "If the owners like what he's doing, either have the other lawyers do it or don't. But he can keep writing his memos." He waved the back of his hand toward us in a gesture that made it clear the conversation was over.

Jim and I got up and left Jack's office, me following a safe distance behind. I wanted to be happy about my "victory," but a little voice of warning inside me said I'd given up more than I realized to get it. Toward the end of the day, Jack came by my office and said: "You don't want to get too comfortable here. I'm clear that you have a lot of ambition, and I don't see you being around for more than a couple of years before you move on to bigger things." He added that most of the other attorneys saw the job as something they planned on retiring from and that I wasn't winning friends by doing things that reminded them that I had greater aspirations.

Jack was right. I could either temper my ambitions and win more friends in the workplace or gain notice and points with the team owners. I chose the latter because I still harbored the dream of reaching that top job in the NFL, and this small victory made me believe it was at least remotely possible. And I made the decision mostly because I was competitive. I did not like losing, and I viewed this job as a competition in the same way I was trained to compete as an athlete. Winning became my mantra in my professional life. I was always competing against white people. Winning against them was how I measured success.

My relationships with the other attorneys, never congenial as with my players' union colleagues, cooled. We were cordial to one another and even shared a laugh or a beer after work on occasion, but I never became close friends with any of them. A distance developed. Perhaps I had revealed my soft underbelly; I was no longer the young, innocent black attorney to whom they could offer beneficial advice. I had revealed that I wanted to be a competitor, and I surmised that they now viewed me as competent competition—and arrogant.

In December 1987, a couple of months after the memo incident, the entire Management Council legal team went down to Palm Springs, California, for an NFL owners meeting. We went to dinner one night at a popular pricey Italian restaurant that the owners had been frequenting throughout the week of meetings. We had a large group at our table that included Jack, Dennis Curran, and Jim Conway. The restaurant was chic with a dark, you-have-to-be-really-rich-to-appreciate-it decor. As a black man it was an unwelcoming, you-are-definitely-in-the-wrong-place decor. The players' strike had recently ended, and everyone in attendance, mostly old, stuffy white NFL power brokers, was in the mood to celebrate.

Georgia Frontiere, owner of the then Los Angeles Rams, and Jim Irsay were in such a good mood that they were sitting together at a nearby table as she jokingly serenaded him. She was about seventy years old at the time, and I wasn't aware that she had been an opera singer in her earlier years. At some point, Jim Irsay looked over, saw our table, and waved. A few minutes later, a waiter appeared with an expensive bottle of Bordeaux for us, saying Jim had sent it over. Dennis looked over toward the table, waved his hand, and nodded his head as a gesture of thanks. When the waiter realized Dennis thought the bottle was being directed to the entire table, he said, "Mr. Irsay wanted me to tell Mr. Huyghue that this is specifically for him."

The table fell completely silent. Feeling uncomfortable with all the attention that had suddenly turned to me, I quickly thanked the waiter. Finally, Dennis piped up and jokingly asked, "What the hell did you do that Jim is sending you over a bottle of wine?"

"I just helped him with a grievance," I said, downplaying

the gift. But I reveled in the unspoken statement Jim was making by sending that bottle of wine. His action said to me that he and I both may have been outsiders, but we shared a bond. Another wedge had been driven between my coworkers and me. Jack's muted smile indicated that he saw clearly what was going on and found the moment a bit fascinating and entertaining. A seasoned negotiator, he knew a power move when he saw it.

Fortunately, there was so much goodwill being shown by the owners toward the Management Council attorneys that no one dwelled on the moment. The league was just a few weeks past a dramatic labor dispute that had threatened to cost millions of dollars and end the 1987 season. Jack and other members of our legal team had helped the owners design a strategy that brought the players back after a twenty-four-day ill-fated strike. It had been a nerve-racking few weeks, and every move on either side had been scrutinized and analyzed fifty different ways by the media. We all knew—players and owners alike—it could have been much worse. The entire season could have been ruined had things played out differently.

At the heart of the dispute was the players' demand for unfettered free agency once their initial contracts were up. The NFL's revenues were continuing to grow, but they weren't seeing any of it. Plus, the average player's career lasted only three to five years, so whatever money they earned during that time often needed to last many years after retirement. Gene had sold the players on the concept of becoming "free." The restraints owners had on player movement was the target that promoted their walkout. If players felt the owners controlled their freedom, Gene knew he could lead them to walk out. It was a matter of respect, not too dissimilar to Kaepernick taking a knee.

The owners wanted as much control as possible over the movement of players between teams to keep salaries down and retain as much profit as possible. They would not give in.

Technically, NFL players had had free agency since 1947, but none of them ever tried to test the waters until 1962, when R. C. Owens, who was black, left the then Baltimore Colts after his contract was up to go play for the San Francisco 49ers. Fearful that the move would set off a wave of players seeking better-paying opportunities and drive up salary costs, the team owners pressured the league to implement a series of rules that pretty much made free agency an impossible option for players. One of the rules remunerated the team that lost a player to free agency by allowing it a compensatory pick—meaning the team that lost its veteran player was able to take a first- and possibly second-round draft pick from the team that had wooed the player. As a result, few teams were willing to risk losing two prime new talents with ostensibly longer careers in the making to pick up one veteran player at a premium cost.

The players had been trying for more than two decades to get rid of that and other restrictions on free agency by the time the 1987 contract negotiations rolled around. Black players in particular wanted to see an end to the restrictions, because on average they were making less money than white players. San Francisco 49ers cornerback Ronnie Lott, who'd recently lost a finger to a game injury, and Reggie White, a defensive end who had been picked up by the Philadelphia Eagles after the United States Football League (USFL) collapsed in 1985, were among the staunchest supporters of the free agency effort and the resulting strike.

Training camp started in July as usual that year, even though the players and owners were locked in intense negotiations around the contract. It was set to expire at the end of August. The players had gone on strike during the last negotiation in 1982, so no one really wanted to see another one. That walkout had also been over earnings-related issues. Among other things, the league had signed a lucrative broadcast deal with major networks at the finish of the 1981 season, and the players wanted 55 percent of the gross revenues from that deal. The owners balked, so after a week of games, the players began a two-month-long strike that cost both sides more than $250 million in lost revenue and wages, which forced the owners to pay back more than $50 million to the networks.

For all the trouble, the final 1982 contract didn't include any revenue sharing for the players, nor was the request for unfettered free agency part of the package. Instead, they got a onetime $60 million payout, some additional benefits, and an increase in the minimum salary. Five years later, with so little resolved to their satisfaction during the last negotiation, the players were threatening to walk again unless they finally got a free agency arrangement that was more in line with what they wanted.

Two weeks into the 1987 season, the NFLPA and the NFL Management Council still hadn't reached an agreement. There didn't appear to be any room for compromise on either side, so on September 22 the players walked out. This time, with the Management Council under the leadership of Jack Donlan, the owners had a plan to take more aggressive steps to break the strike and force the players back onto the field. With the third week of games canceled, the owners hustled to put together replacement teams; scabs, as the union referred to them, would play out the season if necessary. No one was certain the networks or the fans would go for it, but the owners were determined not to lose the kind of money they'd lost five years earlier.

By week four of the season, teams made up of motley players who'd been cut during training camp and the off-season, players from the recently defunct Canadian Football League and USFL, and veteran players who refused to support the strike (which included New York Jets defensive end Mark Gastineau, Dallas Cowboys defensive end Ed "Too Tall" Jones, and Cincinnati Bengals linebacker Reggie Williams) were on the field.

Some of the replacement players had been picked off assembly lines, construction crews, grocery checkouts, and at least one—Washington Redskins replacement quarterback Tony Robinson—had been allowed a work furlough from prison, where he was serving a nine-month sentence for accessory to attempted cocaine distribution, to play for the team. He actually proved to be one of the better players.

The decision to field replacement teams was a risky

move, but on the business side at least, it largely worked in the owners' favor. Fearful of losing advertising revenues, the networks agreed to air the games, which kept the owners from having to pay back the broadcasters as they had in 1982. And because they were paying replacement players far less than veteran players, the owners were actually earning more money per game, even while the number of fans showing up for games dropped by about 70 percent. It wasn't a completely painless financial win, however. The franchises did have to reimburse the networks for the canceled games during week three of the season and some lost revenue as a result of advertisers' pulling out of their planned ad buys during the games.

Reaction to the strike varied wildly on all sides, and that caused a lot of drama publicly and behind the scenes. The press documented a raucous walkout that had all the markings of a big labor dispute. Players, black and white in unison, walked the picket lines, in some cases flanked by fans, and dared the replacement teams to cross them. In Cincinnati, Bengals quarterback Boomer Esiason sat down in front of a bus filled with "scab" players to prevent the driver from crossing the picket line. And when New York Jets defensive end Mark Gastineau showed up for work, he ended up getting into a fight with his striking teammates while trying to enter the stadium's facilities.

While the owners put on a unified public front, there was a lot of bickering behind the scenes at the Management Council. I showed up for work one morning about two weeks into the strike and was once again summoned by

Jack to the conference room where he was meeting with the same group of team owners who'd sent me on the boondoggle errand to place a horse bet a few months earlier. I could feel friction in the air the minute I walked into the room.

Though they'd gotten on board, not all of the owners agreed with Jack's tactic to field replacement teams. Council members like Pittsburgh Steelers owner Dan Rooney and Oakland Raiders owner Al Davis, who were from union towns, thought the move was polarizing. They weren't particularly sympathetic to the players' cause, but they feared Jack's plan would bring a lot of bad press and backlash from fans. Dan and Al also were leery of the racial undertones that the dispute had taken on.

When the players went on strike in 1982, the NFLPA was under the leadership of Ed Garvey, an attorney who had helped organize the association and began directing it in 1971, when the majority of players were white. Gene, who had been with the NFLPA since the late 1970s, took over leadership in 1983. By that time, the racial composition of the league's players had shifted to blacks making up the majority. But despite the NFL's financial gains during that time, black players weren't earning as much as white players. The absence of pay equity was partially the result of black players being relegated to lower paying positions and advertisers being less likely to offer black athletes the kinds of lucrative endorsement deals that their white counterparts were receiving. As a result, black football players were particularly disgruntled when it came time to negotiate the contract for the 1987–1991 seasons.

Gene was keenly aware of the players' dissatisfaction, so in preparation for the forthcoming negotiations, he had his staff poll the players to find out what was at the top of their wish list for the new contract. True free agency was the resounding response. Although five hundred players had achieved free agency status by 1987, only one had been offered a contract under the system. By then the players believed revenue sharing was a nonstarter issue for team owners, so they felt pushing to relax the rules governing free agency was their best chance at increased earnings.

Gene knew it would be a hard fight, and on some level he not only anticipated that race would become a central theme of the battle, but he also attempted to use it to his advantage. He believed the optics of a majority of black players under the financial control of all-white team owners could place additional pressure on the Management Council to make concessions. The press was already raising the issue, so Gene hardly saw reason to sidestep it. Plus, no one could dispute that there was a pay equity issue for black players. Therefore, when the Management Council broke off contract negotiations, Gene publicly accused the group of having a "racist attitude" and of portraying him as "a black militant" who had "misled the players."

The accusation didn't gain Gene the traction he was looking for in the negotiations, but that didn't mean it was without merit. Raiders owner Al Davis, who was on the Management Council's advisory committee and who in 1967 drafted Gene to play for his team, remained a close friend to Gene even though the two were often on opposite sides of the negotiation table. Al used to relay some of the unsavory comments the owners would make during meetings, but the slights never seemed to rattle Gene. He was more intrigued by another fact Al shared, which was that the owners feared Gene had the power to unite the black players in pushing for long-sought concessions. And with the team rosters becoming browner each year, the owners feared they would eventually have to cave.

Jack, however, was confident he could crush the NFLPA and end the 1987 strike in short order. He and Gene had been friendly up until that point and even hung out on occasion, but eviscerating the union was essentially what he was hired to do, and he intended to get on with the business of doing that. He was furious over rumors that some of the Management Council's advisory committee members had gone behind his back and broken the moratorium on talking with NFLPA representatives in an effort to broker a deal. He felt it undercut his authority and weakened the owners' position.

Jack suspected it was Al and Dan who'd been doing the talking. I'd heard the rumors around the office, so it was clear to me when I got called into their meeting that I was there for two reasons: to give the "black" perspective on whether the racial rhetoric had gotten out of control; and to try to reassure the owners that based on my experience at the NFLPA, the union had neither the fortitude nor enough player support to continue the strike.

When I walked into the conference room, Jack summoned me over to stand next to him. He never asked me to sit, however, so I stood there to his right, my hands clasped behind my back, so no one could see them trembling. "You know you two have got to be some of the dumbest sons of bitches around!" he yelled at Al and Dan, wagging an accusatory finger toward each of them. "We distinctly told you *not* to talk to Gene, and you go right behind my back."

I tried not to show it on my face, but I was dumbfounded by Jack's reprimand of two men who were essentially his bosses. But the situation also taught me a lesson about the power of NFL politics, and more importantly about who Jack was. I realized that my having stood my ground with my own boss about the case memos a couple of weeks earlier had probably earned me some brownie points in Jack's eyes. He valued someone who'd speak his mind—as long as it was informed—to whoever was asking, regardless of rank. But I also realized that as a black man I was afforded less latitude to challenge authority, so I'd have to pick and choose my battles more strategically than someone like Jack—who also happened to have a proven track record, something I still needed to establish.

For their part, Davis and Rooney felt the season would be ruined and management would be severely hurt if the strike lasted for another month. In the ten days or so since it had begun, more than 225,000 tickets had been refunded, and in cities like Detroit and Philadelphia, Gene had convinced union leaders to urge their members to boycott the games.

It didn't help that the first set of games with the replacement teams had been a colossal mess by almost any standard. For starters, the teams were incredibly mismatched in terms of the players' abilities. Also, some teams had a larger number of existing players cross the picket lines to suit up, resulting in games that were complete blowouts in some cases. The mismatches made for comical football but hardly competitive games. When asked by a reporter what his team's game strategy had been, Jim Crocicchia, who stepped in as a receiver for the Giants, said it was to stay in the huddle for as long as possible because he and his teammates were having a hard time catching their breath.

The sideline antics also proved entertaining. During an away game in New York City, Cornell Burbage, who was a replacement receiver for the Dallas Cowboys, was caught on camera reaching up into the stands to grab a package that he then shoved under the bench. It turned out to be a box of laundry that his sister had washed for him since he couldn't afford to pay for the hotel's laundry service.

Then there were the unflattering nicknames, such as Chicago Spare Bears, New Orleans Saint Elsewheres, and Seattle Sea Scabs, that the fans had given the teams as a result of all the field mishaps.

The disparaging names, the on-field play, the contentious negotiation accounts being published by the press, and, most important, the lost revenue were causing nerves to fray on all sides. Finally, about seven or eight minutes into his admonishment of Al and Dan, Jack turned to me and said, "Michael, you worked for the union. Do they have what it takes to hold out several more weeks?"

The shakiness that I'd felt in my hands suddenly jumped to my stomach. As Jack pointed out, I'd been working on behalf of the union and its players only a few months earlier, so I had some conflicted feelings about the dispute. My gut, however, told me I wasn't standing in a moment that allowed for equivocation. "No, they'll cave," I said, choking back what felt like betrayal. I knew what I said was true. I always thought Gene had underestimated how individual circumstances would factor into players' solidarity, and the union had no funds put aside to help the players weather the strike. But confirming that Achilles' heel to the Management Council felt traitorous even though I knew that my loyalty lay with the owners by virtue of my job. "From what I've seen, most of the players are living hand-to-mouth," I continued. "I think the pressure from their wives, families, and all the other people depending on them is going to be too much."

The room fell silent for a second after I offered my take on things. Jack had turned to face me while I was talking, and I could see the hint of a smile on his face, letting me know that I'd said exactly what he'd needed me to say. Finally, others in the room started peppering me with questions about Gene, about my take on what the media were saying about the owners' position on free agency and the league's treatment of Gene.

I remember clearly thinking during that moment that as much as we are sold the story of football being a team sport, everyone in the business—from the players to the coaches to the owners and all the others who keep the sport thriving—is in it for himself or herself. Being in it for yourself is what's encouraged when you're negotiating a salary, trying to set a record, or playing to get the ball across the goal line. The battle over the players' contracts was no different. I was certain the strike was going to fall apart and that once the players were back on the field, the public would be content to return to their usual programming.

"I think at the end of the day, players are taught to be selfish, and Gene is hoping for group mentality," I said, hoping they wouldn't continue to press. I didn't believe I had any additional insight to offer beyond what I'd already said. I looked around and saw that the men sitting at the table seemed to be satisfied with my answers. Jack thanked me and told me I could leave.

I'd walked into that conference room feeling nervous, but I walked out feeling simultaneously triumphant and nauseous. My worth had risen a bit in Jack's eyes. I'd been able to help him make his case and show that I had valuable experience—that he'd been right in taking a chance on me. Yet I felt as though I needed to take a bath to wash off the slime of providing information about the players and about Gene, who'd been my mentor. I reminded myself that all I'd actually given the men in that room was my opinion—a neophyte one at that. I hadn't provided any details about the NFLPA's strategy. I didn't have any knowledge of it, so there was no danger there.

As an attorney, I'd done exactly what my fiduciary duties required me to do—act solely in the interest of my client. I cashed their check every week, and, like it or not, I owed them that duty. It didn't feel right, but it was my job. However, I couldn't help but feel that as a black man,

I'd somehow acted against the interests of folks who were more like me than the men in that conference room. And why, I wondered, was this the first time the owners had solicited my opinion? More humble pie.

The episode wasn't quite over. I learned quickly that Jack liked to use carefully crafted perception to gain the upper hand during a negotiation. He'd fielded the replacement teams so that the players would perceive themselves as easily expendable. He'd tamped down on individual owners communicating with the NFLPA so that the union would perceive itself as insignificant in the players' decisions to either continue striking or cross the picket line. And he'd summoned me to the owners' meeting to help bolster the perception that he had an inside track on the way the strike was likely to play out. A few days later, I was reprising my role, this time in DC at the NFLPA offices.

Even though I had no involvement in negotiating the contract between the two sides, Jack asked me to attend a private negotiation meeting with Gene. If I wasn't initially certain of the part I'd play, it became clearer once we were there. Where a week earlier I'd been brought into a room and left to stand, now Jack had me sit right between him and Gene. It was his not-so-subtle way of suggesting he had an advantage in the form of an adviser who had knowledge of the NFLPA's endgame and reminding Gene and others at the union that they'd lost a recent, albeit small, battle when the Management Council lured me away. I thought the suggestions were overstated given my lowly status. I didn't think Gene paid any attention to the optics.

What initially began as a working relationship had morphed into a mentor relationship. Jack was in charge of my career. He decided for whatever reason to assume the role of guardian. Something he saw in me, perhaps; I never knew. It was crucial, though, for me to be able to advance within the league. Without someone like Jack there to deflect the bullets, I would not have the chance to take risks. I would have been stuck under the control of my immediate boss and could not have escaped the claws of the general counsel. There was no avenue for someone of my race or disposition to advance. In a casual meeting conversation with several NFL attorneys, I'd heard a problem that needed a solution described this way: "Guys, we have to find the nigger in the haystack here." Nobody batted an eyelash.

We all shook hands before taking our seats. My stomach was churning, because I knew exactly why I'd been trotted out to the meeting. It was difficult seeing Gene. I smiled and shook his hand firmly, and he was friendly, showing no signs of resenting my recent defection, but the irony of the circumstances wasn't lost on me. We were there in hopes of settling a strike where players were being forced to choose between standing with their picketing teammates or defecting and being labeled scabs. In that moment, I felt like a scab.

We got down to the business of rehashing the players' contract demands and the owners' unwillingness to give in to a few of them. Among other demands, the players were pushing for an end to the compensatory draft pick rule attached to free agency and that players be unrestricted in their ability to entertain offers from other teams after four years. They were also asking the league to double the annual pension contributions to $25 million and for an increase in players' minimum salary. Gene was willing to explore what kind of concessions in the free agency demands the players might be willing to make, but Jack, confident he had the union on the ropes, refused to entertain the topic. We were nearly three weeks into the strike, and we were hearing more and more rumblings about players who were ready for the strike to end.

We left the negotiating table with no agreement and little if any sign of progress, but as Jack gambled, it ultimately didn't matter. The players' will was dissolving just as he'd predicted, and the owners were content to let the situation continue for a while longer once they realized that even with the ticket refunds, they were making more money because they were paying the replacement players an average of only $1,000 per game. Plus, the union was in my opinion losing the public relations battle: Gene had spent a lot of time traveling around to build player solidarity concerning the free agency issue in the days leading up to the strike, so he hadn't been available to sit with the owners to duke out the specifics of the contract during that time, instead leaving it up to his legal staff. A lot of football fans perceived him as having been unwilling to sit down earlier in the negotiations, when the situation could possibly have been avoided.

A few days after our meeting with Gene, the strike truly started collapsing. The Management Council began getting calls from the teams' general managers, who said players were phoning them to say that they didn't want to cross the picket line, but they were willing to come back if an end could be called to the walkout. Also, more of the players— even ones who'd been among the most supportive of the strike in the beginning—were crossing the picket lines.

Dallas Cowboys running back Tony Dorsett had nearly gotten run over by his teammate Randy White when he stood in front of the lineman's truck to try to prevent him from crossing the picket line around the second week of the strike. But Dorsett was forced back to the field himself the following week when Cowboys owner Tex Schramm sent out notes threatening that striking players would lose a sizable portion of their annuities if they didn't go back to work.

By the fourth week of the strike, about 15 percent of the regular players were back on the field, and many more were saying they'd be heading back the following week even if the dispute wasn't settled. On Thursday, October 15, the players voted to go back to work, and three days later, Gene took to national TV to announce the end of the walkout.

The announcement was a huge victory for the owners, who right away began calling the Management Council asking if they could put the returning players back in the games that were scheduled for the following week. We advised them to hold off and play one additional week of games with the replacement teams. The league had established a rule that any striking players who wanted to suit up needed to be on their team's roster by Tuesday of the previous week in order to participate. Since the vote took place on Thursday, bringing the striking players back right away would have required the owners to pay both the replacement players, who were already on the roster, and the returning players.

Plus, we needed to be certain that the players' agreement to return was real and not a strike tactic: that they weren't going to suit up, come onto the field, and then refuse to play, which would have done serious damage to the NFL's TV deals. Also, we needed to figure out an orderly procedure for transitioning the teams. My job during that time was to communicate to the clubs what the process would be and what they needed to tell the players about how we planned to handle their return.

It was several days before the Management Council staff could actually breathe a sigh of relief, but our celebrating began the following Thursday right after we finalized details for the transition. That afternoon, we broke out the beers. Eddie LeBaron, a consultant and former quarterback for the Dallas Cowboys who became a lawyer, gave a toast congratulating Jack for a great strategy. It definitely felt good to be on the winning side of the dispute, but I felt we'd won largely because of circumstances, not strategy. Management Council attorneys spent a good deal of time admitting our own surprise at how quickly the strike had splintered.

The strike's fast demise signaled to the owners that they had a tremendous amount of leverage in negotiating what would be the final collective bargaining agreement covering the next five years. Changes in the free agency policy were completely off the table. The owners okayed some cosmetic givebacks on the benefits side, and they didn't penalize the striking players' pension contributions. But beyond that—with the exception of the mandatory drug-screening policy—the contract largely mirrored the previous agreement.

That defeat is in large part I believe why the NFLPA, even today, some thirty years later and under the new leadership of DeMaurice Smith, a polished, well-educated black attorney from a buttoned-down national law firm, will on occasion use thinly veiled threats against the owners but ultimately will not make walking out a viable player strategy. Deal making instead is the norm today for the NFLPA brass.

The regular teams were back on the field by the last Sunday of October, less than four weeks after the walkout took place. The world of professional football was ready to see the season and the promise of all its spectacular excitement unfold. I couldn't help but feel, however, that most of the drama had already played out. It's startling to think back to the average players' salaries in 1987, which were then about $200,000, with the minimum salary at $50,000. The first salary cap for NFL clubs was introduced in 1994 at around $34 million per team. In 2018, the NFL salary cap is a whopping $177 million per team. The minimum player salary in 2018 is $480,000, and the average player makes just shy of $2 million per year.

CHAPTER 4

Making the Team

In the late 1960s the NFL first established itself as the number one rated sport from a television ratings and viewership perspective, surpassing Major League Baseball. Weekly ratings dramatically eclipsed any other sport in the United States. Viewership outside the US, however, was minimal, and television coverage almost nonexistent. Commissioner Tagliabue reasoned that international coverage of the NFL was the next frontier and a source of untapped revenue.

Since the mid-1980s, the NFL had been promoting its brand of "football" in exhibition games overseas, where soccer was the dominant sport. Tagliabue believed that while soccer would always be king across the pond, there was nevertheless a market for American football. These series of exhibition games typically featured two of the most successful and recognizable franchises in the league. Called the American Bowls, the games were intended to make a subtle dent in those television markets while stoking fan interest.

The games were played primarily in popular European markets like London and Frankfurt. The games in the United Kingdom, for example, were played at the world-renowned Wembley Stadium and were perennial sellouts.

Recognizing that the payments by US television networks to the NFL for broadcasting rights were likely reaching a saturation point, the owners were concerned about long-term revenues. In professional sports, television rights account for about 70–80 percent of all gross revenues. Tagliabue was intent on exploring European television markets for revenue. Historically, the league had received meager television payments dating back to the early 1970s when the National Football League and the American Football League first merged. A decade later, though, television revenues jumped into the then astronomical market of $420 million per year (or $15 million annually per team).

Then, in 1990, intense bidding competition among the networks (over the air and cable) for the NFL package skyrocketed the league's annual revenues to a whopping $900 million, or $32 million per team. In turn, the league divided its coverage by conference (AFC and NFC) to the NBC and CBS networks, respectively. Sunday night was split in half between two cable networks, TNT and ESPN. Monday nights were a mainstay of the ABC network, which also added a Thursday night package.

As a result of Tagliabue's influence, a small group of owners was designated to establish a new spring international league in 1989, which would initially be called the World League of American Football (WLAF). The mission of the league was ostensibly to expand the game of American football overseas and to tap into those potential rights fees. Some observers, though, were less certain about the financial prospects and saw the league solely as a developmental step for marginal NFL talent. The league was the perfect buffer to antitrust attacks from the NFL Players Association, who were suing the league at the time for its alleged anticompetitive tactics as a monopoly. Adding a new league contradicted the monopoly argument and gave the league squatter's rights against any other entity that might seek to establish American-brand football overseas. The NFL saw professional football as its property and didn't want anyone else profiting off its business.

The WLAF initially consisted of ten teams in North America and Europe. Only twenty-six of the twenty-eight NFL owners contributed $50,000 each to the start-up costs for the league. The NFL owned about half of the teams, and the others were sold as franchises to individual owners outside the NFL. The NFL had control over the coaches and players who participated in the league and loaned its shield and logo marks to the new WLAF owners. The teams were located in Birmingham, Alabama (Fire); Sacramento, California (Surge); San Antonio, Texas (Riders); Montreal, Canada (Machine); New York, New York (Knights); Orlando, Florida (Thunder); Raleigh–Durham, North Carolina (Skyhawks); Barcelona, Spain (Dragons); Frankfurt, Germany (Galaxy); and London, England (Monarchs).

I had spent two and a half years at the NFL Management Council at that point and had established a solid reputation of doing good work. Jack had taken an interest in me and shielded me from obstacles, but then suddenly and unexpectedly, that changed. During one of the long-term negotiating sessions with the NFLPA, Reverend Jesse Jackson contacted the league to voluntarily insert himself into the players' fight for free agency. Gene presented free agency as a freedom issue, and that stoked the flames of leaders like Reverend Jackson.

Jack wanted nothing to do with Jesse Jackson's involvement in the negotiations, and I believed his disdain for Jackson was in part racially motivated. That made me question whether this man whom I considered my mentor held the beliefs on race I thought he held. Did he not respect blacks in general with the same level of regard he had shown me? I wondered. I understood that allowing Jackson or any outsider to have a role in the process would potentially displace the control Jack had over the situation, but I began to view Jack's critique of Jackson more as an affront to him as a black man.

I had allowed myself to trust Jack, and aside from the mentoring, I felt that we were friends. We played tennis together on weekends at the West Side Tennis Club at Forest Hills and coed softball on Sunday mornings in Central Park. Jack had strong Boston, Irish roots that belied any prior close friendships with a black man, but I sensed he felt a bond with me, and that feeling was mutual. I suspect he saw me as different from what he knew about and saw in other black people.

After the Reverend Jackson situation, however, my trust

was broken. I believed he did not respect me as a black man but viewed me as "an exception." Many successful black folks relate to being seen as "super Negro"; while blacks as a whole are disparaged, an individual black person might be held in high regard and considered "not like the rest of them." I remembered this feeling years later, when while working with a team, an owner relayed to me that a head coach had described an upcoming potential team college draft choice as "the best character black player [he] had ever recruited."

I felt bitterly disappointed by the insensitive words he'd reportedly spoken, and it hurt badly. *Never again*, I thought. *Don't trust anyone.* It was time for me to leave. Jack had told me the first week of my tenure at the Management Council that I would be gone in less than three years. And as with most things—he was right.

This would be only the first of many other incidents throughout my career in the NFL where racial epithets were bantered about among senior executives, attorneys, head coaches, and even owners as normal parlance. At times race was spoken of offhandedly and off-the-cuff, without regard to even political correctness, let alone genuine respect. Only one such comment was made in my direct presence, but others were relayed to me by white colleagues who respected me and felt the need to confess the derogatory conduct of their peers, as if to apologize on their behalf.

White colleagues who had never previously experienced racism observed it firsthand in my presence and underwent an awakening. Typically, they became enraged at the conduct—for example, a hostess refusing to offer an available table at an exclusive restaurant or always being seated at the least desirable table in the restaurant—and lashed out at the person. Having only briefly observed life from the lens of a black man, these friends began to appreciate the impact and effect of racism, if only vicariously. Throughout my career, confessions from white colleagues served as a constant reminder to me that while culture certainly accounted for a portion of the insensitivity, structural and institutional racism were built into the fabric of the NFL organization. My eyes were wide open from the beginning, though. I knew I was up against obstacles of race and would have to kick through many glass ceilings. Football was a contact sport on the field, and I understood that it would be equally as combative for me off the field.

I received a call in early November 1990 from Mike Lynn, who was the new president of the WLAF. Mike was also the owner representative and general manager of the Minnesota Vikings (another one of the teams I spent a lot of time defending while staff counsel for the Management Council). Lynn was a mover and a shaker and someone I got along with but always kept a cautionary eye on. Lynn had also been unflatteringly famous just one year earlier for trading five players and eight draft picks to the Dallas Cowboys in exchange for then Dallas Cowboys star running back Herschel Walker and four future draft picks. You don't have to be a football guru to know that one player—no matter who—is not worth giving up thirteen players for.

Herschel Walker lasted only a couple of seasons on the

Vikings squad with subpar years before bouncing around with two other teams and ultimately landing back with Dallas. Dallas became a dynasty in the NFL, converting its Walker windfall picks into Super Bowl victories with players like Emmitt Smith and Darren Woodson, both Pro Bowl players.

Putting Mike Lynn in charge of the WLAF may have been his punishment for making such a disastrous trade. Still, it piqued my interest that he was contacting me about becoming a general manager in the new league. "Which team?" I asked during the brief call. "Birmingham," he replied. "It's a bit of a formality, but you will have to meet with the owner, Gavin Maloof, before it's final," he said, as if it were a certainty that I would accept his offer. I accepted on the spot. Three days later I was on a plane to Albuquerque, New Mexico, to meet with the Maloof family at their home compound. Gavin would move to Birmingham to run the team.

Jack was out of town at the time I accepted the offer. I didn't discuss it with him in advance, which clearly broke protocol. In fact, he hadn't returned to the office by the time I had to leave. I spoke with him a few days later by telephone and reiterated what he had originally said about moving on to greener pastures sooner rather than later. We both understood, though, that I was brazenly moving on without his permission or blessing. I was on my own; steering my own course was where I always felt most comfortable. I wasn't one of those black guys who saw the world through the prism of my white mentor's eyes. I owed Jack a great debt of gratitude for mentoring me, but it was time to move on.

I was unimpressed by southwestern culture on my first trip to New Mexico. It just wasn't my taste. The Albuquerque airport was small, and most of the gates were on the tarmac in an open-air facility. It seemed rinky-dink and a long way from New York City in all respects.

I hadn't known much about the Maloof family, who had purchased the franchise rights to the Birmingham team. I did some research and learned that the family patriarch, George Maloof Sr., had recently passed. He had built a dynasty through beer distributorship rights with the Coors Beer company. His widow, Colleen, was now head of the family, which included five children: Adrienne, Joe, Gavin, George Jr., and Phil. Gavin was just five years older than me and was designated by the family to run the new football venture.

It was a muggy morning when I met with Gavin at a local and nearly empty restaurant. I thought it odd that we didn't meet at his home. It would have been a more intimate way to begin our journey together, but I shrugged it off as meaningless. Gavin was a relatively short guy with a stocky athletic build. The way he walked and spoke was hyper. His voice rose with inflection whenever he felt excited, which was often. He also laughed at the end of most of his comments in a self-effacing, almost apologetic way. He was a little uneasy during our conversation, but he was a laid-back type of guy and likable. Our closeness in age made the initial meeting less awkward. Gavin wasn't exactly comfortable, in my opinion, hiring a black man for this position. It seemed like a new experience for him.

I discussed my background information with him and what I hoped to bring to the city of Birmingham and to the new team. I was articulate, eager, and self-confident. Gavin complimented me, though I surmised that he had probably not previously met a black man with my self-assuredness. I grew accustomed over time to reading expressions and watching the looks on his face, which translated into almost disbelief.

I knew the NFL had already dictated to the Maloofs that I would become general manager of the team and this meeting was a formality, but I still worked hard to earn his respect. I met with his mother, Colleen. She was cordial, but again very close to the vest. With the father's recent passing, the family seemed to have closed ranks, and outsiders were not easily allowed into their inner sanctum. As we spoke, I learned that I was not their first choice, but in the end Gavin and I got along well enough that they posed no objections to the NFL brass. Hiring a black general manager was, I believe, a mandate from the NFL. At that time—1990—there had not been a black general manager in the NFL, and when Mike Lynn offered me the job, I understood the significance of race in my hire. I understood that in taking this position I was making history. Some opposed my hiring simply because of my race, and I received many hateful letters calling me "Monkey" and "Nigger."

But this was what I wanted—not the hateful letters but the opportunity to prove my worth; to compete. I was officially on my way to Birmingham and stepping into a much larger arena, a national one. My performance would be scrutinized and critiqued by local and national sports media. The commissioner dream lurked in the back of my mind even as I was determined to be the best general manager in the WLAF.

I arrived in Birmingham the first week of December, and on the sixth we held a press conference to announce my position as general manager. Birmingham was a die-hard football town. They'd experienced a previous foray into professional sports in the United States Football League, the spring league rival to the NFL that ultimately went belly-up in 1985 after three seasons. The Stallions were one of the most successful franchises in the USFL, however, and always had strong attendance at Legion Field, their featured stadium in Birmingham. Rollie Dotsch, a former top assistant with the Super Bowl–winning NFL Pittsburgh Steelers, was the Stallions coach. The town was also split almost evenly in their passion for college football between the Alabama Crimson Tide and the Tigers of Auburn University. Football was in the blood that flowed through their veins.

The press conference was scheduled for 9:00 a.m. at a local sports museum. Everything about the place seemed outdated and uncomfortable. I arrived a half hour early with a few prepared remarks about the rich history of Birmingham and how I was looking forward to upholding their tradition of fielding winning teams.

As I stepped up to the podium after introductory

remarks from Gavin, the two cameramen from local television stations literally pulled their heads from their lenses,
mouths wide open. "We have to stop the press conference,"
one of them called out. "We didn't know he was black," I
heard him say more softly. "We need to call our stations
and get more of the region on this announcement." That
was my introduction to Birmingham. Shock—that a black
man was hired, in Birmingham of all places, to lead their
new football team. I shrugged my shoulders, grabbed a
bottle of water, and walked off the podium.

The press conference reconvened about four hours later.
Now with a dozen or so live cameramen and a roomful of
writers, the introduction by Maloof was repeated. I took
the stage, gave my remarks, and then held individual side-
bars with local and regional writers for almost two hours.
I hadn't realized then that I was actually the *first* black
general manager of an NFL-sponsored professional football
team. And at age twenty-nine, I guess I also was among the
youngest. The local newspaper headline the next morning
read: "First Black Football GM Named in Birmingham."
That would become a regular theme attached to many of
my subsequent positions.

There had been a sprinkling of black assistant coaches
and scouts in the NFL and even a black coach in 1921—
Frederick Douglass "Fritz" Pollard. But outside the white
lines, blacks were heavily underrepresented. Staffs of most
NFL teams contained about thirteen coaches in those days.
(They have about nineteen today.) Typically, a black assistant
coach would be assigned only to the running back position,

the wide receiver position, or potentially, the cornerback position. Not surprisingly, those were also the positions almost
exclusively played by black athletes. They were called "skill
positions," in contrast to the offensive line and quarterback positions, which, in addition to being played by large
numbers of white players, were referred to as the "thinking
positions." This same coach/race scenario was common for
personnel scouts, those charged with the responsibility of
evaluating and grading the talent of college and professional
players. Most NFL teams in those days had only one black
person, if any, on their staff of six to eight scouts.

I had little time to invest in this "first black" issue,
which was perhaps the most newsworthy element of my
hiring. I focused on finding an apartment and started to
build a staff. Many offered me assistance in getting situ-
ated; however, not one black person of authority was in that
group. Someone the Maloofs hired said she had the perfect residence for me in a suburb named Mountain Brook.
Few black people lived in the suburb in 1991. Black people
in Birmingham were in the downtown area, where white
flight had occurred. I was concerned that black folks would
view me as a "sellout" if I accepted her offer to live in the
suburbs.

I arrived in Birmingham not fully aware of the long
racial history of the city. Of course, I knew its role in
the Civil Rights movement, and I was familiar with the
1963 bombing of the Sixteenth Street Baptist Church that
resulted in the killing of four young black girls. I also knew
that Dr. Martin Luther King Jr. penned his famous "Letter

from Birmingham Jail" while incarcerated there. And Birmingham was at the center of the black struggle against segregation during the Jim Crow years that ultimately led to the signing of the Civil Rights Act of 1964.

What I didn't realize was that little to nothing had changed for black people living in Birmingham since that time in its sordid history. Had the Civil War not ended? I felt depressed. I still saw "Whites Only" signs with faded paint scattered throughout downtown, remnants of what had been the norm only thirty years earlier. However, it appeared to me that Jim Crow was alive and well. I felt like a time traveler walking along the streets of downtown. This was my first real taste of the good old South, and it was unappetizing.

I acquiesced and moved into a small apartment on top of Red Mountain in Mountain Brook. I never saw another black person there. I constantly asked myself: *What the hell am I doing here? Is this really the price of admission to leadership in the NFL?*

This was also just after the famous Shoal Creek Golf Club hosted the PGA Championship in August 1990. At the time, Shoal Creek, a top-rated Jack Nicklaus–designed private club, had accepted no black members dating back to its inception in 1977. Hall Thompson, its founder, was quoted just prior to the start of the tournament as saying, "This is our home, and we pick and choose who we want," indicating that the club would not be pressured into admitting a black member. A firestorm of controversy ensued, and the PGA considered moving the event.

Just a few months after my move to Birmingham, I was approached about an honorary Shoal Creek membership. I knew enough not to insert myself into that hornet's nest and politely declined. I was already uncomfortable making national news by being an NFL "first black," and I had moved into the whites-only suburbs. I didn't want to add another token to my name.

The first order of business in building the new team in Birmingham was finding a coach. In my two-plus years at the Management Council, I'd had the opportunity to work closely with every general manager in the league on injury and noninjury grievances. I trusted several of them and began the search with a call to my closest ally, John Beake, the longtime general manager of the Denver Broncos. The Broncos had enjoyed only marginal success the last few years under head coach Dan Reeves. Reeves played professionally for the Dallas Cowboys back in the late 1960s under legendary coach Tom Landry and later worked as an assistant coach for the club. His first pro coaching job had come nearly ten years earlier, in 1981, with the Broncos under owner Pat Bowlen, a Canadian native.

During my conversation with Beake about potential head coaches, he recommended Chan Gailey, who was their current offensive coordinator. Any time someone recommends that you take personnel from their own team, you worry about their value. NFL clubs are not generous about giving up coaches and players they depend upon. However, I had worked on several player grievances with Beake and always found him to be a straight shooter. Notwithstanding my skepticism, I booked the next flight out to Denver to meet with Gailey.

Interestingly, during my research, I learned that both Reeves and Gailey played quarterback collegiately in the Southeastern Conference. Reeves played at the University of South Carolina and Gailey at the University of Florida. Reeves first hired Gailey in 1985 to work for the Broncos as tight ends and special teams coach. At the time, Gailey had just finished his second season as head coach of Troy State, a small college just outside Birmingham, Alabama. That was an important connection for me. Ironically, Gailey had also attended the same high school (though many years later) in Americus, Georgia, that Reeves attended, and both had played quarterback. Gailey stood six foot one, with a stocky, almost heavyset build, broad shoulders, and reddish-colored hair.

I would come to learn that in the NFL coaching ranks, job opportunities were almost always conditioned upon networking and familiarity. Black coaches seemed not to be part of that in-group. And here I was utilizing that system to find my first head coach. *What good is being the first black anything if no other black people benefit?* I asked myself. I reasoned that I first had to become successful and then I could effect change, that it simply could not happen right out of the box. However, I grew to learn that was flawed thinking. When a person of color gets into a position of authority, that is *exactly* the time to reach out to other minorities. First, you may not get another chance to make such a hire; and second, that is often the only way to facilitate that door of opportunity opening for other minorities. When I later became commissioner of the United Football League, I would make hiring minority coaches a priority from this lesson learned.

Gailey worked his way up from tight ends coach to offensive coordinator (OC) in the 1989 and 1990 NFL seasons. In his first season as OC, the Broncos finished first in their division with an overall record of 11-5. With star quarterback John Elway, the Broncos advanced that year to the Super Bowl, only to get crushed by the San Francisco 49ers by a score of 55–10. The next season, though, the Broncos finished last in their division, reversing their prior year's record to finish at 5-11. Was the last year's misfortune the reason why Beake was recommending Gailey to me?

On December 18, I arrived in chilly Denver and met with Chan in a small private conference room at the Broncos facility. I thought about asking Reeves first for permission, which was a league rule, but I wanted to decide if I would even consider Chan as our coach before I opened that can of worms. Beake had recommended him, which technically qualified as permission under the league's tampering rules. After just a few hours of background and general coaching philosophy conversation, it became clear to me that Gailey would be a great fit. He had already been a college head coach and had a strong understanding of the pro game as an offensive coordinator. He worked under a brilliant, offensive-minded head coach in Dan Reeves and had been part of an NFL team that in his first year as OC he led to the Super Bowl.

He was also very comfortable around me, which I interpreted as being comfortable around black people. I could tell from the look on his face and our first handshake that race was not a factor. That was critical for me in the hiring decision because my success would be tied to the success of the head coach. His staff would take their cues from him as head coach; and if the players sensed from him even a scintilla of disrespect or lack of sincerity working with a black man as GM, then it would be difficult for me to earn their respect. If I had to convince the players that I was the man in charge, I would already be defeated, but if the players could immediately recognize the good relationship Gailey and I shared and see him afford me respect, I could be effective. This was critically important. Gailey understood that and accepted his role.

Gailey was humble and had a strong religious background. I perceived him as a man who believed in giving another man respect as long as he earned it, regardless of his color. Although he grew up as an athlete in the Deep South, he was a sincere and fair man. I felt that sincerity emanating from his core. We were from different backgrounds but grounded in the mission that we had a job to do, and we both obviously wanted to be successful. We needed each other to accomplish that outcome.

Then I asked Chan Gailey why he would leave the NFL for a start-up spring league. Even if things were on rocky ground, he could surely get another NFL assistant job after only one subpar season with the Broncos. Why would he consider coaching in a new developmental league? Chan said he believed we would make a good team. Neither of us had any personal agendas, and he believed I would do everything in my power to help him win. That's all he was looking for. Besides, he said, he wanted to be a head coach in the NFL and wasn't afraid of taking a nontraditional route to get there. I knew he was the right choice. He had the perfect background and the local connections to Birmingham, having coached at nearby Troy State. It was our shared ambitions that made us the perfect team.

Although I had not intended to do so, I offered him the job on the spot and he accepted. A brief conversation with Coach Reeves ensued, and it was clear to me that he felt very close to Chan. Reeves told me that I was getting "a great coach and an even better man." He and Chan later embraced in a father-and-son manner, which fostered momentary thoughts of my former mentor Jack Donlan. I doubted I would ever have the close relationship that Reeves and Gailey shared with any mentor in the NFL. I didn't even enjoy that kind of relationship with my own father. Old wounds I will describe later had already convinced me that throughout my career, I would in all likelihood be a party of one. As I watched their embrace, I tried to put mentorship out of my mind.

Much of the lack of diversity in the NFL hiring ranks stems from lack of mentorship. Almost all of the most successful head coaches in the NFL chose assistant coaches they had mentored. Coaches like Bill Walsh from the San Francisco 49ers and Bill Parcells from the New York Giants have proudly watched dozens of their assistant coaches promoted to head coaching jobs. The "coaching trees" of prominent head coaches is the pipeline for advancement up the NFL coaching ranks. Unless and until black assistant coaches find a way into that inner sanctum of top head coaches' staffs, they will remain largely on the outside looking in.

The same is true for general managers within the league. If general managers fail to hire black assistants, the pool of applicants that owners will consider for promotion will be tiny. Later in this book, I discuss my work on the NFL's diversity initiative to increase the number of black coaches and front-office personnel at the league office and club levels. But what is still missing is an effective mentoring program that identifies, educates, and supports young minority candidates for these positions. Only with mentoring will the league become truly diverse. This means not just networking but linking young minority coaches and front-office people to experienced, successful mentors within the league. That will spur real change.

Chan and I made a joint call to Gavin, who was excited to learn of Chan's quick acceptance. Gavin and the family would a day later conduct a perfunctory "interview" with Gailey, but the job was already his. On December 21, we held a press conference in Birmingham, introducing Gailey as our new head coach. There was no need for any interruption from the cameramen when making his announcement. In the South, having someone with local ties is about as good as it gets. Chan also spoke with a heavy southern drawl and local jargon like "might could" and "fixing to." The good old boys loved him.

After the press conference, I flew with Chan to Seattle for their last two games, as he was still working for the Broncos. We flew coach class because we didn't quite have the same first-class budget I had been accustomed to working for the NFL Management Council. This was a start-up league, and every penny mattered. I adjusted my lifestyle to the realities of this new league, which in part meant being seated in the back of the airplane.

The long flight afforded us the opportunity to start carving out a calendar to schedule the hiring of assistant coaches and a litany of other pressing matters. We worked nonstop for five straight hours in those uncomfortable seats. I wondered how Chan would be able to switch gears so effortlessly and call plays for the Broncos game the next day against the Seahawks. I felt bad that the Broncos ultimately lost that game 17–12. However, they won their final game the next week against the equally struggling Green Bay Packers, 22–13. I wanted Chan to leave on a positive note, although I hadn't done so in either of my jobs—with the players or the owners.

I had left my two previous jobs without much concern for the optics or the final impressions I left. No, I did not purposely walk out the door as if waving my middle finger in the air, but my focus was forward-looking, toward the new opportunity. I never wanted to burn bridges, but I felt I was going it alone and had no thoughts of looking back. There was no safety net to pull me back. No second chances.

Now things were different. I hired Chan away from an existing position with an NFL team. I was not violating the

NFL's tampering rules, as I had the prior permission of the GM and the head coach. Still, I didn't want my recruitment of Chan to lead to any diminished attention toward finishing his coaching duties, which would be attributed to me.

Chan and I assembled a coaching staff and began the long hours of preparing for the upcoming player draft, which was to be held in mid-February 1991. Working almost ninety hours per week, we reviewed videotape of players, made calls, and assessed every player eligible for the draft. The highlight of that work was the selection of Brent Pease, who had previously been the third-string quarterback behind the legendary Warren Moon of the Houston Oilers. In Birmingham, we held a contest and selected "Fire" as the team nickname. I always chuckled at how the local fans called us the "Fur."

Opening night was March 23 at Legion Field against the Montreal Machine. Black fans in the community took unusual interest in our new league and frequently approached me about their sense of pride in having a black general manager. "It means a lot to this community, Mr. Hugie, that we have a black man in charge," one older black gentleman told me, slightly mispronouncing my difficult last name, which rhymes with *fugue*, as in Bach's Fugue in G Minor. Another fan came to our offices with his three young children and asked if they could just quickly shake my hand. I received stacks of letters with prayer wishes and other congratulatory messages. I also received a handful of letters that began with "nigger go home."

I was willing to work harder than any other GM to see

our success realized. I got to the office every day before sunrise and stayed each evening until late at night. I understood coaches' and players' mind-sets. I was aware of how to motivate them and how to apply both sugar and spice. I knew being present for every meeting, every meal, every long bus trip was important. Being all in was the recipe for success.

Having a black general manager was a unique experience for the black players as well. On a regular basis, black players would saunter up to my office and drop in just to have idle conversation, something they'd never do with a white GM in the NFL. One black defensive player knocked on my door and entered before I invited him in. "What's up?" I said in a welcoming tone. "Nothing, Boss, just wanted to see you in your spot." Taking a spin in my large leather chair, he said, "Damn, you gotta have your shit together for them to give you this gig." Then, without skipping a beat, he got up and walked out.

That did not happen in the NFL. Players understood not to cross the line when it came to management. Here in a developmental league, it was different. Players both black and white stopped by my office frequently to ask questions, get advice, or just hang out. At times, I had to politely ask them to leave so I could get work done. And although it was only a developmental league, many of these players were previously on NFL rosters but had never seen a black man in charge. The change in the office color scheme was an uplifting novelty to the black players, and they made it a point to let me know that. I also found it interesting that white players were fairly nonplussed by my hiring. I was the boss; that was fine with them, and so be it. I wasn't expecting anything different, but it was nevertheless encouraging.

We drew incredible fan interest, with more than fifty-three thousand fans attending our opening game night. We hired Jerry Lee Lewis to entertain at halftime with twenty pianos on the field playing his hit tune "Great Balls of Fire." Local "experts" had told us to anticipate a crowd less than half that size. But they came from every corner, and for many who were black, it was their first time at Legion Field. The crowd was so large that the game was delayed for more than twenty minutes to handle the flow of people into the stadium.

Unfortunately, we lost the game to the Montreal Machine by a lopsided score of 20–5, despite having the largest opening game attendance in the league. The Maloofs were shaken. Gavin approached me with a panicked look immediately after the game. "What happened?" he pleaded.

"We lost, Gavin," I said in a matter-of-fact tone. "The players are still learning the offense, and it's going to take some time," I added, trying to reassure him. "Chan is a good coach; just trust him!" It was only the first game, and I already sensed knee-jerk reactions from Gavin. He was never going to be patient about the results.

We bounced back the following week and beat the Sacramento Surge 17–10. Still, the Maloofs were uncertain about Chan and his play calling. "We are too predictable," Gavin told me following our first win. Gavin was relying too much on what was being written in the newspapers and said on sports talk radio. I tried to keep him supportive, but because I was essentially hired by the league and had hired the coach without his input, our relationship was tenuous. The Maloofs still seemed comfortable relying on my judgment but doubted Chan's coaching abilities.

We lost a few more games, and the fans became restless. "We only support winning teams here in Birmingham," was a constant refrain. I implored Gavin to resist listening to the pundits, but he couldn't. Fortunately, we made a strong final two-game push with wins that earned us a first-place divisional finish and a play-off berth. We lost 10–3 in the semifinal round of the play-offs to Barcelona at Legion Field to wrap the season at 5-6. The London Monarchs went on to win the World Bowl 21–0 against Barcelona in June before sixty-one thousand fans in Wembley Stadium.

Making the play-offs curtailed some of Gavin's anger. I remained confident in Chan because he had such great character and integrity. In my NFL experiences, I had observed that the key to building a winning team started and ended with excellent coaching. Players—even the great ones, to some degree—were fungible and interchangeable. This was evident also in the mind-set of the NFL owners during their disputes with the players. The owners believed the teams and the venues were the game and that players, while they generated fan interest, were essentially replaceable. That they could be injured at any moment meant they might need to be quickly replaced. This viewpoint ultimately was a control-of-the-game issue for the owners. It was the bedrock of their collective bargaining negotiation strategy.

I studied all of the NFL teams closely during my tenure at the Management Council. Representing the teams afforded me the opportunity to fully examine their underbellies and learn why some teams succeeded over the others. The common ingredient was not just good players; instead, it was superior and consistent coaching. Chan was my guy.

The coaching staff Chan put together was also strong, but pressures from the colleges to lure them away at much higher salaries was mounting. A week after the World Bowl ended, I met with Gavin and asked that he modestly increase the assistant coaches' salaries to thwart competitors who were making strong advances. Gavin, still a bit bitter about the outcome of our season, resisted. "Why do we have to pay them more when they didn't win?" he reasoned. "Because we are building something here, Gavin, and success takes time and patience," I responded. Gavin wouldn't budge. The only way we could be successful was to retain our staff, who were primed to depart for higher-paying jobs but agreed to stay for only slight increases.

If the Maloofs couldn't understand that rationale, then I concluded we had little to no chance of improving. I drafted a letter to Gavin and the Maloof family pleading my case for increasing the assistant coaches' salaries. I also let them know that I would not remain GM if they didn't support my recommendation. The first black GM in pro football, I was threatening to leave after one season. I wasn't trying to play poker, and I'm not sure if principle, arrogance, or not liking them very much caused me to be willing to move on if they shunned my request.

Gavin was noticeably bothered by the tone and approach of my letter, but he was willing to allow me to stay on as GM, provided I backed off this coaches' pay issue. I had purposely kept Chan out of the loop so as not to poison him against the Maloofs. I gave myself twenty-four hours to think things over and the following morning announced my resignation. I knew it was the right decision, even though I had no immediate plans for employment. I was following my rule: Don't be afraid to walk. It was a principle embedded in the souls of the players as well. "Play me or trade me" is often the motto expressed by players. "If you don't think I am good enough to play here, then someone else will." I was no different. If the Maloofs were not willing to support me under my terms, then I would find someone else who would. I didn't know exactly who that person or job was, but I was not afraid to take the leap to find out. Ultimately, that brash fearlessness was my greatest strength early in my career, just as it is on the field for many successful players.

I was fortunate that on each occasion I decided to walk, the result was a better opportunity and position. But when I walked, there was never a guarantee. I made those decisions fully prepared that I might have to take a step back before moving forward again. What these moves did for me, though, was give me absolute confidence, a belief in myself even among uncertain outcomes. It was not easy to jump, but once I took the leap—first from the players union, then from the NFL Management Council, now from the Birmingham Fire—that became my modus operandi.

CHAPTER 5

Coming Home

I contacted Commissioner Tagliabue, and he summoned me back to the league office to help oversee the WLAF. Mike Lynn had just resigned as president; and Joe Bailey, the chief operating officer and former Cowboys assistant general manager to Tex Schramm, had assumed Lynn's duties. Tagliabue wanted me to work directly with Bailey and Roger Goodell, who then was Tagliabue's right hand, and represent the league's interests. I packed up my belongings, and in less than two days I was back in New York working out of league headquarters. I had been gone a mere ten months.

The WLAF was hemorrhaging financially, having lost more than $7 million in its first season. The owners were reluctant to continue funding the league. No major player development success stories had manifested in the first season. Interest from European television companies was nonexistent. Many of the owners saw the European foray as a

Tagliabue pipe dream, and some were refusing to ante up for the second season.

Only six months prior to the kickoff of the second season did the NFL owners finally commit to fund the league. Things didn't get any better. After that second season, the WLAF suspended operations. Undeterred, Tagliabue announced that the WLAF would come back solely as an international product, which would subsequently be called NFL Europe, an all-European league with no teams in North America. In hindsight, the biggest stumbling block for the WLAF was that it had no true purpose.

Some of the NFL owners wanted a developmental league, and others merely wanted to block any potential competition to the NFL in Europe. The WLAF could not meaningfully do both, and as a consequence it eventually failed. Perhaps the best mission was as a true developmental league for players, coaches, and front-office personnel. The threat of a competitive and rival league sprouting up in Europe wasn't likely. It was a missed opportunity. Even today the NFL toys around with the concept of starting a developmental league.

Kim left her firm in DC where she was doing banking and regulatory law work to follow her mentor Timothy Ryan, who was appointed by President George H. W. Bush to head the Office of Thrift Supervision (OTS). OTS at the time was a division of the US Treasury assigned to cleaning up the mess created by the banks and the savings and loan industry. Ryan was widely criticized for his take-no-prisoners style of leadership against many of the faulty banks. Kim described him as a hard-nosed Irishman who took no crap. He sounded a lot like Jack Donlan.

Closer proximity and the separation of time had rekindled Kim's and my relationship, and I found myself most every other weekend on the shuttle from New York to DC. Maturity and a concentrated focus on my personal life allowed our relationship to grow. Kim was a woman who always had my back. She might disagree with me in private (as she was often prone to do), but in public she was there to support me. For the first time in my life, I finally let my guard down, revealed my vulnerabilities, and trusted someone fully and completely. This was the woman I wanted to marry. I realized I needed her support and that, frankly, I could not be successful going it alone. Kim knew me better than anyone, and I trusted her advice and opinions completely. She not only was my biggest supporter, she was also my most trusted counselor.

In my observation, personal relationships in the world of the NFL did not last very long. The nature of the business was such that players, coaches, and front-office personnel spent so much time away from home that it was difficult to keep relationships from fraying. Coaches were first married to their jobs. Front-office personnel were constantly in the hot seat and knew the job had to come first, even over family, in most cases. The players were mostly young and rich, with temptations not ideal for supportive marriages.

As they evolved as young men, many players had difficulties staying with a wife whose personal life was not advancing at the same pace as her husband's. Too often, the pressure was just too much for everyone. The constant blowouts where either coaches or players were at each other's throats bred a climate of high testosterone and physical violence. It was difficult for many to leave that negativity at work. It regrettably often spilled over into domestic violence, philandering, and neglect in family lives, and the results were damaging to all.

I went into marriage with Kim knowing full well that the odds weighed heavily toward difficult times ahead, but I was undaunted. I loved her. I needed her, and that was all that mattered to me.

On November 3, 1992, I proposed. I had a clandestine plan, first sending a limo to her DC office with only instructions from the chauffeur that she "leave work immediately and get in the car." Kim thought I was still in New York, as we had just spoken by telephone. (I had forwarded the office number to my cell phone and was actually already in DC.) An attorney, and perhaps more important a black woman, Kim wasn't guaranteed to cooperate. She told me later that she went along because if she were being kidnapped, at least she knew the abductors had money. That's my girl.

She was driven to the Morrison-Clark Historic Inn and Restaurant, a nineteenth-century Victorian mansion located a short distance from the Capitol Building and the White House. There she was offered champagne and a seat in a private waiting area. Minutes later she was ushered to a private table in the dining room in front of a fireplace where I was already seated. I suspect she knew what was coming at this point, though my purposeful demeanor suggested exactly the opposite. "Hey, babe, I am just in town on last-minute business and thought I would surprise you with a nice dinner."

Uncertain of my intentions and slightly puzzled, she asked, "Is the driver coming back? I left my briefcase in that limo." Dragging it out even longer, I waxed poetically about politics (as it was election night) and the prospects of Bill Clinton winning the presidential election. Kim excused herself abruptly to use the ladies' room.

Maybe I am taking the deception a bit too far, I thought to myself. While she excused herself, I gave the 1.4-carat slightly imperfect diamond ring (purchased with my entire life savings) to the head waiter. She returned to the table looking slightly frazzled. We finished a lovely dinner of duck and red wine and began to look over the dessert menu.

As we mused over the possible choices, the waiter arrived carrying a covered dish and said to Kim, "Compliments of the house." She lifted the cover off the plate, and there sat the ring box. I gracefully got down on one knee and asked her to marry me. It was perfect. Not because of the theatrics but because I had found the woman I loved, and I knew she loved me back. She said yes.

We spent the night in the honeymoon suite at the hotel eating chocolate strawberries and drinking champagne. We called our families and friends as the election results rolled in over the television. Clinton won, and we were engaged.

It was a great night. The limo took her back to her office the next morning, where a dozen roses were waiting at her desk, and I headed back to New York.

With the WLAF having suspended operations in the United States and being focused on owning and controlling the remaining teams in Europe, my job was to negotiate settlements with those owners and retain the league's intellectual property rights.

The Sacramento team was owned by Fred Anderson, who had made the bulk of his money in the lumber business. Fred decided to hold on to his team and move it into the Canadian Football League. He released the WLAF marks outright.

It was quite satisfying to contact the Maloofs and strong-arm them into turning over their ownership rights to the Birmingham team. We paid an amount that was fair but most likely not much more than it cost them originally to purchase the team from the NFL. Gavin didn't fight me on the transaction. Other owners followed suit, with Raj Bhathal, a swimwear magnate, turning over the rights to the Orlando franchise; and Larry Benson, owner of the San Antonio franchise (and brother of NFL New Orleans Saints owner Tom Benson), doing the same.

The only team the league didn't own outside the US was the Barcelona team that was franchised to Jose Figueras. Mr. Figueras lived in a castle in Barcelona and invited me to his home to negotiate the settlement. I was caught off guard by his hospitality, because I was told by other team executives that he had inquired about black players fitting

in with the Barcelona community and had even asked if
the team was "required to recruit black players" because
that would not go over well in Barcelona.

I arrived on a sun-filled October afternoon and stood
in awe at the front gates of his estate. Servants showed me
to my quarters, where refreshments of water, sliced apples,
and cheese were provided. I nibbled on a few snacks and
was soon told Mr. Figueras would see me in the study.

Mr. Figueras spoke Catalan, the native language in Barcelona, along with Spanish and broken English. It was easier at times for me to speak to him in Spanish, which I had
learned in school and from a bilingual father. Mr. Figueras,
as he preferred to be called, chatted briefly about the "bue-
nos tiempos" with the WLAF. Servants then announced
that dinner was prepared and just the two of us were seated
at a table that could easily have accommodated fifteen to
twenty people. We ate a light meal of pea soup and a white
fish. After dinner we drank red wine, moving to seats in the
living room in front of his massive fireplace. Mr. Figueras
was married, but his wife lived in a separate home in the
downtown area. I never inquired into the reasons. For most
of our time together, he just sat quietly and observed me.
To say it was awkward would be an understatement.

The next day I worked with local attorneys we had
hired to negotiate with Mr. Figueras's attorneys to settle
the dissolution of the team. All parties spoke in Spanish
(as a courtesy to me) throughout the three-hour meeting.
Ultimately, we agreed on a fair price and shook hands. Mr.
Figueras never participated in the discussions, and I didn't

get to see him again before heading back to New York. Less than a year later I heard he had died of unexplained causes, though he had been previously been in good health.

The last team to settle was the New York/New Jersey Knights. The owner was Robert F. X. Sillerman, a media and entertainment billionaire from New York. Bob and I got to know each other during my time with the Birmingham team and while working in the league office. He had a very strong personality, and most people found him not too easy to get along with. He invited me to his home in the Hamptons and graciously sent his helicopter to Manhattan to transport me.

I arrived on the helipad at his estate and noticed the four collectible cars, including a vintage Bentley convertible, in the expansive driveway. As I knocked on the door, Bob was just putting a robe on over his Speedo bathing attire. He had been lounging at the pool and, strangely, left the robe partially open, as if he wanted me to notice his fit-for-his-age physique. I just thought it was weird.

This was the precursor meeting where Bob was to inform me what the league would pay him. He walked me through his digs, and motion-sensor lights came on intermittently. It was my first experience with a smart home, and I played the role of being amazed during this tour of his wealth. But I was on to him; frankly, I was sizing him up. I had been in many situations where a counterpart had never squared off against a business rival who was black. For me, it was business as usual, and that always gave me an upper hand, the advantage.

Bob ultimately agreed to a follow-up meeting in New York at league headquarters, with his attorneys handling the negotiations. Every so often during that meeting, though, they excused themselves to make phone calls, which were obviously to Bob. There was no question he was pulling the strings. In the end, we agreed to pay a bit more than we wanted but still within the parameters the league had given for the settlement.

Bob, who had been impatiently waiting in a nearby area of the building, came into the room and we shook hands. "One more thing," Bob said to me. "Sure, Bob, what's that?" I asked, hoping he wasn't reopening the deal. "You guys are going to pay for my dinner tonight," he said with a straight face. "We'll [meaning Bob and his lawyer] be at the Quilted Giraffe," he told me. After a long pause I responded, "Sure that's fine, Bob."

The Quilted Giraffe was a four-star restaurant located in midtown just a few blocks from league headquarters. I waited in my office for three hours before Bob appeared with a receipt for $450. "Nice dinner," I said, a little perturbed. "You're lucky I like you. I went easy on the wine," he said. A few minutes later he signed the documents and the deal was done. It didn't bother me to let Bob have that petty, unimportant bit of victory. I was interested in the finish line, not the sideshow. It did teach me that those of his stature and wealth never fully lose in a deal.

Not much was left to be done now that the WLAF had disbanded and settlements with the franchise owners had been made and the league's intellectual property rights had been regained. I had an impending wedding in July, and I knew I needed to look for my next opportunity, one that would work for both Kim and me.

Our wedding was scheduled to be held in her hometown of Detroit. Kim wasn't a big fan of New York City, and I was somewhat eager to consider working for an NFL team. We considered Washington, but Charley Casserly, a former assistant to Bobby Beathard, had taken over as GM. I knew Beathard very well because he was one of Jack Donlan's closest friends among the senior executives who worked for the NFL teams. Beathard and I were friendly, and had he still been there I would have jumped at the opportunity, but I didn't feel the same amiability with Casserly. I asked Commissioner Tagliabue if he knew of any other opportunities among the teams. He mentioned that Russ Thomas, the longtime Detroit Lions GM, had recently retired, and his former assistant Chuck Schmidt, a finance guy, was assuming his role. "I think they are going to need someone with your football experience along with salary cap management," he offered.

"Detroit," I said aloud to myself. This was just too coincidental. Kim was raised in Detroit, and we both had attended the University of Michigan Law School. I wasn't keen on the weather, but I had managed to survive my three years of law school in nearby Ann Arbor. The Lions played in a domed stadium in Pontiac, a suburb about forty-five minutes north of Detroit. Because of the hours I needed to work, living in Detroit would not be feasible. Instead, we found a beautiful two-story brick home with an acre of land in Rochester Hills, just ten minutes east of the stadium and our offices. None of the players, coaches, or front-office personnel lived in Detroit proper. Everyone was nestled in somewhere closer by, like the suburbs of Auburn Hills or West Bloomfield.

I contacted Chuck Schmidt, whom I had met one time briefly during a grievance hearing in Detroit. He seemed excited on the phone and asked me to immediately meet with him at his offices inside the Pontiac Silverdome, about a forty-five-minute drive north of Detroit. The team was owned by the automotive scion Ford family, led by William Clay Ford Sr. Mr. Ford was the youngest of four children of Edsel Ford, his father, and grandson of Henry Ford, who started Ford Motor Company. William Clay attended undergraduate school at Yale University and captained both their tennis and soccer teams. I figured the Ivy League connection (I had attended Cornell University) might help build a rapport.

Upon my arrival at the team's offices, Chuck greeted me in the lobby and personally escorted me to his office. Chuck was a tall man who was very fit and dressed conservatively: no fancy watch, modestly priced clothes, and durable shoes. I knew he was paid well, so it was obvious that he chose to be practical in his spending. Normally an assistant would handle the duty of greeting me at the door, so it impressed me that Chuck did so himself. I asked about meeting with Mr. Ford, and he shrugged off the question, telling me the owner rarely appeared at the team offices. It was clear to me that Chuck would be making the hiring decision alone.

We chatted briefly about my role with the World League and at the Management Council. "I heard very positive things from almost everyone I talked to about you," he said. "Almost," I repeated jokingly, knowing I had passed the initial screening test most common in the NFL. Someone always has to vouch for you. In my case, that meant someone white.

Chuck mentioned that he had played baseball in college and that he knew I had played both baseball and football at Cornell. "What school did you play at?" I asked. He paused briefly—signaling that I should have known—and then replied, "The University of Michigan." Oops, I hadn't done my homework. "A Michigan man," I said with pride, hoping to partially cover my tracks. Our shared alma mater worked to my benefit.

Every opportunity in the NFL hinged on connections. Whom you worked with, where you went to college. These were the key factors for access. Without them, you remained on the outside looking in. First, it was my connection at Cornell that got me to Buck Briggs and the NFL Players Association. Then an off-chance meeting with Jack Donlan in the copy room with résumé in hand got me to the Management Council. Being low man on the totem pole and having to handle the plethora of injury grievances that the Minnesota Vikings had filed against them got me to Mike Lynn and the World League. Now it was the University of Michigan connection that was guiding me to the Lions.

But therein lies the rub for diversity in the NFL. I had attended predominantly white universities and was trained within their network. The vast majority of African Americans, however, are not privy to this network. Many are educated at historical black colleges and universities, which, while great centers for learning, are not interwoven into the NFL network stream. This is in part why so many white executives at the NFL will say they would love to consider hiring more minorities, but they simply don't know any. The network is systematic and works against blacks in particular, who frequently attend schools and participate in organizations outside the NFL's built-in network.

Chuck mentioned that Russ Thomas, their former GM, had a poor relationship with the players. The NFL had by then suffered several defeats under antitrust law challenges from the players in the federal courts and through givebacks in collective bargaining negotiations. The owners had reluctantly agreed to a modified form of free agency for the players, so teams now placed a greater emphasis on their ability to recruit free agent players. After five years of service, players could now choose the teams they wanted to play for rather than being restricted in their movements by the owners. For the first time, players could select the teams they wanted to sign with. Building relationships with players as opposed to having unfettered control over their rights was the new norm for the NFL.

Chuck was a finance guy, but he wanted me to manage the salary cap and negotiate all of the players' contracts. I could tell that in addition to my legal skills and prior experience as a GM in the World League, Chuck thought my race would be among my biggest assets. Having a black man in the front office would surely assuage any residue of player resentment toward the former general manager. My title was senior vice president of football operations, as well as general counsel. I accepted the position and called Kim to tell her we were moving to Michigan. She was happy to be coming home. Once again, the stars were in alignment for me.

I started in December 1992, just after the team finished a sobering 5-11 season following the prior year's astonishing 12-4 record (a first since 1970). The NFL mantra, though, is all about "what have you done for me lately," and there was a palpable sense of anxiety around the office. The team put me up in a Hawthorn Suites hotel directly across from their offices. I parked my car outside in the open-air lot each evening and found it remarkable that every morning for thirty straight days I had to scrape snow off the windshield in frigid temperatures. I was undaunted, however; at thirty-one, I was determined to make a significant impact on the club.

Wayne Fontes was the head coach. Fontes was a robust, colorful man of Portuguese decent who had played briefly in the NFL as a defensive back in the early 1960s. A Michigan State graduate, Fontes worked as an assistant coach in the NFL for thirteen seasons before gaining the head job with the Lions midway through the 1988 schedule. The star player on the Lions was unquestionably Barry Sanders, a prolific running back whose explosive speed and agility made each carry of the ball a highlight-reel tape. Fontes, partially because of his ethnic background and mostly because of his own unique personality, was well liked by the black players. I felt at the first handshake that he was very comfortable with me.

In addition to overseeing the salary cap and negotiating player contracts, I was second in command to Chuck Schmidt, which meant oversight of the other departments in the organization: marketing, ticket sales, administration, finance, community relations, and public relations. Most of the managers in those departments, as well as their support staff, had worked there for more than a decade. Despite the frequent changeover on the coaching and personnel side of the football operations, the front-office staff remained relatively intact over the years.

The staff had also remained exclusively white, save two administrative "helpers." Otis Canty was the Tonto to Coach Fontes's Lone Ranger. Otis served as a chauffeur to Mr. Ford in his early years with the organization and then morphed into a role as assistant to the head coach in his later years. It was in my view a gofer position intended for a young man, but Otis held that role late into his senior years. It seemed to me that Otis had learned to survive in the Lions organization by kowtowing to everyone's needs. That likely made him appreciated but certainly not respected. Otis was always friendly toward me, but he never let down his guard. We made small talk, but nothing substantive. I wasn't sure if he didn't trust me or he wouldn't allow himself to confide in another black man.

I was a black man who had grown up in a generation where we could speak our mind; Otis was one who presumably had no other choice but to hold his tongue all of those "yes sir" years. He had spent too long in that role to suddenly start speaking openly and freely to me. I understood and put no pressure on him to act differently. It infuriated me, though, that he appeared to want to placate everyone to maintain his job in the organization. I felt that Otis played the subservient role that is so readily accepted by many white people. He called everyone "Boss" and imposed no threat to anyone. That was not behavior I believed in. It spoke to me of the "yah sir" days of slavery.

The only other African American in the organization was Mai Sellers, a strong-minded woman in her late forties. Her title was office assistant, but she was in essence the office janitor. She cleaned up the offices, sorted the mail, and set up any internal lunches or parties that were held for staff in the offices. Mai was prideful, though, and didn't play a Jim Crow role. She forced no big grin onto her face when tasked with a responsibility; she just did the work and moved on. I could sense her observing me, though we rarely spoke my first few weeks. The remainder of the staff, about thirty-five whites, now reported to me.

My primary focus was to get the football team back on track with a winning record. Still, I could not overlook the lack of diversity in the front office. Chuck had acknowledged to me during our interview that Russ Thomas, the former GM, had a poor relationship with the "players." But what he really meant to say was the *black* players. I knew from my time in Birmingham that a team made up of primarily black players needed to see some diversity in the front office to truly trust the organization.

We couldn't win games unless the players believed in the organization, and our players, I presumed, had very little trust in the organization. The owners' not trusting a black man to have an influential role in the organization indicated to the players that the front office saw blacks as nothing more than performers on the playing field. Players thus grew to distrust and steer clear of management when possible. Lack of diversity in the front office created a chasm between management and players.

Perhaps issues like player protests and kneeling would be averted if there were more dialogue between black players and senior executives within the NFL teams. There would undoubtedly be more dialogue were there more blacks in front offices. This potential for dialogue is lost on the majority of NFL teams.

We held weekly senior staff meetings, and while the staff was cordial, I could sense the distance they kept from me. I was the unknown, and until they got a better read, they would stay bunkered in their respective silos. Often the response to questions was a curt "We have always done it this way." If the culture of losing that had set in was going to change, we had to find another way to conduct business rather than business as usual. Change is always difficult to accomplish in an organization; it is ten times more difficult when the staff is all white and the new manager is black.

Having been in leadership roles for a good part of my life where I was among the only blacks, I was much more accustomed to these workplace racial dynamics then they were. By working longer hours, being more prepared, and making them stay on my pace, the process of change would begin. They would either fit in or get fired. I was comfortable with either scenario, but it was surely going to be uncomfortable for them. I didn't have to spend a lot of time thinking about how they related to me as a black man. I let my work ethic and the expectations I set for them govern our relationship. The rest was left up to them to figure out.

Fortunately, Kim made regular trips to Detroit to begin looking for a house and plan our wedding. I could afford to take off only one week before the start of training camp in July, so the wedding was planned over the Fourth to maximize our time.

That was how life was in the NFL. You scheduled everything of a personal nature around the football schedule. Between training camp in July and the end of the season in January, there were no days off. When the season ended in January, the staff immediately began scouting college players for the April draft. We also spent January through April restocking our rosters with free agents and other veteran players. The month of May was typically the time players reported back for organized on-field practices and weight training that ended in late June. That left about two weeks open in July for vacation. That was also the busiest time for me to get the draft choices we'd selected in April signed to contracts before the start of camp. Kim didn't like the hours I was working, but she knew the schedule and tolerated it.

Most nights I worked long after everyone in the administrative staff had gone home. Mai would routinely come by my office around 7:00 p.m. and clean out my wastebasket. I would see her periodically throughout the normal business hours, but I was always too preoccupied to stop and engage her in a conversation. One evening, Mai came into my office and looked me straight in the eyes. "You know these folks are going to have a hard time adjusting to working for you. They don't feel comfortable working for a black man," she said.

I sat motionless as she continued, a smile on her face: "Just watch yourself and know I am praying for your success."

In my normal nonwhispering voice, I replied, "Mai, these people *are* going to have to adjust to me. I appreciate your support. I didn't come here to fail. But just for the heck of it, I would appreciate it if you would keep praying."

Mai laughed loudly and then went back to work.

Each day after that Mai offered a comment in support of my mission. She became my eyes and ears within the organization. She had a wealth of knowledge of the inner workings of the office. She recommended that we send a group package of Federal Express items to the league office each day, as opposed to the four or five separate packages each department was sending, which yielded substantial savings. She suggested we limit the amount of free drinks we stocked in the lobby area, as the assistant coaches were basically taking them home for personal consumption. She advised me that most of our staff travel was booked last-minute with the travel agency rather than meeting advance-purchase deadlines that would result in reduced airfares. Mai was saving the organization tens of thousands of dollars.

I rewarded Mai for her good work with a promotion to office manager. While the rest of the support staff did not have to report directly to Mai, she had more authority than they did. And I raised her salary commensurate with the position. Suddenly, Mai rose from wearing an apron to work each day to sporting fashionable office manager business attire. She not only looked the part, she deserved it. It also gave her direct access to me, which immediately changed the office dynamics and how the rest of the staff interacted with her. No longer was she inconsequential. My promotion of Mai sent a message to the rest of the staff and made the network system work to the advantage of my people for once. Step 1—check.

I began interviewing candidates for the position of director of player programs. Chuck had recommended a few former Lions players but left the hiring decision mostly up to me. I knew from the start that I wanted a black person for the job. The position was designed to build a bridge between the players and the front office, to be a liaison the players could trust. The racial complexity of our team, like most NFL teams, was about 75–80 percent black. The relationship between the players and the front office was already strained, and I believed the players would view a former white player in that role as a spy for management. They needed someone they could trust.

Ultimately, we agreed on Larry Lee, a former Miami Dolphins offensive lineman who had done some work in scouting and had front-office aspirations. Offensive linemen were always among the most intelligent players on any team's roster, and Larry was no exception. He was big, confident, and black. In a very short time frame, the Lions organization was adding some much-needed color. Step 2—check.

Larry and I spent a majority of our office time together. We enjoyed each other's company. While Mai was my office liaison, Larry kept me abreast of all the subtle issues confronting the players. Typically, players never let management see their vulnerabilities. You might have a player on your roster for four years and never really know anything about his personal habits, only what he wants you to see.

Players are taught at a young age by other players not to cozy up to coaches and managers with their personal issues: "You keep your shit to yourself." I learned from my own experiences as an athlete growing up in Connecticut that other athletes could sniff out bullshit a mile away. As we front-office staff and execs passed by players in the hallways, we got a lot of "yes sirs" and "no sirs" and nothing more. Larry was able to genuinely relate to the players because he truly cared about them. More important, he wasn't being asked to spy on them.

If you pandered to players, the smell of it reeked in the air. It was a stench that athletes were attuned to because someone was always trying to take advantage of them. Larry was no sellout and easily passed their sniff test.

Wayne Fontes recognized the benefits the players would gain from having a black voice within the top ranks of the organization. Technically, I reported to Chuck, while

Wayne and I held lateral positions within the organization, yet Wayne invited me to attend every practice and sit in on the coaches' meetings. At practice, I would occasionally send in hand signals from the sideline with Dan Henning, our offensive coordinator, indicating the offensive plays to the quarterbacks. Wayne often exaggerated my role by openly referring to me as "Boss" in front of the players. "Guys, here's the new boss man Chuck hired to run the team," was the way he first introduced me to the squad.

Wayne and I never addressed the exaggeration of my role that he used with the players. I fully gathered that Wayne knew the culture of black players enough to know that if they perceived his boss and the top man to be a black man, they would be pleased and more invested in the organization as a whole. This was particularly true when the former head guy, who was white and had been distant from the players, was being replaced by a black man. It would give confidence to the players that the organization understood the importance of diversity and in particular black player issues.

More important, we knew our primary and mutual goal, the endgame, was to win by building a cohesive team. Breaking race divisions was an integral part of that. I ate lunch every day with players and quickly bonded with many.

We had three players competing for the starting QB job: Rodney Peete, Andre Ware, and Erik Kramer. I spent a large amount of time with each of them, getting to know their competitive spirit firsthand. On any football team, the quarterback is typically the leader, and I wanted to be certain who that was on our team.

Peete, a black man, had played his collegiate football at the University of Southern California. Peete was the starter and had the most overall talent of the three. Ware, also black, was a tall and strong-armed quarterback who had played at the University of Houston, shattering all their records and winning the Heisman Trophy in 1989 as the most outstanding college player. The Lions drafted him in the first round (the seventh overall pick) with the hope that Ware would become their franchise quarterback. Unfortunately, in his transition to the pros, Ware didn't enjoy the success he'd had at the collegiate level. Some refer to it as the curse of the Heisman, which befell many former Heisman-winning quarterbacks who didn't pan out in the NFL. Kramer, a white cerebral player, and I often practiced speaking Spanish over lunch.

Barry Sanders was the team's star running back. His athleticism defied the laws of physics. He could start and stop on a dime in ways that made defensive players fearful of breaking an ankle just trying to tackle him. He was among the league's most talented and recognizable players and was single-handedly the key to our offense. Barry played college ball at Oklahoma State University, though he was raised in Wichita, Kansas. In his junior year of college Barry broke almost every rushing and all-purpose yards record and won the Heisman Trophy, even though he stood only five foot eight and weighed two hundred pounds. In 1989 he forfeited his senior year to enter the

NFL Draft early and was selected by the Lions as the third pick in the first round.

Barry's contract was up for renewal my first year in the organization. I checked with Chuck to see if he wanted to participate in the negotiations, as Barry was the team's franchise player. "No, you handle it," he said without hesitation.

Mr. Ford just happened to be in the office that day, so I quickly ran down to the locker room and asked Barry to come with me to visit the owner. Barry seemed nonchalant about the meeting; wearing team-issued shorts and a Lions T-shirt, he walked with me into the executive offices. I asked Barry to wait outside as I walked in alone to see Mr. Ford, who was smoking a cigarette at his large empty desk. I politely interrupted him and said, "Mr. Ford, we are redoing Barry's contract, and I just wanted to bring him in to visit with you briefly to reassure him that we will treat him as fairly and respectfully as he deserves."

Mr. Ford squinted his eyes as he looked at me equivocally and motioned his hand to indicate permission. I called Barry in, and he and I sat opposite Mr. Ford as he continued to smoke. Barry greeted Mr. Ford and stood to shake his hand. "I just wanted to bring Barry in to visit briefly, Mr. Ford, because we are about to start discussions on a new contract," I said to start the conversation.

"It's good to see you, Barry," Mr. Ford offered sincerely. "Yes, we will get your deal done, so don't you worry one minute," he continued, as if he were instructing me in addition to speaking with Barry.

"I know you will be fair, Mr. Ford," Barry responded.

Mr. Ford stood up and shook his hand a second time and the meeting was over.

This was a little awkward, I thought to myself, but I rose out of my chair and walked with Barry back down to the locker room.

"He's a pretty good guy," Barry said, almost as if he were saying it as a question.

"Yes, he is a good man," I replied

"That's the first time I've ever had a meeting with him in his office," Barry said, as if impressed with the occasion.

"Really?" I said in disbelief.

"Yep, first time," he continued as he began changing into his practice uniform.

Barry was entering his fourth season with the Lions. He had already established himself as a future Hall of Famer, and yet this was his first time meeting with the owner! It seemed unfathomable to me that Mr. Ford had never gotten to know Barry on a more personal level off the field.

I then understood the disconnect between the players and the front office. If Barry Sanders couldn't earn the respect of the owner, there simply wasn't any respect to be given out.

I've noted that the kneeling NFL players in 2017 felt disrespected. Instances like this are the reason I know how they feel. Paying the players big salaries is one form of respect. How you treat them and the racial makeup of the team's coaching staff and front office are other compelling displays of respect.

Barry was represented by two separate agents: Lamont

Smith, who had established a prior relationship with Barry's father during his college recruiting days; and David Ware, whom Barry had developed his own bond with. Both men were experienced and highly successful African American sports attorneys. They represented a surge of new black attorneys who had begun to enter the sports and entertainment field, which gave black athletes and entertainers the opportunity to be represented by individuals who looked like them.

Lamont was not quite as buttoned down as David with his Ivy League demeanor, but he was equally as bright. I scheduled the first meeting at our Pontiac offices. We had begun the initial meeting exchanging customary pleasantries when suddenly Lamont interrupted and asked, "Where is Chuck Schmidt?"

"Chuck turned over the contract duties to me," I explained. "I will be handling the negotiations."

A frown came over Lamont's face, and he audibly muttered, "Great, we got the B-team."

I let the comment go and assured Lamont: "Barry is the top priority for the club, and I do not anticipate any problems reaching a fair deal." I told them both that I wanted to keep our discussions out of the media so as not to contaminate the process with outside factors.

David concurred immediately. Lamont seemed disinterested in continuing our discussions, merely nodding his head. It was too early to discuss numbers, so I asked that we reconvene in a week to present initial proposals.

As they gathered their personal effects, I asked David

if he could remain behind for a brief minute. Lamont was eager to leave, so he hurried himself out of the room.

David spoke first, telling me that he was "comfortable with the process" and that he was concerned only about getting a fair deal for Barry. It was abundantly clear, after only one meeting, that David was the good cop and Lamont the bad, even if not intentionally.

That evening, not even eight hours after our meeting, one of the regular NFL sports beat writers penned an online story that read "Discussions under way between the Lions and Barry Sanders; team using a rookie executive to negotiate the deal." The article had Lamont's fingerprints all over it.

Indignant, I fired off an e-mail to both Lamont and David, indicating that "leaking information to a writer was a direct violation of the terms I set out for our discussions." I figured Lamont would go ballistic when I added accordingly, "I am removing Lamont from our next meeting until such time as he can abide by my directives."

I had to establish control of the negotiations and make clear my authority. I knew David and Lamont were joined as partners, not by mutual consent but rather by circumstance. David, I suspected, would quietly enjoy my admonishing of Lamont. I planned to use their good cop / bad cop roles to my advantage.

As expected, Lamont responded with a lengthy diatribe via e-mail, dressing me down and threatening to go directly to Barry. He even suggested filing an unfair labor charge against me with the NFL Players Association for not bargaining in good faith. The letter was clearly hastily written, with grammatical errors and typos that he would not normally have made.

Seizing an opportunity, I circled the mistakes in red ink and attached it to an e-mail reply to Lamont further reiterating my position and requesting that he take more time when drafting responses, as his e-mail was replete with errors. I copied Barry on the e-mails and placed copies on his locker where he could not miss seeing them. David remained silent throughout.

Barry approached me the next day, turned his head to the side, and smiled, indicating he was enjoying the banter between Lamont and me. It was risky sending that e-mail, and it could have easily backfired. Both David and Lamont could have ganged up on me, gone to the media, and made me out to be unprofessional and petty. In hindsight, I admit I went overboard, but when I am in a fight, I don't punch with pillows. I hit hard. "Fuck 'em and make it retroactive," to again quote Jack Donlan from the NFL Management Council.

David and I met separately and made some good progress. A week or so later I invited Lamont to participate in the follow-up discussions. His demeanor was much more congenial.

It was not lost on me that here we were, negotiating a contract for perhaps the greatest running back in the history of the game, and we were all African Americans. Why, then, did we have to bicker with a "crabs in a bucket" mentality, pulling one another and the group as a whole down in petty fighting? It was as if there were an unwritten rule that there could be only one black man at the top, so everyone fought for that spot rather than supporting one another.

Some refer to this as the HNIC (head nigger in charge). *Is that the dynamic going on here?* I asked myself. Being a black working with other blacks generally served my interests well, particularly in NFL-related matters where we front-office blacks were such a small minority. Was this fight with Lamont strictly a business violation of the terms of our negotiation, or was there a crab smell to it? That both agents were black did not alter the situation. They were the competition, and that was all I let matter to me.

Several weeks later we reached an agreement and decided we would hold the story until the press conference the following morning. Just a few hours later, though, the story broke over several media outlets with quotes from Lamont on how he'd secured the "highest salary for a running back in the history of the game." Touché, Lamont! I was happy to have the deal done.

Barry and I grew closer through the process and respected each other a great deal. Months later Lamont and I also buried the hatchet and found common ground. More players approached me on a regular basis, often just asking for advice on personal matters. I guess I passed the sniff test and they trusted me. That was an important next step for change in the Lions' front office. Step 3—check.

Shortly after inking Barry's contract, I found myself negotiating what would likely be the last contract extension for Lomas Brown, our All-Pro left tackle who was already thirty years old. Lomas hailed from Miami, Florida, but he had a country boy's natural strength. A stout black man standing six-four and weighing nearly three hundred pounds, Lomas was the senior statesman of the team, an unofficial team captain. Lomas spoke softly for his size but always with purpose. He also had two agents, both white attorneys from the same firm.

We were in the final stages of negotiations and no longer making progress. It seemed likely to me that we were headed toward an impasse. I told both agents that we were essentially deadlocked and that my authority to move any further was exhausted, which was the truth. I might have been able to squeeze out a slight bit of wiggle room but nothing substantial.

Lomas was also seated in the team conference room during the negotiations, which was somewhat unusual. His agents perhaps presumed his imposing presence might chill my temperament and give them the advantage of intimidation. Instead, it allowed me to demonstrate my command of the process, something I hoped Lomas might notice.

His agents began packing up their briefcases as if to say, "No deal"—something none of us wanted. They motioned to Lomas to leave with them, but instead he sat still. After a brief moment, he said, "You guys wait outside the room. I want to speak with Michael privately."

I quickly interjected: "Lomas, they are your representatives, and they really should be present during any negotiations. It's actually unethical for me to initiate a discussion with you independent of them."

Lomas collected his thoughts and said, "Well, you didn't initiate this request, I did."

He's one clever son of a bitch, I thought to myself.

Looking disturbed, his agents reluctantly walked outside the conference room. Once the door closed, Lomas looked me dead in the eyes and said, "Now you tell me, Michael. Should I take the deal you are offering?"

"Lomas," I began, "you know I work for the club. You have hired lawyers to advise you on whether or not you should take the deal. It's not appropriate for me to say."

"Yes, I know all of that," he said. "I trust you. If you say I should take the deal, I will take the deal."

Not sure what to say, I decided to just go with the truth: "Lomas, what you have on the table is essentially the best we can do. If I were advising you, I would tell you to take the deal."

Lomas must have sensed as much, because a big smile came over his face. He stood, towering over me, and reached out his massive hand to shake. "We have a deal," he said.

I was pleased, but I also knew his agents would be furious. "Lomas, your agents are going to be pissed off, and I may well have violated some ethical rules in speaking to you like this," I said.

"Don't worry about them. Remember, they work for *me*," he said wryly, smiling again.

It was inspirational to me that one promotion could start an avalanche of change within an organization. When I promoted Mai Sellers, her all-white peers were forced to change the way they treated her. Albeit reluctantly, they related to a black woman on equal footing. My senior staff learned to move out of their comfort zones and accepted working for a black man, something they might never have previously envisioned. Larry Lee, our new player programs director, was the spark that allowed the players to see change and build trust with the front office.

Our head coach, Wayne Fontes, understood how impactful it would be to his players (both black and white) to see a man of color in one of the highest positions of Lions authority, and, while he was my peer, he embellished that impact by assuming a subordinate role in front of them. Black lawyers representing Barry Sanders put aside, after some sparring, the crabs-in-the-bucket mentality to find common ground and mutual respect. Lomas Brown was willing to accept the word of the team's contract negotiator over his own hired guns to determine whether or not to accept a new contract.

Diversity was the tool that brought about change within this organization. In one short season, we had changed the culture and the character of that organization for the better. The final step—check.

I ended up staying only one and a half seasons with the Lions; the team jumped off to a quick 7-2 start before ultimately finishing the year at 10-6 and earning a play-off berth after winning the NFC Central Division. The Lions have not replicated that divisional championship again to date since that special 1993 season.

CHAPTER 6

Expanding the Field

I first heard there was such a position as commissioner of the NFL when I was a ten-year-old kid watching the NFL on television and learned that then commissioner Pete Rozelle had been the general manager of the LA Rams prior to being selected as commissioner. I loved playing Pop Warner football at the time, but I had decided on the spot that one day I would become commissioner of the NFL—after first becoming a general manager. What an absurd aspiration for a black kid from Connecticut with no exposure to or connections with the professional sports industry!

My family was middle-class, but our ambitions ran high. Leading the charge was my father, who left his own parents' home at age fifteen and essentially raised himself, acquiring his formal education later in life. He met my mom in the inner-city neighborhood of Hartford where they both grew up. Neither of them had any basis upon which to foresee a future where they could raise a family in a much more affluent lifestyle and enable their children to attend some of the most prestigious colleges and universities in the country.

They made it happen, but the toll of raising three highly driven kids while still catering to their own relationship proved too demanding. Looking back, I understand that the foundation of our family was so focused on accomplishment that we forgot to build the basic fundamentals of love and support. Our household engaged a crack-the-whip mentality to garner results, which even in horse racing isn't always the best strategy. We needed more sugar cubes along the way. I was spared much of the emotional baggage, as my two older siblings, a brother and a sister, suffered the brunt of my parents' constant demands of finishing first. The result was a win-at-all-costs burden on them.

As the youngest, I was a third wheel and not the central focus of their edicts. Still, I felt somewhat neglected, not being forced to bring home perfect grades and other honors. Perhaps my family experience enabled me to understand the stories of many NFL players. Although my father worked hard every day to provide the comforts of life for our family, and he loved me very much, he was not the person who served as my primary mentor during my early childhood. Much of that came from various coaches I had in junior sports.

I loved my father, but I learned many of my life lessons from surrogate dads, which has been the experience of many of the black NFL players I have come to know over the years.

In 1961, I became the youngest of three, stairsteps, with a sister and a brother each older by one year. My parents were determined to live, even if vicariously through their children, the American dream they felt was denied them. That dream was predicated on their philosophy that "anything white people can do, we can do." My brother and sister were under the persistent watch of my dad to become overachievers.

Later in life I understood how my birth order proved to be my saving grace. Instead of being fed a constant dose of "You have to perform twice as good as whites," I was left to dream and imagine my own future at my own pace. My less-than-stellar report cards were not heavily scrutinized, and there was much less pressure to excel, a blessing in disguise because my parents were emotionally unprepared to provide the sugar-and-spice approach to raising prodigies.

Neither of my parents had quite come to grips with their own unresolved childhood shortcomings. Both my brother and sister resisted, buckled, and as young adults gradually fell from their Ivy League perches to employment opportunities down the road that were less representative of their lofty skills and abilities. I, the odd man out, was largely unaffected.

We spent the first six years of my life living in a rough, predominantly black section of Hartford. Crime was rampant, and the public school system was among the worst in the state. When my dad realized I could barely read at a first-grade level, though I was receiving solid As on my report card, we moved to Windsor, an almost exclusively white suburb of twenty thousand people.

Growing up in Windsor was challenging. For the first time, I confronted racism. I found myself regularly in fights provoked by white boys. I didn't have much of a choice but to fight back, and it came naturally to me. When the odds were stacked against me, I found creative ways to level the playing field.

Once one of the main bullies announced during second-grade recess that he was going to beat me up after school. He was a fat redheaded kid named Steven that nobody liked, so he played the bully role to get attention. The other kids seemed interested in watching me get beat up, so I anticipated an audience. I was already on probation with the principal for earlier altercations, so I told the kids I would fight Steven at my bus stop—off school property. That reduced the number of kids who would witness my beat-down, and it put me on my home turf. Steven was enjoying the buildup and ego boost, so he readily agreed.

We rode the bus home, and as we got off at my stop, Steven was slow to gather his belongings. That was my opportunity; I turned and ran as fast as I could toward my house. Steven, sloppy and out of shape, opted not to bother and got back on the bus.

It hadn't shamed me that I ran. I had been in plenty of fights, and I hadn't feared losing. I smartly avoided the likely outcome of an unwinnable situation—getting suspended. I also realized, for the first time, that I was a damn fast runner.

A few months later, one of the boys, a Jewish kid named Wayne Dobrutsky, asked me if I was going out for the Little

League baseball team. I had never played any organized sports in Hartford, but I assured him that I was. His dad agreed to pick me up and actually signed the permission slip for me to try out. My dad was running for city council, and that, in addition to his job as an executive with the insurance company Cigna, occupied the majority of his time.

I wore jeans and a T-shirt, but I didn't have a glove or a baseball cap. Wayne loaned me one of his hats, which fit my Afro like a beanie. The coach, an older white man named Jim Blanchard, asked me if I had ever played baseball. "Oh, sure I've played baseball," I lied. Mr. Blanchard paused at my reply and told me to go to the outfield to catch some fly balls with the other kids. As I started to run toward the line of kids, he stopped me. "You're gonna need this," he said, and with a worried look on his face, he handed me a glove.

I watched intently as the other boys circled under the fly balls before catching them with what looked like both hands fully extended over their heads. I put on the baseball mitt and waited my turn. "Okay, 'Huey,' your turn!" Coach Blanchard yelled, trying to pronounce my last name. I chose not to correct him, and suddenly the nickname was born that I carried throughout the rest of my childhood. I was Mike Huey, or "Huey" for short.

As I approached the fly ball, instincts I didn't know I possessed took over and I reached up for the ball and caught it cleanly. Problem was, I caught the ball with my bare right hand, forgetting to use the glove on the opposite hand. I hadn't focused yet on the incredible sting that was radiating from the palm of my hand down my right arm until Coach Blanchard praised me: "Great catch, Huey. Don't forget to use your glove, though," he added, chuckling with the other dads who were assisting.

In a very short time, I was catching balls all over the outfield and developed enough skill to become one of the better hitters on the team. No longer was I getting in fights. Now I had teammates who actually treated me like a friend. I was hooked; I'd found an activity that I could excel at and avoid the antagonism of racism from the regular students, although the racist sentiments didn't go away. Racism was just put on hold. I was an athlete now, part of a somewhat protected class. When we finished the baseball season and took a team picture, you could identify me from a distance as the only dark face.

My parents still expressed little interest in my participation in sports, so Mr. Dobrutsky continued to drive me back and forth to practices and games. Wayne and I became good friends. And Big Al, Wayne's pop, became my surrogate sports father.

With each new season, I embraced the current sport—football, basketball, baseball, and even tennis. All that mattered to me was to be on a team. Competition and sports was my vehicle to establish a more level playing field among my all-white classmates. I still wasn't treated as an equal, but it was far better than the alternative, which was to be a black nobody: ignored, overlooked, called names. I didn't just want to fit in and be part of the norm; I wanted to lead. I am certain that without athletics I would not have had that ambition. Nor would I have developed the positive outlook on life that I have today. I likely would have been angry. Rather than striving to be a change agent in the sports industry, I probably would have distrusted the system.

As a top athlete, I gained not only self-esteem but a clearer focus. My childhood wasn't geared toward academics like my brother's and sister's; rather, I was "Huey the athlete." Even at an early age, I knew athletics would play a key role in my life and determine my career path.

Prejudice ran strong in the late 1960s, and many of the families in our neighborhood were openly racist. During Thanksgiving break, boys my age all gathered to play tackle football in an open field in the neighborhood. I was routinely invited to play with the other boys, but I had to remain outside when they went inside certain families' houses for hot chocolate and cookie breaks.

Some families wouldn't allow black people into their homes. I couldn't even come onto their property. I sat on the curb outside their houses until the other boys finished their cocoa and then went back to playing football. Not one of my friends ever chose to remain outside with me. Feeling guilty, some of my "closer" buddies would sneak a cookie or two for me on the way out. They'd offer it, crumbled up in a napkin from their pocket, but I never accepted. I was hungry, too, but I had no appetite for that bitter taste of racism.

We also had sleepovers where we camped out in one another's yards in tents. A teammate named Don Lareau and I were good friends. Whenever he wanted to sleep over, we had to put up a tent in my yard and one in close proximity to our property, so that the boys whose parents wouldn't let them stay in my yard could still join in by staying in the adjacent yard. Brian Beetle lived next door to us, and his more liberal family agreed to put up their tent. We danced around this racism game my entire childhood. The overt hatred and bigotry of these boys' families wasn't lost on me; I just found a way around it as best I could. I wondered if my white friends agreed with the way their families treated black people or whether they considered me an exception. I was too fearful of their answer to ever ask.

By the time I entered high school, I was recognized among the school's best athletes. I was also a top student, earning National Honor Society recognition. At the end of my junior year, I was selected by my school administrators to participate in a program sponsored by the American Legion named Boys State. It is a program intended to teach top academic students about the inner workings of government on the local and state levels. I was chosen with two other students from my high school. They told me five hundred boys across Connecticut would attend Boys State.

The weeklong event was held at the US Coast Guard Academy in New London, about an hour's drive from our house. I met boys from all across the state and participated in everything they had to offer. I was the editor of the daily newspaper, ran for office, played an instrumental role in getting a candidate elected to the position of governor, and played in the organized athletic games every day. One kid I hit it off with was Mike Okun. He was my height and weight with short curly hair. He lived in Wallingford, an upper-middle-class town about thirty-five minutes from Hartford. Mike was one of the best athletes at Boys State, and we teamed up together to win most of the contests. He was Jewish, just like my buddy Wayne Dobrutsky.

At the end of the week, the administrators asked each delegate to place votes for the kid who most exemplified the attributes of Boys State. It was called the Boys Stater Award. I voted for the boy we elected governor, who was from Simsbury, a wealthy suburb.

When they announced my name as the winner of the Boys Stater Award, I was in complete shock. I was even more surprised when all of the boys stood in applause as I accepted the award. The organizers of the program had selected me as one of two boys to represent our state at Boys Nation.

If there was an inspirational "aha" moment in my life, that was it. I was the first black boy in the state of Connecticut to be selected to attend Boys Nation, a program begun in 1946.

Unlike most of the other boys, neither of my parents were on hand to watch me win the awards. In fact, my dad was supposed to pick me up but at the last minute chose not to make the long drive. My mother, who was always there for me, was forced to pick me up, and by the time she arrived, all the other boys had left. I remained an hour or two alone on the steps of the auditorium waiting.

On the drive back, I casually mentioned that I'd been selected to attend Boys Nation. "That's nice," my mom said sincerely, but she was nonplussed and unaware of the award's significance to me.

A few minutes later she inquired: "It doesn't cost anything to attend, does it?"

I paused, choking back tears. "No, Mom, it doesn't," I said softly, and changed the subject. I knew she would have been very proud of me; she just was naturally preoccupied with her marital issues. As painful as it was, I understood.

A few weeks later I arrived in Washington, DC, as one of two delegates representing Connecticut at Boys Nation. We stayed on the campus of American University, my first time on a college campus. The weeklong program was designed to teach us the inner workings of the government on a national level, with each delegate serving as a "senator" from their respective states.

Although the formal program and team exercises were enlightening, I was more heavily immersed in developing friendships with the other boys. Kenyon Draughon, who was white, was one of the first boys I met. He was from Graceville, Florida, a small town located in the western portion of the state and very close to the Alabama state line. I presumed he was a redneck, but he nevertheless sought me out.

Ken knew at an early age that he wanted to be a preacher, and he held small group devotionals each evening. Short and slim, he didn't have the frame of an athlete, but he didn't come across as a nerd, either. To my surprise, I felt compelled to attend. I became completely immersed in the devotionals, connecting with others on a spiritual level for the first time in my life. Ken and our small group of boys talked about the promise we had as future leaders and the great responsibility that came with it.

This was the first time I'd allowed myself to trust someone other than myself. I sensed I was not alone in life and that perhaps there was a plan for my life designed by a force much greater than myself. How else could I explain the circumstances of my selection to this program? Most of these boys had achieved Eagle Scout status, were brilliant students in the classroom, were entrepreneurial, and came from privileged and affluent families. Almost all were white. I shared none of their backgrounds, but Ken made us all feel equal and humbled by the honors bestowed upon us.

I left Boys Nation with a renewed purpose to my life, filled with a tremendous sense of self-confidence and determination. I saw myself in a more mature and focused manner. I was unwilling to revert back to the status I'd held among my friends back in Windsor. I no longer felt apologetic or uncomfortable about my race. I had a sense of confidence that surpassed race. I believed I was capable of achieving anything, and race was no longer going to be a barrier for me. I knew I would always face racism, but I was determined to not let it defeat me. And I no longer felt the need to hide behind athletics to fit in.

I understood at the time that my life had been changed for the better by my Boys State and Boys Nation experiences. It was almost surreal when, thirty years later, my seventeen-year-old son, Tyler, was selected to attend Boys State in Florida. His maturity following the completion of that program was eerily similar to my own and seemed to zoom.

My senior year was a bit of a blur. I excelled in everything, earning all As in my classes and giving my best performance in every varsity sport I participated in (football, basketball, and baseball). I was elected in that overwhelmingly white school by my peers as the "Student Most Likely to Succeed" and "Best Athlete." Boys Nation had launched me to a new level of belief in myself, a level beyond what I could have ever envisioned.

I applied to colleges primarily in the Ivy League—following most of my fellow Boys Nation delegates. My parents were mostly AWOL for my college selection process, but my mom did come to one meeting. Once the representatives from the University of Pennsylvania discussed the costs, she looked at me, exasperated, and told me it was time to leave, stating, "We don't have that kind of money, Michael!" She hoped to steer me away from a huge disappointment.

I reassured her, saying, "Don't worry about the costs. I'll figure that part out."

My school guidance counselor didn't present any of the brochures for the top-ranked colleges and suggested instead that I set my sights far lower, perhaps the University of Connecticut. I thanked him and located the Ivy League applications myself. Recruited by the Ivies as an athlete, I was afforded the opportunity to visit their campuses. I decided to attend Cornell University, where I would participate in freshman baseball as a third baseman and star on the varsity football team as a wide receiver. Choosing Cornell wasn't an exact science; it may have rested in large part on the fact that they had the best meal service of all the Ivy schools I visited.

My parents' marriage was deteriorating at that time, and so my college acceptance experience was somewhat subdued. For my high school graduation in 1975, my dad bought me my first car—a 1972 white Chevy Vega that he paid about $2,000 for. It leaked so much oil that I kept a full case in the hatchback, grateful to just have wheels.

My brother's and sister's tuitions had exhausted any savings they had left, so I was on my own at age eighteen. My dad had earlier told me how he felt when he left home at fifteen. I understood how he felt: empty and alone but determined.

I thanked my dad for the car, shook his hand from a full extended arm's distance, and loaded up all my belongings to make the six-hour drive to Ithaca, New York. After leaving, I made only the occasional, isolated holiday visit; that was the last time I was home with any frequency.

My dad wanted me to succeed and did the best he could with the resources he had. He was also dealing with his own job insecurities, his failing marriage, and the challenges all black men unfairly face in some form or fashion in corporate America. I wasn't bitter; I was just disappointed deep down that he was not the mentor I had sought—the mentor I found in my youth sports coach, Big Al Dobrutsky, and later in Jack Donlan.

CHAPTER 7

Tying the Knot

Kim and I were married on July 3, 1993, in a beautiful ceremony; a reception followed at the Ritz-Carlton in Dearborn, Michigan, with 350 guests (mostly her family). Following a honeymoon in Saint Martin, we settled into our new expansive brick home in Rochester Hills, a suburb just ten minutes from the Pontiac Silverdome. Kim's parents and a majority of her relatives were still residing in Detroit, and visiting them helped occupy her time since I was at the office every day from early morning to late evening. We also learned shortly after our honeymoon that our first baby girl was on the way.

Having won our division, the Lions were optimistic about another winning season heading into the 1994 schedule. In February, we were preparing for the upcoming Indianapolis Combine, where some three hundred draft-eligible college players would convene to take extensive physical examinations and undergo positional skills workouts for the thirty-two NFL clubs.

The league now comprised thirty-two teams because both Carolina (Panthers) and Jacksonville (Jaguars) had recently been awarded expansion franchises, in October and November 1993, respectively. I hadn't been following the expansion process closely, but I knew Jacksonville was a surprise winner. Their group, led by shoe magnate Wayne Weaver, beat out Baltimore, St. Louis, and Memphis in the eleventh hour based upon a commitment from the city of Jacksonville to spend $121 million to update the Gator Bowl stadium. Also, Weaver's group reportedly had sold ten thousand club-seat tickets with a five-year commitment in a record ten days. That apparently sealed the deal for the NFL owners, who wanted expansion into the Southeast, notwithstanding Jacksonville's rather small television market.

I found a message on my desk to call the "Jaguars." Oddly, the number wasn't local. Ford Motor Company had purchased Jaguar a few years before, and Coach Fontes was driving one of their luxury models as a company car. I was driving a regular Ford SUV as a company car and assumed I was being upgraded to a Jag by the club after our successful season.

I hurriedly returned the call and reached someone named David Seldin, who was with the Jaguars football team but not the car company. "Hi, Michael, this is David Seldin, and I am president of the Jacksonville Jaguars," he said assuredly, as if it were a team with a long history in the league.

I paused, first coming to grips with the fact that I

probably wasn't going to be driving a new Jag. "Uh, oh, hey David, how are you?" I responded. "I heard you guys were up and running. Something I can help you with?" I asked, assuming he wanted to pick my brain about something.

"Yes," he said. "We would like to speak with you about running football operations for our club. Would you be interested in meeting?"

Visions of all the previous jobs I had departed so abruptly suddenly popped into my head. I jumped ship in less than a year from the NFL Players Association to join the NFL Management Council. Then, without proper notice, I quit my position there after just a few years to join the Birmingham Fire. After one season, I left again to work in the headquarters of the World League for a year and a half, only to then depart to join the Lions.

I had been with the Lions for only one season, and so I immediately felt guilty but also intrigued. "Uh, David, I don't know how that works exactly," I stumbled. "I think there has to be some formal request and permission by the team for me to even have this conversation."

"Oh, yes indeed," David replied casually. "You came highly recommended to us from the league office, and we have already gone through all the appropriate protocols to initiate this conversation. We have permission from your owner to speak with you."

"Wow," I said to myself out loud, relieved. "So, they gave you permission?" I was not quite sure of the implications.

"Frankly, they cannot deny permission when another club offers an elevated position," he informed me.

"Elevated?"

I didn't say anything to Kim right away about the phone call. She was very comfortable in Detroit, and our baby girl was due in April. Before I had a family, I would not have hesitated to make a spontaneous move. Now I was a husband and would soon be a first-time father. I was still going to make the decision based upon my career aspirations, although I knew that wasn't completely fair. I trusted that Kim would support me and my decision.

David and I met at O'Hare Airport in Chicago, in a private club so as not to draw any unwarranted attention. David had a slim build, stood about six feet tall, and was perhaps a couple of years my senior. He wore intellectual-looking glasses and dressed in an open-collar shirt, gray trousers, and a blue blazer. His leather belt was expensive, as were his designer-label shoes. I was able to catch a glimpse of his watch, too, a Patek Philippe, Swiss-made, very expensive and classical. He had impeccable taste despite a disheveled demeanor.

He seemed at ease and completely comfortable around me as a black person, displaying none of the awkward discomfort I can quickly pick up on. *Aha*, I realized, *David is Jewish*. I found it very easy as a black man to relate to Jewish people, having been partly raised by the Dobrutsky family. I had gone to Wayne's bar mitzvah and could recite the Jewish blessing over bread before a meal in Hebrew. Leading up to Wayne's bar mitzvah, I knew it better than he did, much to the chagrin of his mother, Elaine.

We made small talk about our backgrounds, and David

noted that he'd graduated from the University of Pennsylvania Wharton Business School and was working in private equity for the Pritzker family in Chicago. The Pritzker family was one of the wealthiest Jewish families in the country. They were most prominently known for owning the Hyatt hotel chain. David explained that he was brought in on behalf of the Jaguars ownership group to put the expansion deal together and to help oversee the construction of a new stadium. He acknowledged that he knew very little about sports in general and needed someone with my expertise to run the football part of the organization.

David asked many questions unrelated to football and in large measure about current events. He was definitely a liberal, and we shared similar political views. We seemed to communicate in a similar fashion. I had known the first time I met Gavin Maloof in Albuquerque that it was going to be difficult to relate to him. David was the complete opposite. I was fairly certain I would be comfortable working with him.

We left the airport after meeting for three hours and agreed to schedule a follow-up with the owner, Wayne Weaver. David said I would find it very easy to get to know and like Wayne. This time, I did my homework. Through research I learned that Weaver was a shoe magnate owning both Shoe Carnival and Nine West, two companies I had never heard of. Kim owned a bunch of expensive shoes, so it didn't surprise me that someone could get that rich selling women's shoes.

Weaver had grown up in the South, in Columbus,

Georgia, not too far from where both Chan Gailey and Dan Reeves lived. He was currently living in Darien, Connecticut. Connections were mounting. Weaver was the lead owner of the Jacksonville group that had paid the NFL a whopping $140 million along with Carolina in expansion fees to purchase their teams. The last expansion of new teams in the NFL had been in 1976, when both Tampa Bay and Seattle were started. Those teams paid the NFL expansion fees of only a paltry $16 million.

A week later Weaver and I met in the Delta lounge at LaGuardia Airport in New York. Weaver was athletic-looking, about six-one, slightly overweight, and losing his hair. He had a robust, slightly red face that was friendly. His handshake was overly strong. The blue-collar nature of his walk belied his net worth of almost half a billion dollars. I could tell he hadn't grown up with money and still held on to traditional values. I perceived all of that even before we spoke. "Nice to meet you, Mr. Weaver," I said, extending my hand.

Almost embarrassed, he responded, "Oh, please, call me Wayne."

Wayne didn't spend much time on the normal pleasantries. He was eager to get down to business. "Everyone we spoke with says you're the guy to run our football operations," he said in a somewhat nervous manner, as if seeking my confirmation.

"Well, I outwork most people and I have a reasonable degree of intelligence, Mr. Weav—er, Wayne," I replied, still awkward about using his first name. I had a work ethic as good or better than any of my peers in the league. I wasn't the most intelligent, nor did I think I needed to be. I'd succeeded in law school among many other students who were much smarter than I was because I had a knack for figuring things out.

In the NFL, I didn't have to be a genius to succeed. In fact, others were sometimes put off by the appearance of being too smart. The presumption was that if you were too intelligent, you couldn't relate well to coaches, players, and, in some cases, owners. I had often seen Commissioner Tagliabue trying to dumb down to the group he was addressing and took careful note of that.

Wayne smiled. "Do you think we can build this team with college players, or do you think we need mostly veterans?" he asked.

"Well, the most important question, I think, starts with who the coach is. If he comes from the college ranks, I would focus on younger players initially. If he's a longtime NFL veteran, then I would focus primarily on veterans and mix in younger players."

He stared off into the distance for a minute. "That's a very interesting perspective," he concluded. "I hadn't necessarily tied the age of the player to the background of the coach." He asked which type of coach would be best for "our" team.

I reflected for a moment and said, "I would look for the best college coach you can find. Young players given the opportunity to play right away will be hungry and disciplined. Veteran players will see an expansion team as purgatory and resist what they will perceive as a second-tier team. Most people recall how poorly both Seattle and Tampa performed as expansion teams early on, and there won't be much different expectation for Jacksonville and Carolina." I had previously looked up those expansion teams' records in their first two seasons: Seattle went 7-21, and Tampa was a pathetic 0-24.

Wayne seemed impressed, as if my answers were right in line with his thinking. "We are exactly on the same page! In fact, it's not public knowledge, but I just offered the coaching job to Tom Coughlin, the Boston College coach," he said more softly, as if someone might overhear our conversation.

I hadn't met Coughlin, but I certainly knew his reputation as a highly rated coach. He had been mentored under legendary coach Bill Parcells of the New York Giants and was considered by most to be a strict taskmaster. I wasn't worried about getting along with Coughlin. Putting ourselves in the best position to win would be a recipe right out of Coughlin's playbook. Just as Wayne Fontes had seen me as the vehicle to give his black players a sense of pride in the organization, I figured Coughlin would also utilize me to help corroborate "his" message to the black players. A white head coach in the NFL has to make black players a primary concern, as they represent almost 80 percent of a team's roster. Coughlin would know it takes a lot more than cracking a whip to get the support of black players.

Weaver had many more questions, but they were mostly

perfunctory. I assumed he was already convinced in his decision to offer me the job. I presumed someone at the league office had instructed him to interview a black person for the job. My sense was that he was looking to make a hire of a black man if he found one he felt was qualified to do the job. If not, he most certainly would have looked elsewhere, having spent $140 million on the franchise. Wayne didn't play the waiting game; he offered me the job right there in the airport and said David would work out the financial terms.

"Welcome aboard," he said as he put one hand firmly on my shoulder and shook hands with the other. I hadn't officially acknowledged my acceptance, but we both understood that I would.

I returned home later that evening, which was less than a week before Kim's birthday on the twenty-fifth. Our little bundle of joy was still working her way toward an expected late-April delivery. We were lying in bed watching the baby kick when I broke the news. "Honey, I think I am going to accept a job with a new expansion team in Jacksonville," I said, hoping the shock wouldn't cause any premature contractions.

She looked at me, puzzled, and said, "Jacksonville, what?"

"Florida," I replied sheepishly.

She jumped out of bed and went to her desk to search for something.

"What are you looking for?" I asked.

She didn't respond. She flipped through a book and then scanned her eyes down the page. "Here it is," she said. She was holding an almanac.

My first reaction was *Who keeps an almanac in their bedroom?*, but I decided it was best not to voice that. "There is a new expansion team there, and they want me to run football operations," I continued. "I would essentially be the general manager and report directly to the president or the owner of the team."

She hadn't changed her expression, so I kept selling. "I think they will double my salary," I finished.

Still no change. "But look, if you are totally against it, I am sure there will be other opportunities," I said.

"Never been to Jacksonville," she said with a smile. "I am sure we are going to like it," she said softly, rubbing her expecting tummy. In that moment, I realized how special she was. I realized she didn't want to go to Jacksonville, but she never let it show and was supportive of me. We had just bought the perfect home, were living a short drive from her parents' house, had our first child on the way, and still she was willing leave it all to follow me to a place she'd never heard of. I committed to myself then that I would never let her down. I called David Seldin the next morning. As expected, his offer more than doubled my salary. I officially accepted.

The press conference was held a week later in Jacksonville at the chamber of commerce in a rather small and unimpressive building. There wasn't quite the same shock or fanfare as in Birmingham, fortunately, though I was now among the highest-ranking African Americans in the NFL. My title was vice president of football operations. I was the third hire in the organization, behind President David Seldin and newly hired head coach Tom Coughlin.

Tom and I got along well right away. He could smell bullshit from a distance and was convinced early on that I had no hidden agenda. We needed to trust each other if we were going to be successful as an organization, and we did so from the beginning. Both Wayne and David stayed completely out of the football decisions, leaving it up to the two of us. Wayne said if we got into a situation where the two of us could not come to a mutual agreement, then and only then would he step in. Tom had the authority to select the players, but I had the authority to determine what we paid them. Ultimately, we had to agree. It was a forced marriage, but one that both of us desperately wanted to work.

The two expansion franchises of Jacksonville and Carolina didn't begin play until the 1995 season. That gave us a year to prepare (and to get the Gator Bowl stadium rebuilt). Tom wanted to prepare as if we had an active team during that prep year. So we analyzed rosters, studied players, and designed game plans as if we were actually competing in the 1994 season. We built a mock roster and even contacted agents about potential contracts—which made them think we were partially insane.

"You want me to pretend to negotiate a contract with you," Frank Bauer, an agent from Stockton, California, who was representing Green Bay Packers backup quarterback Mark Brunell, said in disbelief.

"Yeah. What would it take to acquire him?" I asked.

Tom had already done his research and believed Brunell, only twenty-four years old and in his second pro season, would never see action as the third-team quarterback behind Ty Detmer and superstar Brett Favre, who was only twenty-five at the time.

"Well, he's on Green Bay's roster, and you guys aren't even an official team yet," Bauer said, as if I were unaware of the obvious. "I'll tell you what: if Brunell ever becomes available next year when you guys are a real team, then I will give you a call," he said, snickering under his breath.

"Okay, fair enough," I said, and hung up.

I even attended the Heisman Trophy ceremony in December of that year to visit with some of the top agents who were on hand representing the top-rated collegiate athletes. At the time three of the finalists, Ki-Jana Carter, Kerry Collins, and Steve McNair, were prospects we were considering for our inaugural 1995 college draft. Carter was a stout, explosive running back out of Penn State University. Collins was a straight-from-central-casting, strong-armed, white-thinking-style quarterback also out of Penn State. McNair, whose nickname was "Air McNair" was a black athletic and improvising quarterback out of Alcorn State in Mississippi. All three were quite different yet equally impressive choices.

Back in Jacksonville, Wayne began relocating some of his staff from Connecticut to oversee the financial and business operations for the team. He wanted people he was familiar with. I had barely spent time with any of them, but I did notice they were all white. I felt a certain coldness from many of them, so I just kept my distance. Our roles barely intersected. I was sitting in the audience of the theater for the Heisman Trophy presentation (the highly coveted award given to the most outstanding college football player each year) when I noticed an urgent message on my phone to call the office right away. Not unusual to have emergencies. I got up from my seat and went to an area where I could make a call.

My secretary mentioned Wayne needed to speak to me and transferred the call into his office. I could tell by the volume that the phone was on speaker as he picked up. "Hi, Michael, how are you?" he said, somewhat curt.

"Just fine, Wayne. I am at the Heisman Trophy presentation in New York," I said, trying to indicate that if it wasn't urgent I needed to go.

"Listen, I have been speaking to some of my staff from Connecticut that are moving down here and they are a bit concerned," he began.

"Concerned about what?"

"Well, I guess it got out that you said you were going to fire all the Connecticut people because you didn't trust them, and it's created some bad feelings."

I paused to take in his comment. "And who in the world said that?" I asked, my voice raising.

"Well, Kim [one of the financial accountants] overheard the story and repeated it to me," he said, as if he was trying to protect her.

"Wayne, I have not had a single conversation about the

Connecticut staff. I haven't even met the vast majority of them. I would never say something as outrageous as that." My heart rate was climbing now.

"Put Kim on the phone and let's get to the bottom of this," I demanded.

I was put on hold for three to four minutes before Wayne came back on the line: "Uh, Michael, I guess there was a misunderstanding. Kim said she never attributed the statement to you. I guess there was just some gossip of sorts going around. I tell you what, don't worry about it and enjoy your time in New York," he said, hoping to end the debacle.

"Sure, Wayne," I said. "Just understand, though, if you ever have another conversation with me about something of this nature, I will quit on the spot. I think I deserve better," I added, and ended the call. I didn't even pause to reflect on the fact that I had just chastised my boss and could have ruined my relationship with him for good. It didn't matter. Survival in this industry for me as a black man meant eating a lot of humble pie to accommodate white people's idiosyncrasies, but my integrity and my sanity depended upon my ability, without fear, to simply walk. Wayne never addressed the incident again with me.

My wife, Kim, made a few house-hunting trips to Jacksonville, and we found a lovely Georgian-style brick four-bedroom home in the suburbs at a place named Marsh Landing, in Ponte Vedra Beach. The gated community location was pristine, with multi-million-dollar homes, boat docks, an exclusive golf course, and a wildlife sanctuary.

Neither Kim nor I had ever lived in a gated country club community. What it offered was privacy and security, and that is what most sold us on the property.

When a black family moves into an exclusive enclave like Marsh Landing, everyone knows your name and what street your house is on. No matter which neighbor I met for the first time, they always knew us and our full background. I was accustomed to this from my stint in suburban Birmingham, but it caught Kim off guard. In one such first-time meeting, a couple greeted us and introduced themselves. I started to say my name, and they quickly interrupted: "Yes, Michael, of course, we know who you are. And Kim, I didn't meet you, but I saw you in the golf shop the other day buying golf balls."

It took Kim's breath away! Were these people spying on her? Taking note of her comings and goings? "Watching our every move!" Kim said to me afterward, feeling really uncomfortable.

"Yep," I said, "Lucky you were buying expensive golf balls or the word on the street—I mean, cul de sac—would be that you were cheap," I joked. Kim ordered customized window blinds the next day to replace the ones that originally came with the house. They provided more privacy. We've lived in that same house we bought in Marsh Landing in 1994 ever since.

Both the Professional Golfers' Association (PGA) Tour and the Association of Tennis Professionals had their world headquarters there. We were Marsh Landing's first black family. Tom Coughlin later moved into the same community on the same street. I remember early on being unsure how to navigate by car around the seven bridges that make up Jacksonville to get to our new home. One time, I asked a random middle-aged black man near our temporary downtown offices if he knew which bridge I needed to take to get to the beach.

"Where are you headed?" he asked again, as if he didn't hear me correctly.

"The beach. I am thinking about moving out there," I said.

"Oh, son, someone is playing a joke on you," he said. "Black folk don't live out at the beach. It's only white folk out there. You better check that address."

Welcome to the South, I thought to myself.

As a surprise for Kim, I hired people to move in all our furniture from Detroit plus all the new items she'd purchased online. The movers unpacked all the boxes so that when she and Kristen Nicole, our two-month-old beautiful baby girl, arrived, everything was moved in and ready. It didn't hurt that we went from the frigid cold temperatures of Detroit to the warm, sunny (albeit humid) days of a Florida beach community. Kim was comfortable, and taking care of Krissy consumed all her time. Kim's mother, Judith, came to visit for a few weeks, and the transition was relatively smooth.

There were a few unexpected hiccups, though. One evening, Kim and I went to dinner to give her some much-needed time away from the house. We chose a chic new restaurant called Sterling's in the artsy Avondale section of the city. The small parking lot was private and attended to by an older, gruff-looking white gentleman. As we approached the lot, the man began waving feverishly at us. "Can't park here; can't park here!" he shouted toward us. I continued into the lot, ignoring his antics. We parked and started walking toward the restaurant.

"This is only for restaurant parking. I'm going to have your car towed for sure!" he yelled from a distance.

Kim hadn't heard him clearly and asked what he'd said. "He was talking to someone else," I said, knowing damn well what he'd said, as we continued into the restaurant. Inside, we were given a nice table because the manager recognized me. He was polite. The meal was excellent. The restaurant was full. We were the only black couple. In fact, almost every time we went out to eat at a nice restaurant in Jacksonville, we were the only black couple. Having lived in New York City, DC, and Detroit, it was unusual to be the only black people in a restaurant. Sometimes at exclusive restaurants in those places, if there was another black couple or two, I would subconsciously count. Living at the beach in Ponte Vedra early on, we never had to count. It was always just us.

We paid our tab and headed to our car. It was now evening and dark outside. I opened the car door for Kim and then pretended to have recalled leaving my credit card inside the restaurant. "Oops, gotta get my card," I said. "I will be right back." Kim closed her door and locked it.

I went directly to the older man's car where he sat casually with the window down. I reached inside and grabbed him by the neck. "You ever disrespect me again like that and next time you'll be in the hospital," I said, squeezing a bit tighter. The man looked at me in fear but said nothing. I turned and casually went back to my car.

"Get your card, honey?" my wife asked. "Yep, sure did," I said, and drove on. I reflected on the ride home how crazy that stunt was. I could have been arrested and possibly fired from my job. He could have been carrying and shot me. He could have filed an assault charge against me with the police. Someone could have witnessed it and reported it to the media. There were a whole host of outcomes that would have been horrific for me professionally. It was irrational, but also in my mind completely necessary. It was the only way I knew to maintain my sanity in that racist environment. I just wouldn't look the other way and ignore it.

I gained national recognition for my position with the Jaguars, again, the "first" black general manager in the NFL. At that time I began mentoring large numbers of black students and working professionals both within and outside the NFL. I was contacted on a regular basis by young black NFL coaches, scouts, and front-office personnel who aspired to advance in the league. They wanted my counsel and my advice. If someone knew a black person interested in a career in the sports industry, they often contacted me. There were a rare few of us in top positions within any of the professional sports leagues at the time, and I considered it a responsibility and my duty to help any person of color who reached out to me. I always made myself available; I still do today.

As we prepared for our first draft in the 1995 season, Tom ran every scenario of available prospects. He knew exactly what type of player he wanted at each and every position. His formula required a big up-front (offensive and defensive linemen) strong running game led by a big running back, a mobile and very smart quarterback, and bigger-than-normal wide receivers who could win a jump ball contest in the end zone over their defenders.

Friday, April 21, the evening before the college draft, I was about to leave my office at 9:00 p.m. when the phone rang. Already exhausted from many nights of little to no sleep, I considered not answering but finally picked up. "Yeah, hello," I said, almost rude. "Hey, Michael, this is Frank Bauer." *Why would he be calling?* I thought.

He continued, "You mentioned once last year that you were interested in negotiating a contract for Mark Brunell. Well, he's available if you are still interested. The Packers are willing to trade him for a third- and a fifth-round pick. We just need to work out a new contract. We were negotiating with the Philadelphia Eagles, but they are demanding a four-year deal and we only want a three-year deal. You have about thirty minutes if you think you can pull the trigger."

Brunell was the quarterback we wanted, but we'd had no idea the Packers were willing to trade him. They had shrugged off our earlier overtures. Tom had already left, so I quickly phoned him. "No time to explain, but I have a deal on the table to acquire Brunell for a third- and a fifth-round pick. Three-year deal; likely less than a million per year," I rattled off over the phone.

"Unbelievable," Tom said, the excitement palpable in his voice. "Go get it done."

Twenty minutes later, the Brunell deal was done and I was on the phone speaking with our newest arrival. A call beeped in during our conversation and I clicked over, thinking it was Coughlin.

"Michael, this is Jeff Lurie. Not sure how you guys got in the middle of our deal, but we had already verbally agreed to sign [Brunell] with the agent." Jeff Lurie was the owner of the Philadelphia Eagles, and I was shocked that he would personally call.

"Well, Mr. Lurie, the agent called, I guess after an impasse, and we were able to strike a deal," I said, hoping to satisfy his concerns.

"That's not true. There was no impasse," he said.

"Oh, well, that's what we were told; sorry it worked out that way for you."

There was an awkward pause. "Listen, we'll give you $1 million to revoke the trade and let us complete our deal," he said. I wasn't sure if he meant me personally or the team. Either way, it didn't matter. We wanted Brunell, and we certainly weren't going to give him up.

"I am sorry, Mr. Lurie, but we really want the player."

He hung up the phone. The situation felt like another blessing of serendipity. I had been fortunate to be in my office when Bauer called. Otherwise, the deal would have never happened. But it wasn't serendipity that earned us Brunell; rather, it was hard work. Had we not played out

Coughlin's mock year, I would never have made the initial call to Bauer to put him on notice.

We selected ten players in our inaugural draft, which was headed by our first overall pick, Tony Boselli, a mammoth-size offensive tackle from the University of Southern California (USC). Boselli was considered the next great offensive lineman by most of the pundits, who compared him to Anthony Muñoz, perhaps the greatest offensive lineman in the history of the game. Boselli had not given up a quarter-back sack during his collegiate career at USC, which was in and of itself an amazing accomplishment. He stood six foot seven inches tall and weighed about 322 pounds. Even more impressive, he was fast. During minicamp, when all of our draft picks report for spring workouts, Boselli finished first in all the sprints, even ahead of the skill-position running backs and wide receivers. He was special.

Like most offensive linemen, Boselli was highly intelligent. I invited him into my office during a break at minicamp just to let him know how I would approach getting his contract completed. He was represented by Jack Mills, a sports lawyer from Colorado who had earned the trust of Tony's father during the agent recruiting process. Jack was among the better agents in the league, and we shared a friendship. I wanted to size up Boselli to see how strongly he might participate in the contract negotiation process. He was twenty-two years old at the time, so I wasn't expecting too much sophistication.

To my surprise, Tony walked into the meeting in his

hulking way and plopped down in one of my brand-new conference chairs—which I wasn't sure could support his weight. He was carrying one of those scientific calculators I've never understood how to operate. A person used those calculators, I imagined, to figure out cosines and interest rates at a push of the button.

I had spent a few minutes circling around the deal when Tony interrupted: "So, were you thinking six years in terms of length?"

A bit surprised, I said, "Well, yes—six years seems about right. It might have to be five years and an option for signing bonus proration, but it's essentially the same thing."

Fully comprehending, Tony continued, "Okay, that works; and how about signing bonus—do you have a number in mind yet?" Negotiation 101 says don't give your cards away first, but we seemed to be making real progress.

"I can't go over $6 million and make the rookie pool number work in the first year," I said.

Tony began entering numbers into his fancy calculator. After a few minutes he looked up and said, "Okay, we are pretty close, so that will work." He stood, shook my hand, and went back to the locker room.

I never told Jack about our conversation. League rules and legal ethics required me to contact the player's agent prior to initiating any type of direct negotiations with him. In this case, I had a sliver of protection because the player had "initiated" the conversation. Still, Jack would have expected me to advise the player that he needed to first contact his agent. I knew Tony wanted to have a face-to-face relationship with me and that ultimately it might help me reach a better deal. It was a "bend but don't break the rules" relationship.

I told Tony I wanted to do something special with the first draft class, and as the top pick he would have to agree. I wanted to sign all ten players on the same day, a month before they were scheduled to report. Traditionally, drafted players sign intermittently throughout the summer, with the top picks agreeing normally closer to the start of training camp at the end of July. No team had ever signed all of its draft selections en masse. Pulling it off would send a message of team unity and perhaps a little personal bravado. Tony agreed, and off I went to lock in the other draft choices. Some of the agents initially resisted, fearful that there would be repercussions from rival agents criticizing them for working to help the team. I bullied them into compliance, and on June 1 we signed all ten players at a televised press conference. Tony signed a six-year deal with a $6 million signing bonus.

While there was a true benefit to our signing all ten players at once, it stood out in stark contrast to the norm. Other NFL owners questioned their GMs about the wisdom of such a strategy. Once again, I had stepped outside the customary boundaries of my counterparts. Several articles quoted anonymous GMs calling the move a gimmick and braggadocio. Some suggested my arrogance would bite me in the rear end down the road. I didn't appreciate their criticism, but it didn't change the way I conducted business. Fuck 'em and make it retroactive—the mantra I learned from Jack Donlan.

Did I showboat in signing all ten players? Perhaps. I was climbing a ladder. Any GM could try to accomplish the same goal. While I wasn't trying to make enemies, I wasn't in the job to acquire friends. I was among the few black people in my role in the entire NFL. If following the system worked, then there would have been more black people in my position. But there were not. The system did not work the same for blacks; instead, it heavily benefited white men. They were the only ones who were rewarded by the system. It was a system I had no confidence in, nor the luxury to support. I could either sit back quietly, not bucking the system, or play the game by my own set of rules. The latter carried a hell of a lot of risk from haters, but I was committed to my plan of being not just a black face but a game changer, and there was no turning back.

Our inaugural season in 1995 started even slower than we expected at 0-4, and we had also lost our first preseason game to our expansion rivals, the Carolina Panthers, 20–14. Fortunately, our first victory came in week five against the Houston Oilers with a nail-biting 17–16 finish. The Panthers didn't notch their first victory until week seven of the season. Weaver was getting anxious; Coughlin had well-publicized run-ins with the players who were forced to adhere to his military schedule, which was uncharacteristic in professional football. The players resisted, and Coughlin dug in deeper as disciplinarian.

My role shifted to that of a buffer. I was the buffer between the strict micromanaging style of Coughlin and the agitated players. I was the buffer between our increasingly impatient owner and Coughlin. If the players didn't show to up to meetings five minutes early, Coughlin considered them late and would fine them accordingly. He also fined players for every infraction one could think of: wrong tie, improper shoes, loud music, and a host of others. NFL players were not accustomed to this type of behavior from a head coach. Whenever a player was fined, I drafted the fine letter and copied the finance department to deduct the amount. That afforded me discretion. In many instances I would simply approach the player, have him acknowledge the error, and then serve the written notice as a warning rather than an actual fine. I did this routinely, never letting on to Coughlin that I had done so.

In one such instance, we held a forty-five-minute non-uniform walk-through where players staged personnel formations on the depth chart in various situations: kickoff, punt team, and punt return. It is a practice formality with no running or contact. Our star quarterback, Mark Brunell, participated in his normal attire, except he wore flip-flops rather than sneakers.

After completing the short practice, Coughlin approached Brunell: "What the hell are you wearing, Brunell?"

Confused, Brunell replied, "What do you mean, Coach?"

"What's on your feet?" Coughlin persisted.

"Oh, flip-flops, Coach," Brunell said, now fully aware of the intention of Coughlin's query.

"They aren't what you are supposed to be wearing, so you just earned yourself a fine," Coughlin said as he walked away dismissively.

In that instant, a look came over Brunell's face that I hadn't seen before. There was no better team leader than Brunell, and he would make any personal sacrifice on behalf of our team. I could sense the anger mounting in him. I quickly went up to Brunell and, smiling, said, "Jeez, Mark, you can't even get the walk-through attire correct."

Brunell's expression did not change.

"Listen, you know Tom is a stickler for wearing the correct team gear," I continued. "Plus, it's just his nervous energy. I will waive the fine, but promise me you won't wear flip-flops in a walk-through again."

Almost immediately the red disappeared from his face and a gentle smile ensued. He let out a deep breath and said, "Okay, Michael, no problem—and thank you." He ran off with the other players as we boarded the flight for our game. Brunell ended up having one of his better games that next day, throwing for more than three hundred yards and two touchdowns in a convincing victory.

Tom sat next to me on the bus ride back to the airport to catch the team charter flight. "You see, you are always talking to me about fining the players, but Brunell got my message yesterday and look how well he performed today," he said with confidence.

I just nodded my head and said, "Yeah, I see what you mean, Coach," and left it at that.

Weaver was reaching a boiling point with Tom and had even considered taking personnel authority away from him. Perhaps it was too much to handle along with his head coach/offensive coordinator roles. I could have stepped in and acquired more authority at that time, but it would have been viewed as an act of betrayal by Tom. I assured Wayne that Tom could handle both roles and asked for his continued patience. Tom and I spoke on the field following my conversation with Wayne, and I assured him that the owner had full confidence in him, never letting on that he had almost been stripped of personnel authority.

After the first ten games of that inaugural season, our record stood at 3-7. The Panthers, always our comparison, were 4-6 but had just completed a four-game winning streak. Wayne continued to grow impatient with our sluggish results. The following week we played our in-state rivals in Tampa Bay and scored a touchdown in the final thirty-seven seconds of the game to come within one point with the score of 17–16. We could have kicked the extra point to tie the game and essentially go into overtime or go for a two-point conversion (which had just been added to the NFL rules the prior year in 1994). Momentum had been on our side as the game started out 10–0 Tampa and then stretched to 17–10 just before the final score.

Tom wanted the players to buy into his aggressive style of play, so he opted for the controversial and risky two-point conversion, which failed as our receiver Jimmy Smith caught the ball just out-of-bounds in the corner of the end zone. We retrieved the ensuing onside kick, but our Hail Mary pass was intercepted as time ran out.

Weaver was livid. He marched down from his suite into the locker room, first locating me. "What the hell was that all about?" he demanded. "We had all of the momentum and we go for two instead of tying the game? We blew the game!" He wasn't waiting for a response, and I chose not to give one. After a few moments of deadening silence, he turned and walked out. He was pissed off in a way I had not seen before.

Tom finished his routine postgame press conference with the media and walked over to me. His emotional energy seemed spent from the full drama of the closing minutes of the game, but he was otherwise upbeat. "Well, we sent a message to the team that we are going to be aggressive and play to win," he said, still justifying his decision to himself.

"Absolutely, Tom," I said, trying to reassure him. "It was a gutsy move, but it was the right call."

Tom looked around the room and turned his glance back toward me. "Did Wayne stop by?" he inquired in a softer voice.

"Oh yeah," I said. "He had a large group flying back on his plane, so he had to leave. He said it was a bold move and one he fully supported. He told me to tell you to stay positive," I lied.

Tom took in my comments and then moved closer. "See, that is why we are going to win. We have an owner who gets it," he said. Tom went into the coach's shower area, got dressed, and took his normal seat next to me on the bus ride to the team charter plane. We didn't speak on the ride, but Tom patted me on the shoulder twice as he stepped off the bus.

By the time Weaver got back to Jacksonville, he had finally cooled off and come to grips with the decision Tom made. He was ultimately supportive of the decision once he had ample time to fully digest the situation. I was able to communicate to Tom what Wayne would have wanted to say. I absorbed the added pressure of Wayne's in-the-heat-of-the-moment words. That was my job. I was the buffer. We finished that first season at 4-12. Carolina finished 7-9. Our owner and even our fans were supportive and optimistic about our future.

CHAPTER 8

Cap Jail

Tom and I generally saw eye-to-eye on the decisions we made. More times than not when there were differences of opinion, I would try to sway him toward my view. If he was locked in his position, I would normally concede and try to find a way to make his position work. On one occasion, though, we simply could not agree, and I was unwilling to give in. It was just before the start of training camp in our second season, and our wide receiver crew consisted of two solid players in Jimmy Smith and Keenan McCardell. The problem was, we had nothing but first-year players to fill the third receiver position. Coughlin was adamant that we needed another veteran receiver. At the time, the best available player was Andre Rison, a twenty-nine-year-old former first-round pick of the Indianapolis Colts who was later traded to the Atlanta Falcons. Rison was an outstanding receiver, finishing second in most receptions league-wide for six seasons.

183

The problem with Rison was his off-the-field behavior. He had a well-publicized but often rocky relationship with female rap star Left Eye Lopes of the popular R & B group TLC. I felt he was not likely to fit into Tom's disciplinarian style of coaching.

Tom finally went to the owner to plead his case. He explained to Weaver how Rison would provide the third element to our receiver core that was predicated on three- and four-wide formations. Wayne, thirsting for a better season, was inclined to agree with Tom. "What's your concern with Rison?" Weaver asked me as he and Coughlin sat in my office.

"The agent wants a two-year guarantee, and I am certain he won't last that long," I said. "He's not the type of player who I think will buy into our system."

Wayne understood my concerns and accepted them at face value, knowing Tom's penchant for excessive team rules off the field. "Tom, are you comfortable saying this player will be on the roster for two years?" Wayne asked.

"Look, he might be our best receiver. I know how to handle these types of veterans," Coughlin said. Tom was willing to take the risk, not fully appreciating the financial implications.

As we all sat around my desk, Rison's agent, Charles Tucker, called.

"Put it on speaker," Weaver directed.

"Hey, Mr. Huge," Tucker began, mispronouncing my name as he always did. "Rison only wants to play for your coach. He said with 'Coughlin,' he could make the Pro Bowl." Tucker was playing to Coughlin's ego.

"Well, we think so, too, Tuck, but we can only guarantee the first year," I said.

Tom sat closer to the desk, his face showing mounting angst.

"We gotta do two years, Mr. Huge, but I promise you are getting a steal at this price," he said. "We got two other teams willing to do the same deal, so we have to know now."

I put the phone on mute and again reiterated to Wayne and Tom that we couldn't afford the risk.

Wayne looked at Tom and said, "Well, if you are sure, Tom, then okay."

I took the phone off mute, said, "Tuck, it's a one-year guarantee or no deal, so call me back," and hung up the phone.

Tom rose out of his seat as if he was going to swing at me. He said, "Great, you just fucked our team," then stormed out of my office.

Wayne looked at me in disbelief, trying to absorb what had just happened. "I hope you know what the hell you are doing, Michael," he said. "Tom is pissed off."

Angered myself, I said, "Yeah, well, Tom is always pissed off."

Wayne wasn't quite sure what to make of our behavior. He stayed in my office, hoping the agent would call back. I told him there was no guarantee he would call back. "I wasn't bluffing," I said.

Weaver frowned.

Five minutes later, I received a call from Tucker. "Okay, Mr. Huge, one-year guarantee. Dre is on his way to Jacksonville."

Whew, relief. I hadn't been sure how the situation was going to play out, but I had been prepared to lose the deal if they hadn't accepted our terms. It would have made things difficult with Tom going forward. Once I told Tom the news, he smiled, but it didn't smooth over the fact that I had challenged his authority in front of the owner. I won in that I got the deal I was after, but I lost in that Coughlin now saw me in a different light.

We signed Rison on July 16, just before the start of training camp. Midway through the season, on November 18, Rison was cut by Coughlin on the team charter headed home from the Pittsburgh Steelers game for ongoing disciplinary reasons.

We finished the season with a surprising five straight victories and a record of 9-7, which was good enough to earn us a wild-card play-off spot. Despite three straight road games, we made it all the way to the AFC Championship Game against the New England Patriots. In the blustery cold we lost 20–6, but we had accomplished a great feat in advancing that far in the NFL play-offs in just our second season of play. Oddly enough, Carolina finished the year at 12-4, also earning a berth in their divisional NFC Championship Game. They lost 30–13 to the Green Bay Packers, also in the brutally cold temperatures. Both expansion teams were one game away from playing in the Super

Bowl in just their second season. Many of the NFL owners were now regretting the extra draft choices the expansion teams were given to balance the lopsided start the prior expansion teams had faced.

The next few years saw our team reach the pinnacle of success. We finished both the 1997 and the 1998 seasons at 11-5. The 1999 season was almost perfect; we lost only to the Tennessee Titans twice, for a final record of 14-2 and another unprecedented trip to the AFC Championship Game. Ironically, we lost that game to the same Tennessee Titans, 33–14. Still, we were considered among the most successful start-up franchises in the history of the NFL. The Panthers' record went in reverse. They finished the 1997 season at 7-9. The next two seasons were 4-12 and 8-8. The Jaguars were the clear winners of the expansion race.

In reaching those milestones, we had sacrificed a bit of our future. Our 2000 season ended at 7-9, and the following season loomed with a salary cap overage of some $30 million, the most in the league. I was in charge of the salary cap, so the burden rested squarely on my shoulders. I understood every nuance of the salary cap and how to fit players into a current year by circumventing the rules or simply pushing financial obligations into future years.

League rules required all teams to remain below the mandated total salary cap for each individual season. If a team was projected to be over the salary cap for an upcoming year, they would be forced to restructure contracts, release players, or whatever they had to do to get under the cap. Otherwise, their roster would be frozen by the league, and hefty penalties would ensue. In short, deep doo-doo. We were so far over the projected salary cap that we internally referred to it as being in "salary cap jail." For four years, I kept pushing salary commitments into future years. I knew there would be consequences to pay in that fifth year, but I believed that by the fifth year, we would go to the Super Bowl and all would be forgotten. I wanted to *win now*. And I wanted to prove to myself that I could manipulate the cap better than anyone else. It was part of my DNA to always be competitive and to win.

During our first five seasons, I was deemed a "salary cap expert" by my peers and the sports media for the Jaguars' ability to keep so many key players on the roster. I was lauded as the new breed of general manager who brought both a business and a personnel background to the position. Legendary sports agent Leigh Steinberg even acknowledged me in his book *Winning with Integrity: Getting What You're Worth Without Selling Your Soul*. He described me as one of the top general managers in the NFL because of my skillful management of the salary cap. I was also twice named to the prestigious *SportBusiness Journal*'s 40 Under 40 Top Sports Executives. I was "feeling myself," and I felt good. I continued to manipulate the cap, expanding our opportunities to win football games.

Tom wanted to keep our star players throughout those years and was a bystander as I found ways to accomplish that. He may or may not have known that my magical cap hands would lead to problems at a later date, but, regardless,

I was the one who pulled the trigger. Weaver blessed the game plan, hoping the win now / pay later blueprint would generate a Super Bowl victory. It didn't, and the deferred bills came due in a big way.

Had we reached the Super Bowl, all would have likely been forgiven. My freewheeling salary cap maneuvers allowed us to keep a fully loaded roster of talented players and twice in our first five years fall just one game short of reaching the Super Bowl. Had my Super Bowl gamble won, my salary cap gambit would have been deemed an acceptable strategy, notwithstanding the long-term consequences.

The accumulated salary cap debt essentially handcuffed our ability to retain many of our star players, and it also precluded us from acquiring talented new players. In retrospect, I understand that winning at all costs always has ramifications. Maneuvering the salary cap functioned like sins of the past coming to light after living as if all that mattered was today. Because of tremendous pressure from their fan base, NFL teams today, some thirty years later, are in large measure operating under a "win now" philosophy with regard to acquiring players and managing a team's salary cap.

Weaver didn't want to blame me publicly for the salary cap fallout, but he didn't want to reward me, either. He told me my contract would not be extended, meaning I could stay on, but without the protection of a multiyear agreement. It wasn't a termination, but it was a message.

I decided to depart on my own terms. I had served seven years as the team's head of football operations. I had originally set a maximum timeline for myself of staying in the job for ten years. In part I knew that the demands of the job would take their toll, not only because of the immense pressure but also because of the personal sacrifice of not being present for my family. Early in my career, I had watched older general managers kneeling down on one knee to time athletes running the 40-yard dash at the Indianapolis Combine for college players entering the NFL Draft and sworn to myself I would not be clocking kids running drills when I was sixty years old. I had decided then that ten years was a good target time to get out. Seven wasn't bad, and I had learned an invaluable truth: winning today at all costs is not an acceptable or sound business strategy or personal philosophy and ultimately jeopardizes long-term plans.

I was leaving believing other black GMs now had a path. I had paved the way for other deserving, talented blacks to earn the right to run other NFL teams' football operations, as head of player personnel and as general managers. Ozzie Newsome of the Baltimore Ravens, Rick Smith of the Houston Texans, Rod Graves of the Arizona Cardinals, and Jerry Reese of the New York Giants all make me proud of my years with the Jaguars. These men were and remain the best of front-office personnel in the NFL. We are our own band of brothers; we continue to stay in touch with one another.

Once again I contacted Commissioner Tagliabue, who told me he had a major role for me at the league office. I agreed to meet with the commissioner in New York and told Weaver I would be leaving the team at the start of the 2001 season, which for every NFL team officially kicks off with training camp in the sweltering heat of July.

Weaver rewarded Coughlin, the coconspirator in our "win now" plan, with a two-year contract extension. I didn't think it was fair, but I was already looking ahead to greener pastures.

As the 2001 season approached, I was focused mostly on my next job opportunity rather than figuring out how to solve our team's interminable salary cap problems. My family had grown to five, with the addition of Kathryn Leigh in 1995 and Tyler Jacob in 2000. Jacksonville was our home. I was not fully comfortable with the prospect of returning to New York. As a family, we had grown accustomed to the warm weather and slower pace of Jacksonville. I wasn't sure what role Tagliabue was contemplating for me at the league office in New York, and though it had to be a senior position, it would mean an entirely new and more complicated lifestyle. The transition would have been easy for me, but not for Kim and the kids. I reflected back on how easily she had given up our life in Detroit to enable me to take the job in Jacksonville. Moving now would mean displacing her once again, *and* our entire family. I wasn't sure I could do it. I had never weighed these considerations before. With this next career move, I realized it wouldn't be fair for me to make a selfish decision based solely on my aspirations.

My family was important to me, but I hesitated when I asked myself, *Is my family a priority even over my career?*

I decided not to discuss the potential move to New York with Kim until I was certain in my mind that I wanted the job in the league office.

Just before the start of training camp in late July, I scheduled the meeting with Tagliabue that he had recommended. We blocked out a full morning to meet in his Covington & Burling law offices in Washington, DC, I assumed to avoid any unnecessary speculation. Before becoming commissioner, Paul worked at Covington, a very prestigious law firm that was the primary outside counsel to the NFL. Paul represented the NFL as its lead attorney for almost twenty years. He had assumed the role of commissioner in 1989, succeeding Pete Rozelle, who had served as commissioner for almost thirty years and was the name I associated with my kid dreams of becoming commissioner.

Seeing Tagliabue become commissioner further enhanced my resolve to someday become commissioner. He was an attorney who represented the owners, much like the experiences I'd had with the NFL Management Council. Paul was not a personnel guy and had never worked for an NFL team. I thought my combined experiences, along with a brief stint at the NFL Players Association, would position me well for such a lofty opportunity at a later time. Perhaps, I thought, my time would come at the conclusion of Tagliabue's term. No one in the queue for the top job had my background at that point.

I felt confident that Tagliabue liked and respected me. He had chosen me to serve on several NFL committees during my stint with the Detroit Lions and the Jacksonville Jaguars.

One assignment was on the football side, working directly with the NCAA (National College Athletic Association) on issues pertaining to college players and rating their draft prospects within the NFL during their junior-year seasons (when they are first eligible to leave school early and enter the NFL Draft). Another committee was called the NFL Committee on Workplace Diversity, designed to address the disparity in hiring of minorities in the league and at the team level. Paul put me in charge of that committee, which afforded me much direct access to him and key black coaches in the league.

In February 2000, I held a meeting with Denny Green, Tony Dungy, Ray Rhodes, and Commissioner Tagliabue to discuss issues pertaining to diversity hiring among head coaches in the league. At the time, Denny was the head coach of the Arizona Cardinals, Tony was the head coach of the Tampa Bay Buccaneers, and Ray had just been fired as head coach of the Green Bay Packers. I asked each of them to give Paul their candid thoughts on how we might improve diversity hiring. I expected them to be somewhat tempered in their remarks with the commissioner, but my expectations were wrong.

Tony and the other coaches made their feelings crystal clear to Paul: "Black head coaches are constantly being overlooked for coordinator and head coaching positons." Tony was particularly blunt about racism playing a role and how the league needed to do more to give black assistant coaches a fair shot at jobs they clearly deserved. All three coaches could instantly name a half dozen coaches they had worked with who were far more deserving of head coaching opportunities than some white coaches selected over the last couple of seasons.

I was struck by the honesty and tone the coaches took with the commissioner. They held nothing back and spoke their minds freely and without regard to any potential consequences. They were advocates, which was what I had realized I needed to be. I was proud of them, and yet they thanked me for providing the forum with the commissioner. They helped me to center my compass and better appreciate the responsibility I had to always speak up.

Paul listened to every word, took everything in, and I believe better understood the plight facing minority coaches in the league in getting their fair shake at promotion. Paul told me, "We are going to fix this."

Paul was less formal than I had expected and didn't pelt me with questions. Instead, he spent the time methodically searching my philosophical thoughts about owners' roles, protecting the NFL brand, and disciplining players. I felt that he was determining whether or not I had the necessary vision to lead the league. I had prepared for questions on what I had accomplished. Paul was more interested in my perspective on the league as a whole. How did I make decisions? What were my personal views on important league issues? He threw me off guard. It seemed subjective and arbitrary, but I knew better. Tagliabue was anything but arbitrary. Paul framed the discussion the way he did to discern my views on expanding the number of teams, building the television coverage both digitally and internationally, and branding the league beyond football.

I expressed my views clearly, but I worried that Paul believed my vision was not traditional enough. The old guard of owners wanted to keep the product "traditional," which was code for "outdated and stale," in my mind. The league had operated that way for many years. "If it isn't broke, don't fix it" was their mentality. I believed that if you waited until it was broken, it was already too late to fix it. The time to make adjustments and improvements was when it was working. My logic would face a steep uphill climb in resonating with the owners.

When I first told Tagliabue that my goal was to become commissioner, I wasn't quite sure how he would react. It was the first time I'd ever told someone in the league office (let alone the actual commissioner) that I aspired to have the job of commissioner. I wondered if he would take me seriously. Was this just a dream I held that no NFL owner would actually consider? I was nervous about asking, but I needed to know the answer. Was it time to pinch myself into reality, or was I really a potential candidate for the job?

Paul paused before answering, which only drew out my worst fear of his eventual response. Instead, he simply stated, "Of course I know you want to be commissioner. I would not be talking to you about a potential COO role here if I didn't believe you had the stock to one day become commissioner. The dynamics of how that will all play out over time, though, involves far too many variables to focus on now."

I was relieved that Paul had expressed this confidence

in me. Whether or not I could truly be given the job was a wholly different story. His words still felt like a validation of my many years of hopes and dreams.

I continued to interview with Paul over the next couple of days. When the opportunity arose, I asked him directly what he thought I would need to do to enhance my chances of sitting at his desk.

"Well," he began, "you will need to have managed one major aspect of the business to gain the confidence of the owners. If, for example, you were in charge of football operations alone, that would not suffice. The owners consider that the technical part of the job. You would need to manage the business side or have a significant role in the negotiations of the television contract. The lifeblood of the league will always be tied to television revenues."

I paused to take in all that Paul had said. "So, you would want me to run the business side of the league?"

"No," he responded. "That will be managed by Roger [Goodell]. He already has a strong relationship with many of the owners and works primarily on the business side with them. You have the football background, and you would continue to oversee that. But you would also have the chief role in negotiating the television agreement. You and Roger would have co–chief operating officer roles."

Roger Goodell was a few years older than me. He was the son of Charles Goodell, the former US senator from New York, and his entrée into the league almost twenty years before had been as an intern to then commissioner Rozelle. He attended Washington & Jefferson College in

Washington, Pennsylvania. I was always impressed with the way he could navigate between owners of strong intellectual backgrounds and others who were more handshake-type guys. Roger had the touch. He was highly astute and masterful at reading people. I pride myself on those skills as well, but it was clear to me that Roger had the advantage.

Managing the football operations of the league was a no-brainer for me. Much of my then fifteen-year career had been spent managing teams, rosters, and the salary cap. I had no experience negotiating television contracts, but negotiating the league's television contracts was handled with outside consultants who spent the majority of their time in that arena. Paul was referring to directing the owners toward a long-term strategy and vision for television revenues, not the technical aspects of negotiating the legalese. It was a role that required business savvy and vision. I began to understand why Paul conducted our interview the way he had. He was assessing whether or not I was capable of that challenge.

I naively thought I had positioned myself for the commissioner's role, yet I had not even fully understood its key responsibilities. All this time I'd thought the job would be about understanding the blend between football and business, when there were already professionals within the organization to handle that responsibility. The commissioner had to set the vision for the league and ultimately generate revenue for the owners. He was the CEO of the league, and the owners were essentially the shareholders and board of directors all in one. It was an "aha" moment for me, but one that still did not deter me from wanting the job. I just realized I would have to step up my game to have a chance to win over these owners.

Paul was scheduled to retire in five years, which meant the commissioner's job would be open in 2006. I would be only forty-five then. Tagliabue said Goodell and I would have comparable positions: I would be running the football operations and working on the television deals, and he would be more directly involved with the owners and running the business side of the league. I imagined that when the time came to choose the next commissioner, after working side by side, Roger and I would compete. My academic résumé and other qualifications would, in my mind, give me the slight on-paper advantage. But I also knew that decisions like this were not reduced to résumés but would be primarily based on trust and relationships. In that analysis, Roger would be the heavy favorite. It was of great import also that Roger was white and I was black. While the vast majority of players in the NFL were black, by then there had been only a handful of black GMs and still no black team presidents or owners. How in God's name could they select a black commissioner?

Paul truly believed in diversity. By putting me in the job of co–chief operating officer, he would be opening the queue for me to compete for the commissioner's job. But I knew he was also very loyal to Roger, who'd had long-time similar aspirations. Maybe if I were single and without family responsibilities, I would have considered moving back to New York, investing five years of my life only to then perhaps be disappointed with the outcome of being chosen as the bridesmaid, not the bride. I also knew that if Roger did get the job, I would not be able to stay under his administration. It would just be too painful to me. No, once the dream came to an end, I would have to move on to something else. I could not accept this position in New York with my head in the sand, knowing there was no viable pathway to my dream of becoming commissioner. For the first time, I was forced to come to grips with the harsh reality of an evaporated dream. It was a bitter pill to swallow, the first real disappointment in my career. The truth sank in, and I immediately accepted it.

Although he never officially offered the job, I said, "Paul, I think I am going to stay in Jacksonville." I told him I appreciated his long-standing support.

At that meeting, I emotionally separated from the NFL. Looking back, this dead end helped prepare me for setbacks I would later confront in my career.

CHAPTER 9

A Free Agent

In November 2001, I resigned from the Jaguars, removing the buffer between Coughlin and Weaver. (At the end of the next season, the Jags went 6-10 and Coughlin was fired.) The month after I resigned, I learned that Tagliabue had promoted Goodell to executive vice president and chief operating officer of the NFL.

Trusting my own entrepreneurial skills, I opened Axcess Sports and Entertainment, headquartered in Jacksonville, Florida. I chose the name Axcess (the proper spelling was already registered) because I had a strong Rolodex and access to many people in the sports industry. I wanted prospective clients to know they would be working with someone who had been on the other side of the bargaining table and fully understood the process from both perspectives. I was the only former general manager from the NFL representing players as an agent. That gave me an incredible advantage. It also afforded me the opportunity to attract other agents in baseball and golf to join my company and broaden our services.

Our offices were located downtown in the Modis Building. It was among the tallest and most prominent buildings in the city. I hired a professional interior decorator to custom-design our office with expensive leather furniture, multiple large-screen, high-definition televisions, and marble conference tables. It looked first-class and was certain to impress any potential client. I took out a loan of $750,000 along with $250,000 of my own money to begin with a working budget of $1 million. I was paid well in my time at the Jaguars, earning about $600,000 per year. We had three kids now, all in private schools, and with college tuitions looming, our affluent lifestyle demanded similar earnings. Taking the personal loan and depleting $250,000 from our personal savings was a big risk, the biggest I had taken so far in my career.

Kim sensed the pressure I was under and immediately decided to dust off her legal skills and informally join the staff as well. She oversaw the finances, working closely with our in-house certified public accountant. She also served as president of our entertainment company, Juba Entertainment. It was surprisingly easy to have her completely immersed in the business. I knew she was there primarily to add support, and I let her know we were in this together. She always had my back.

I hired an initial staff of ten people, most of whom I had known through the sports industry. Although I hired several white employees, it could not be mistaken that we were a minority-owned business. Anyone signing up with our firm would first recognize they were hiring me, a black man.

The loan required me to put a lien on our Florida home. We had purchased a second home a few years earlier in Martha's Vineyard and still had a sizable mortgage on that property. We owned three cars and a small boat. We couldn't afford any financial hiccups. The pressure was not new, though, and I was comfortable betting on myself— and now Kim, too.

Cash was always on my mind. We paid some of our top employees as much as $250,000 per year. At its peak, our overall payroll was almost $2 million per year. We needed to generate significant revenues to stay afloat.

Almost immediately, I was able to recruit top-rated college and pro football players. My prior experience as a general manager afforded me an audience with almost every player I recruited, although the agent community attacked me. They wanted to deter other club executives from getting into the representation business. The agent business can be dirty and cutthroat in recruiting players. Players, or their families, commonly asked for under-the-table cash payments, and less-qualified agents were eager to comply. The highest rated players tended to be uninterested in cash payments, knowing they would soon be earning millions of dollars. They sought out the most competent agents, and I found myself immediately among that select, small group.

At the time I started Axcess in 2002, not a single black agent represented a white NFL player. I wondered, *Do black agents simply not bother to recruit white players? Do white players collectively not trust black agents to represent them?* A large majority of players in the NFL are black, so it wasn't essential that I represent white players, but where was the disconnect? Almost immediately, though, I started receiving calls from current Jaguars players seeking my representation. They were all players I had signed to Jaguars contracts when I was working for the team. Now they were interested in firing their agents and hiring me.

First it was Zach Wiegert, an offensive lineman and former Outland Trophy winner who sought my services. Then Brad Meester, another lineman; and Kyle Brady, a tight end from Penn State and former first-round draft choice. I also signed quarterback and former Heisman Trophy winner Eric Crouch. All white and all interested because of my prior background. My race was not a factor in their decision to hire me.

Black players were slower to reach out to me. Some said they doubted whether a black man would be competent enough to do the job. Others simply no longer wanted to put their trust in a black man, only to be let down, as they came from homes with broken or nonexistent relationships with their fathers and communities without black male role models. I was often told that meeting me raised these feelings because they had never met "someone like [me]." My own issues with my father gave me understanding and compassion for them, and I set my focus on more educated black players, with whom it was easier to relate. Fortunately, I was able to sign black players with relative ease just by being myself. I signed Vince Wilfork, Jon Beason, Adam "Pacman" Jones, and a host of other elite players who were selected in the top rounds of the NFL college draft.

Black and white players were alike in that the most important aspect of their decision in selecting an agent was how well they trusted the person. It was less about race. The litmus test for both black and white players was their perception of the agent's undivided loyalty and support for them.

Within our first six months, I received a call from Bob Dickerson. His son Bubba, a twenty-year-old college golfer in his junior year at the University of Florida, had recently won the US Amateur and the Western Amateur golf championships. He also finished second in the Southeastern Championship. These were the major collegiate golf tournaments. Only a handful of golfers achieved that feat—most prominent, Tiger Woods. Bob asked if I would be interested in representing his son, who was turning pro after playing in the Masters golf tournament as an amateur. I had no idea what was required to represent professional golfers, but I agreed to meet. On the golf course where Bubba regularly practiced, Bob explained that agencies like International Management Group were too big and too focused on Tiger Woods. They wanted someone who would focus primarily on Bubba.

"He would be my first golf client, so I am sure I could allocate the necessary time," I said. "Out of curiosity, why did you call me?"

"I watched your career at the Jaguars, and frankly I

thought you were brilliant. You did an amazing job negotiating contracts, and I knew you could do well for Bubba.
You also remind me of one of my closest friends who was
also a sharp black guy like you."

"Oh, okay. Let's go meet Bubba," I said, perplexed why
someone would call their child what I'd always thought was
a disparaging moniker for dumb country folk. I learned that
people in this part of Florida proudly referred to themselves
as rednecks and that my clients were truly a "redneck"
family. They were very comfortable around me, notwithstanding my own Alice in Wonderland uneasiness. I was
only a recreational golfer, but I still held a single-digit hand-
icap primarily because of my strong athletic background.
I hadn't had any formal golf instruction, and I certainly
was not familiar with the white junior golfers' circuit for
aspiring young golf professionals.

We watched Bubba hit balls on the driving range. He
had a head of fiery red hair and opted not to wear the traditional baseball-style golf hat. "Hey, Bubba, I am Michael.
Nice to meet you," I offered as I shook his hand.

Immediately he smiled and shook my hand as if we had
met before. "I'm Bubba." We decided to go have breakfast
and shortly thereafter shook hands to seal the deal. I was
suddenly in the golf business.

I registered as an agent with the PGA Tour and learned
that I was the first black to register as a "player manager."
Sixteen years later, I am still the only black player manager
I am aware of certified on the entire PGA Tour. As the
2002 Masters Tournament approached, Bubba, as the US

Amateur winner, was paired with the prior year's winner, Tiger Woods, who had now won his second Masters event. I was excited to meet Tiger and watch Bubba compete with him. Bubba seemed completely nonplussed by the overwhelming austerity of the Masters Tournament. In golf, this was the Super Bowl. I still felt out of place, a black man in a vanilla-white industry. Tiger was the only black player in the event, and I was the only black player agent. Walking with Bubba around the pristine facilities of Augusta, I felt as if all the spectators' eyes were on me.

Butch Harmon, a world-renowned golf coach, is the son of Eugene "Claude" Harmon, the head golf professional at Winged Foot Golf Club in Mamaroneck, New York, and Seminole Golf Club in Juno Beach, Florida. Both Winged Foot and Seminole were and remain among the most exclusive private golf clubs in the country. The Harmon name (his three brothers were also teaching pros) was royalty in the golf industry. Butch was Tiger's coach, and together they had rewritten golf's record books. Butch stood next to me as Tiger and Bubba approached the first tee. "Nice to meet you, Mr. Harmon," I said. "I am Bubba's agent, Michael Huyghue."

Harmon, a very friendly man, quickly patted me on the shoulder. "Hey, Michael, nice to meet you. Call me Butch." We walked together for the first nine holes, each following our man.

Although Bubba struggled on a few of the par-three holes, he played fairly well. His final score of 79 did not fully represent how well he played. Tiger shot a two under par and was tied for seventh place after the first day. Tiger and Bubba got along well during that opening round. Tiger was unusually cordial to his playing partner, perhaps sensing something about Bubba that put him at ease. Bubba did a great job overcoming the tremendous pressure of the massive crowds that were following Tiger.

After two rounds Tiger moved into a tie for fourth place and Bubba missed the cut, but Butch was still impressed with Bubba's play. "I only work with a few players," Harmon said. "If you are interested, I would be happy to work with Bubba. I think I can help him with a few things."

I was caught completely off guard. "That's awesome, and we would be honored to work with you," I said.

"There's no fee, just schedule some time with my assistant to come out to my facility in Vegas," he said, handing me one of his personal business cards.

"Will do, and thanks again," I said. I motioned good-bye to Tiger, who waved as he was shaking hands with Bubba.

"He's got a lot of talent," Tiger said. "Make sure you hook up with Butchy."

With the PGA Tour headquarters located just south of Jacksonville, many of the top-ranked PGA Tour and Web .com (the developmental tour) players lived in the area. I began representing about a dozen of these players, including Fred Funk, Len Mattiace, Russell Knox, Steve Marino, and Steve Wheatcroft. Often our political views were widely disparate (they were hard-core Republicans), yet they still sought out my services because they knew and trusted me from my role at the Jaguars.

I was most proud that I represented Tim O'Neal, the only black player on the entire Web.com developmental tour at the time, as well as Jim Thorpe, the lone black player on the Champions Tour (former tour players over fifty years old). Notwithstanding Tiger's worldwide presence in the game, golf remained an essentially all-white sport. The Tour began a strong effort to reach out to inner-city kids around 1997 with its First Tee Program, but the impact in getting minority kids to play competitive golf was minimal. Minority kids could not afford the high costs of the equipment, nor did they have access to golf courses. A large number of kids entering the First Tee Program were actually white. Scott Langley, a white kid from Barrington, Illinois, was the first player to graduate from the First Tee Program and earn his way on to the PGA Tour. To date, not a single black kid from the First Tee Program has earned pro tour status.

We also established a baseball division at Axcess. I hired two experienced baseball agents to run that part of the business, though I remained fully engaged. Doug Rogalski, a former coach at University of North Florida, led the division and quickly signed star players like Ian Desmond, Billy Butler, Gregg Zaun, and Stephen King, along with a host of other highly rated Major League Baseball players. I didn't spend a significant amount of time recruiting baseball players, but I almost always made the closing presentations. I found that all athletes shared a common thread. Having played baseball in high school and college, I was easily able to relate to these athletes. It was a building process, though, as many of these players had toiled in the minor leagues for three to five years before graduating to the major leagues. Accordingly, less revenue was associated with the baseball players we signed in their first few years.

A first-round draft selection in Major League Baseball, just out of high school or college, for example, might get a $1 million signing bonus. Our commission was 4 percent. For the next three to five years, they would play in the minors, graduating from rookie ball to A, AA, and eventually AAA before they earned a chance to play in the big leagues. During those developmental years, the players are paid only a modest monthly salary ranging from $1,000 to $5,000. The agent doesn't really make any significant money until the player reaches the major leagues. In the NFL, though, the agent can retain anywhere from 1 to a maximum of 3 percent of the total value of the player's contract. If an NFL veteran signs a five-year deal for a total of $60 million, paid out at $12 million per year, the agent earns (at 3 percent) $360,000 for each of those five years, assuming the player participates in all five seasons. Once an agent acquires ten or more veteran players, he can likely earn several million dollars per year just on those athletes. That is why football was our core business at Axcess.

Our business was doing well when an old colleague from the NFL named Constance Schwartz called me to inquire if I would be interested in working with legendary rapper Snoop Dogg (Calvin Broadus Jr.) to help him expand his youth football league and to possibly get the NFL to participate. Constance was working with a company called the

Firm, which was representing D O Double G. I was pleas-antly surprised by how quickly so many business opportuni-ties developed for Axcess from contacts I had made during my career. My Rolodex was paying dividends.

Not sure what I could do for Snoop Dogg, I agreed to meet him in Los Angeles. Snoop's adolescence is widely known to have featured alleged gang participation (the Crips) and arrests for illegal drugs, and although he had gained national prominence as a superstar, it seemed highly unlikely to me that the NFL would consider linking its brand to his name.

We met in the W Hotel in West Hollywood. Snoop was completely different from what I had anticipated. He was focused and well-spoken. He explained that he wanted to do something for the inner-city kids in Compton and other rough south-central LA neighborhoods where black boys were being killed and incarcerated in large numbers. Snoop wanted to provide an alternative to gang participa-tion and crime for these kids. His message was sincere and compelling, and I told him I would help. We would need to build a full league with coaches who were required to go through background screening and a training process. We needed venues and equipment. I already had the experience to build a football league, and I felt I could do the same for Snoop.

I contacted Commissioner Tagliabue and asked him to meet with Snoop. I anticipated that Tagliabue's public relations staff would be fully against any such meeting. "Commissioner, I know your staff is going to voice strong opposition to taking such a meeting with Snoop. But I spent some quality time with him, and I can vouch for the fact that what he is attempting to do would also be good for the NFL. Many of the young athletes entering the NFL were raised in similar high-risk inner-city neighborhoods that Snoop wants to reach out to. His message is about spreading the game, and I know the NFL shares that mission."

Paul listened to my pitch and then without hesitation said, "Fine, let's set it up. No promises, but I will keep an open mind." I knew from my own exchanges with the commissioner that he cared about diversity, was keenly perceptive, could gauge the sincerity of Snoop's intentions, and had the power to influence the NFL to look past his prior legal transgressions.

I met Snoop in the lobby of the W Hotel on Lexington Avenue in New York just prior to the meeting with Tagliabue. Yes, Snoop liked W Hotel properties. The league offices were just a few short blocks away, and we could walk to the meeting. Snoop traveled with a security detail of eight bodyguards. I prepped Snoop in the corner of the lobby, reviewing in advance the questions the commissioner would likely ask. Snoop looked at me as if to say, "This isn't my first rodeo." He was not the least bit nervous and shrugged off all my buzzword suggestions for speaking with Tagliabue. "Don't worry," he told me. "I got this."

We walked the two blocks to the league office, Snoop, me, and eight behemoth-size bodyguards. Not very inconspicuous. Motorists driving by began recognizing Snoop.

"Yo, Snoop. What up, my nigger!" a man yelled from his car window. Nodding his head Snoop tipped the brim of his baseball cap to acknowledge the friendly gesture.

I had asked Snoop to dress "appropriately" for the Park Avenue meeting with Commissioner Tagliabue. Snoop interpreted that to mean wearing jeans, a varsity letterman jacket, a baseball cap, and Chuck Taylor basketball shoes. I guess I should have been more specific. I wore an open-collar button-down shirt and traditional blue blazer with black Salvatore Ferragamo loafers. It wasn't quite the Fresh Prince of Bel Air and Carlton act, but it was pretty close.

As more drivers of passing vehicles recognized Snoop with loud honking, shouted greetings, and slowed traffic, I began thinking about the East Coast versus West Coast turf war then going on among hip-hop rappers. The feud was related to the shooting between the East Coast rappers, led by the Notorious B.I.G. and his record label Bad Boy Records; and the West Coast rappers, led by Tupac Shakur and his label Death Row Records. Snoop was part of Death Row Records, and we were on East Coast soil. Even surrounded by his entourage, I felt the sudden need to walk a safe distance behind him as we approached the NFL building.

When we walked into the lobby, I once again assumed the lead position. As we waited outside the commissioner's office, all eyes held a full skeptical gaze on Snoop. NFL brass and onlookers were obviously wary of the meeting, and yet there was abundant curiosity about Snoop. He was a huge celebrity, and the staff couldn't resist their awkward gawking.

After about twenty minutes, we entered the head man's conference room, a place I had been many times before. Not missing a beat, Snoop immediately took the seat at the head of the table. I'll never know whether he was unaware that it might be reserved for the commissioner or making a ghetto power move. Before I could say anything to Snoop about the seating, Tagliabue walked into the room. Snoop jumped out of his seat, smiling, and extended his hand. "What's up, Commish," he greeted him.

Standing a short distance away, I watched as Tagliabue's executive staff looked on with what appeared to be tense body language.

"Hey, Snoop, nice to meet you," the commissioner responded, as if he were often greeted that way. Paul recognized Snoop's seating faux pas and just took a random seat in the middle of the conference table. I stood for the entire brief meeting. He asked Snoop to explain the reasons why he wanted to start the league and what his aspirations were. Snoop hit every buzzword I had prepped him on, to my surprise. He was impressive. I chimed in on just a few points here and there, but this was Snoop's show. Paul absorbed it all and then turned to speak briefly with his subordinates, whom he jokingly referred to as his minions. He cordially then asked them to leave the room.

Snoop never looked to me to gain any insight into how I thought the meeting was going. His demeanor indicated he was self-assured, that everything was going along smoothly. I had hoped so but was by no means certain.

Paul turned to Snoop and said, "You will have the full

support of the NFL. We don't typically allow it, but you can use the league's marks as well for your youth teams' names, in a limited capacity. Michael will work with our team to cover the details. But we will support your league, and I wish you great success." Paul stood and extended his hand. They shook and embraced. Paul left the room.

"That was a home run," I said, congratulating Snoop. "The league never allows anyone limited use of their marks. That was all you, Snoop." Snoop was pleased but acted matter-of-fact. He shook my hand in a way that demonstrated I had earned his trust. I graciously accepted that trust and would later remember that moment when I heard that Snoop told rap artist the Game that I was his "Niggah-Niggah."

I remained at the league headquarters and let Snoop and his bodyguards leave on their own. Yeah, I'm not *that* down with Snoop. Their cars were waiting in front of the building, and Snoop left satisfied and with a smile on his face. Some of the league's senior executives glared at me as if to say, "You'd better handle this situation and not let it come back to embarrass the league." I knew my name was on the line, but I believed in Snoop.

In the fall of 2003 we launched the Snoop Youth Football League (SYFL). Some thirteen hundred kids between the ages of eight and sixteen participated, including Snoop's own sons Cordell and Corde. The teams were given NFL nicknames like the Bears and the Lions, using the league's trademarks. Each year the NFL allowed the top team from the SYFL to play a game during Super Bowl weekend against a local Pop Warner team in that area. The game was called the "Snooper Bowl" and featured major rap artists as part of the pregame and halftime entertainment. The game in Jacksonville, for instance, during Super Bowl XXXIX in 2005 drew an oversize crowd of twelve thousand fans to a local high school stadium. Other Snooper Bowl games drew similar audiences. The kids even got to play in NFL stadiums in Detroit, Miami, and Los Angeles.

Snoop also used $300,000 of his own money to purchase a customized bus for his team, equipped with state-of-the-art video screens and speakers. Other famous rappers like P. Diddy, Nelly, and Luke Campbell also formed youth football teams that we competed against. No shootings, fights, altercations, or arrests of any sort occurred at these games.

The local games were played in some of the toughest crime-ridden areas of Los Angeles. Snoop scheduled a meeting in advance with the leaders of both the Bloods and the Crips to make sure the games would be allowed to go on. I attended. It seemed to me that everyone in the group was carrying a gun. The games were designated as safe zones, and the gangs agreed there would be no violence at these parks. The meeting brought home to me how different my own upbringing had been in Windsor, Connecticut. The kids Snoop was helping lived in what were essentially war zones. Gangs had to agree to allow activities like Snoop's youth football league. Otherwise, parents would not have let their kids participate. Kids as young as ten years old stuffed colored bandannas into the front of their football pants, signifying their allegiance to either the Crips (blue) or the Bloods (red).

Working with Snoop, I dealt with two personalities: the serious, business-minded Snoop, whose creativity and vision were remarkable; and the unpredictable, somewhat abrasive rap superstar. The latter was egotistically driven and played to the audiences that supported him. I much preferred the former, but I grew to understand and respect the performer side. Snoop was a genius. For me, navigating between the two personalities was often very difficult.

One of our youth play-off games was held at night in a small stadium outside the hood in a white upscale suburban neighborhood called Brentwood. We did not play night games at our inner-city venues, as they did not have field lights. We started the game a bit late and were running close to the end of the contractual time to finish. Loud music boomed from the speakers, and Snoop played stadium announcer for the game: "My man Number 34 just took the pitch and for sho' juked three dudes to gain twenty-five yards," was a typical call from Snoop, his voice raised in excitement. It always seemed to me that there was still a large child inside Snoop, and these games were an outlet for that inner child's expression.

A white police sergeant approached the field, looking for someone in charge. I asked the officer if I could help him with something.

"Hey, you guys are past your curfew for the game and the neighbors are complaining," he said in a stern voice.

"You have a bunch of older wealthy people in this area, so they complain a lot," he said in a more professional manner. "If you guys can just bring the noise level down, I will let you finish the game. Otherwise, I have to shut you down."

"Sure thing, Sergeant," I said. "And I appreciate the courtesy."

I briskly walked up the stadium steps to the small press box where Snoop was broadcasting the game on the microphone and selecting music to play. "Church," I said, interrupting loudly, using his close-circle nickname. "The police are here, and unless we bring the noise down they are going to shut us down. Can you bring it down some?"

Snoop looked over to me and nodded his head in agreement.

I had turned back toward the sergeant when I heard Snoop's voice even louder over the microphone: "Hey ya'll, po-po here telling us we gotta be quiet because we're making too much damn noise. So, I guess we gotta tone it down."

I was relieved.

Then he continued, "Nah, we not fin to quiet down. We 'bout to raise the roof on this motherfucker!"

I could feel myself shrinking as I watched the sergeant aggressively head toward his car. Fortunately, the "po-po" didn't shut us down, and the game was a huge success.

Many of the young kids' fathers, who had not been present in their lives, showed up to these games. They were proud to see their sons having success on the playing field. Some even wore T-shirts that read, "My son is # _____."
Snoop knew he was making a difference in these families'

lives, and it was hugely important to him. I saw that up close. This was no performance, no publicity, just Snoop spending his own money and, more important, his time to make a difference in his own community.

The league left an indelible impression on me. I saw firsthand the plight of our young black boys. These kids were hoping, in most instances, just to stay alive and out of jail. And a lot of them failed.

These images were emblazoned in my mind when I first saw NFL players kneeling in protest. I knew many of them had played on fields like those in the Snoop league, where the gangs had to allow the games to go on, where on any given day a young black boy was shot and killed. It was a life completely unfamiliar to many of the people who challenged these NFL players' right to protest.

I grew close to Snoop professionally and personally. As his Niggah-Niggah, I unexpectedly learned life lessons from Snoop: to always challenge the status quo, to not accept the norms of society—especially as a black man. Snoop's life is a testament that moving beyond one's circumstances is more a function of a state of mind than just talent. Snoop consistently pushes the envelope without fear of reprisal or fear of the outcome. He taught me that as black people we are often limited by our own stereotypical views of what black people are capable of accomplishing. I thought I had mastered striving for success. Snoop taught me to press further, beyond the boundaries that were in front of my eyes. His view of the world was almost limitless in terms of going after his dreams and ambitions.

Working with Snoop made we wonder if perhaps I had jumped off the NFL train too abruptly. Might I have changed what I perceived to be an intransigent mind-set among the owners? Maybe I had needed to gut it out a bit longer. Might I have gotten to the doorstep of the commissioner's selection if I'd had Snoop's mind-set? Had saving face and avoiding the pain of failure prevented me from wholly going after my childhood dreams? Had bowing out of the NFL, on what I believed were my own terms, been self-limiting?

I began asking myself these questions because Snoop inspired me.

CHAPTER 10

Diversifying the NFL from the Outside In

About a year after leaving the Jaguars, absorbed in my own business, I continued to receive calls from black assistant coaches and scouts in the NFL about the lack of opportunities in the thirty-two clubs. Over and over again, qualified black candidates were failing to get hired or not even seriously considered. I spoke regularly with Coach Dungy and Coach Green, two prominent and highly successful black head coaches in the NFL, who served on the diversity committee I had previously chaired for Commissioner Tagliabue.

"You were our voice," John Wooten told me, expressing the disappointment that he and other black coaches and executives had felt about my leaving the league. Wooten was a former offensive guard who played nine years in the NFL. He graduated from the University of Colorado with a degree in education back in 1959 and was accepted to Dartmouth and other top universities. He worked in player personnel (scouting) for the league with the Dallas Cowboys for seventeen years before moving to the Baltimore Ravens in 2002 as the assistant director of pro and college scouting. Wooten is a very intelligent man who should have been a general manager in the league a long time ago. But the league routinely passed over black guys like Wooten. Wooten, then sixty-six years old, was the de facto leader of the black coaches and scouts in the league. In 2003 Wooten became chairman of the Fritz Pollard Alliance, an association that monitored and assisted the NFL to promote minority hiring in the league. (Fritz Pollard was the first black head coach in the NFL dating back to 1921.)

I promised John I would contact Tagliabue and do what I could from outside the league to help solve the hiring problem on NFL coaching staffs. I wasn't certain there was much I could do. I was still personally disappointed by the league's glass ceiling in the executive ranks, and I wasn't eager to reengage in that kind of fight for the coaching staffs. But I realized I hadn't contemplated that my departure from the league would affect potential opportunities for other blacks—executives, scouts, and coaches. I had been among the most senior black executives in the league, and others counted on me to open opportunities for other black coaches and executives. I couldn't walk away from that responsibility.

In October 2002, I sent a letter to Commissioner Tagliabue with the reference line "Minority Hiring in the NFL." I outlined the long-standing lack of diversity among the league's head coaches and how qualified and deserving black candidates were being systematically excluded from the hiring process. I encouraged the commissioner to hire me as a consultant to assist in getting to the root of the problem and to design a program that would improve diversity hiring among the league and the member clubs. The league was under intense scrutiny, as both Denny Green and Tony Dungy had been recently fired. Paul agreed and asked me to draft a report outlining measures that would be effective in combating the problem. He asked for my complete candor, and I wholeheartedly agreed. I analyzed the league's overall hiring statistics historically through 2002. The findings relative to minority hiring of coaches were atrocious, given not only the racial makeup of the nation but also that 75–80 percent of the players are black:

1. In 2002 there were only two African American head coaches among the thirty-two NFL teams.
2. There were never more than three African American head coaches in any given year prior to 2002.
3. Only fourteen African Americans in total had been hired as head coaches in the NFL since 1963.
4. Newly hired African American head coaches typically outperformed their white counterparts in the number of games won in the first few seasons.
5. African American head coaches were rarely given a second chance to become head coaches after they were first fired, in stark contrast to their white counterparts.

6. Only five teams have hired two African Americans as head coaches, and no NFL team has hired three African American coaches in their history.

7. Of the sixty-four total offensive/defensive coordinators in the NFL per year, fifty-two of them were white in the 2002 season alone. Thirty-one of thirty-two total were offensive coordinators, and twenty-one of thirty-two total were defensive coordinators. That meant only one black coach served as an offensive coordinator, and eleven blacks served as defensive coordinators.

8. Between 1992 and 2001, there were only sixty-six black coordinators in the NFL, an average of 6.6 coordinators per year of the sixty-four total.

This lack of diversity in the head coaching and coordinator ranks was the result of three critical factors:

- A stigma attached to black coaches among the NFL owners. Blacks were believed to be less qualified intellectually than their white counterparts to coach the "thinking" positions within the NFL.
- The qualification most associated with consideration for a head coaching position was prior experience as either an offensive or a defensive coordinator, positions where black assistant coaches were disproportionately underrepresented.
- Opportunities for head coaches often sprang from mentorship or association with a prominent white

head coach. Blacks were not grafted into these favorable coaching trees.

NFL owners favor promoting assistant coaches who have been mentored by the most successful head coaches in the game. One can often track the pedigree of a new head coach to a well-known head coach he worked under and was recommended by. This networking system has limited opportunities for black assistant coaches; few black head coaches have the same status among NFL owners, and black coaches mentor white and black assistant coaches.

Examples of coaching trees that spawned successful new head coaches are Bill Walsh, Marty Schottenheimer, and Bill Parcells.

These San Francisco 49ers assistant coaches to Walsh were promoted to head coaching positions in the league: Mike Holmgren, George Seifert, Sam Wyche, Denny Green, and Ray Rhodes. All of these offspring proved to be successful head coaches and were in high demand because of their connection to Walsh. Two were African Americans: Denny Green and Ray Rhodes.

New York Giants coach Bill Parcells's coaching tree included Sean Payton, Tom Coughlin, Al Groh, Chris Palmer, Ray Handley, Tony Sparano, Romeo Crennel, and Todd Haley, among many others. Romeo Crennel is African American.

Coach Marty Schottenheimer, who served as a head coach in the league with the Kansas City Chiefs, Cleveland Browns, and San Diego Chargers, was responsible for mentoring numerous assistant coaches who went on to fame as head coaches: Pittsburgh Steelers boss Bill Cowher and three African Americans—Herm Edwards, Hue Jackson, and Tony Dungy—who all landed top coaching jobs in the league as a result of their lineage to Schottenheimer.

Coaching trees matter in diversifying the NFL. Almost half of the black head coaches in the NFL through the mid-2000s can be linked to the coaching trees of just these three coaches—Walsh, Schottenheimer, and Parcells. NFL owners must include black head coaches in that exclusive head coaching network to help propel a larger pool of black assistant coaches into head coaching positions. Black head coaches are also more likely to hire another black assistant coach for a coordinator position, thereby increasing the pool of potential black head coaches. The vast majority of these key referrals from white head coaches, however, are passed on to other white assistant coaches. Black assistant coaches have to land jobs with highly successful white head coaches who have a history of mentoring successful head coaches, or they are further back in the queue for consideration and often unable to be promoted.

I passed my findings on to Commissioner Tagliabue, who convened a larger audience of senior NFL executives and select owners as a working committee for diversity hiring practices. Dan Rooney, the owner of the Pittsburgh Steelers, chaired the committee. My findings debunked the "dearth of qualified black candidates" excuse that owners often used to justify not hiring minority coaches.

These results were also supported by research performed

by Dr. Richard Lapchick, the director of the Institute for Diversity and Ethics in Sports at the University of Central Florida, who gave the NFL a grade of C in 2003 for its diversity practices. That was the lowest grade among the NFL, the NBA, and Major League Baseball. There were only two black head coaches in the NFL during the 2002 season and just one additional in 2003.

The NFL was uninterested in identifying the root causes of the lack of diversity in its coaching staffs. They wanted a quick solution that would counteract this wide disparity in hiring, which was a public relations issue for the league. So many of the players were black and yet so few of the coordinators and head coaches. This raised some very troubling issues.

"Just saying there is bias in the process isn't enough," Tagliabue told me. "We have to do something about it."

The result was the creation of the "Rooney Rule," named after the committee chairman. The rule required all NFL clubs to interview at least one minority candidate when any head coach or senior football operations position became available. Stiff penalties would be applied to any NFL club that failed to adhere to the procedure. The Detroit Lions were fined $200,000 in 2003 when they fired Marty Mornhinweg and immediately hired former San Francisco 49ers coach Steve Mariucci without interviewing any minority candidates. (The Lions claimed it was widely known that they wanted Mariucci for the job, which led all the minority candidates they considered to decline interviews.)

Diversity hiring among head coaches and front-office

positions marginally increased under the Rooney Rule. But the rule was not without its downsides. With no real teeth in the rule, teams only had to "interview" minority candidates. There was no requirement to diversity hiring. Many black assistant coaches felt interviews under the Rooney Rule were often a sham, done perfunctorily merely to comply with the rule. Black coaches described to me what led them to believe the owners were not giving them serious consideration. NFL teams got publicity kudos by announcing these black coaches were being interviewed for the head coaching positions, and it gave the appearance of a fairer process, but many candidates considered it a ruse.

Black coaches who were more likely to be considered as potential head coaching candidates later in their careers felt that taking interviews and not getting the job weakened their chances for serious future consideration. No one wanted to be known as the guy who was passed over for several jobs. So black coaches routinely turned down these interview requests for fear of contaminating their future opportunities.

Finally, the pipeline was still skewed. Black coaches with defensive backgrounds were almost routinely considered for interviews as opposed to their black counterparts on the offensive side of the ball. Owners and decision makers in the NFL seem to be more comfortable selecting black coaches with defensive backgrounds for advancement to a coordinator or head coach position. The result is the perception that black assistant coaches are less qualified to oversee the offensive side of the ball as a coordinator or head coach. This is yet another form of structural racism that limits the pipeline of black assistant coaches, primarily those with defensive backgrounds. Most of the thirty-two teams in the NFL have an even split between head coaches with offensive and defensive backgrounds. Therefore, black assistants are potentially considered for only half of the already limited head coaching opportunities that arise each year.

The Rooney Rule, while flawed, was progress, an initiative that provided more exposure for black assistant coaches. If not for the Rooney Rule, minority coaches would not have had the opportunity to make their pitch in front of general managers and team owners. Even if the interviews were in some measure a sham, it was still a worthwhile endeavor, and there were marginal increases in minority hiring as a result. The Rooney Rule did not create a level playing field for minority hiring in the NFL, but it did produce incremental progress.

CHAPTER 11

An Off-Book Play

The primary focus of our business at Axcess Sports and Entertainment was football representation. Like most top sports agents, we charged 3 percent of the total contract as our fee, which is the maximum allowable under the NFL Players Association rules. I had a staff of seven people working on the football side. Some were agents, some were recruiters, and others were salary cap and contract specialists. As mentioned earlier, we were fortunate to be able to represent some very high-profile players almost immediately. At one point, we were among the top agencies representing NFL players in first-round draft choices.

One such player was Adam "Pacman" Jones. Pacman was a highly rated defensive back and return specialist. He played college ball at West Virginia University. Pacman was a modest five-ten and 180 pounds, but he ran with unbelievable speed and possessed incredible athleticism.

Pacman grew up in a very tough neighborhood where

a Pop Warner coach took a liking to him and kept him away from gangs and drugs. By the time Pac was a junior in college, he had become one of the more highly sought players in the 2005 NFL Draft. He had also recently been placed on probation for a barroom fight he got into with some other students while at West Virginia University. At the time of the NFL Draft in April, there was widespread concern about "character" issues surrounding Pacman. Nevertheless, he was selected in the first round with the sixth overall pick by the Tennessee Titans. Pacman was the first defensive player taken in that year's draft.

I met Pac through a mutual friend of his, Dee, who served as a mentor to Pacman. Pac had originally signed a representation agreement with another agent, but Dee wanted Pac to have an agent who could handle negotiations with the Titans under the circumstances of his prior arrest and other troubling character issues. Dee knew of me from my time with the Jaguars and felt my relationship as a former general manager would potentially disarm the Titans general manager and allow for a fairer deal. I wasn't sure representing Pacman made a lot of sense. He was considered by many insiders to be a "bad guy" and a troublemaker. He was an outspoken black player, wore dreads, and his image, particularly among whites, was that of a "thug." Many NFL scouts and GMs said he would "ruin [my] reputation" if I represented him. I thought he just needed some good counsel and advice. I agreed to meet with him and Dee.

Pac walked into the room and shook my hand and looked me straight in the eyes. Almost instantly I wanted to work with him. Pac was a surprisingly bright kid. I knew he would trust me. Inner-city black kids like Pac who become NFL products are preyed upon by many people. Everyone offers a welcoming hand but *always* want something in return. I didn't need Pacman for his contract fees and certainly not for the incredibly bad publicity he generated, but I could make a difference in his life. I was in this business to work with kids exactly like Pac who came from broken homes, lacked business sophistication, and needed someone in their corner to influence them to make good life choices. I felt I could do that with Pac, even though I would generate bad public relations.

We spoke about his musical interests and the fact that I was working with Snoop Dogg. We chatted about almost everything *other* than football. He was intuitive, street-smart, and highly perceptive, but he kept his cards close to the vest, reminding me of myself at that age. His strength was appearing not to follow a conversation, when in fact, he was directing the conversation. He was like a stray puppy I wanted to adopt.

Negotiating with the Tennessee Titans was difficult. Pac's recent baggage—arrest for assault and battery—gave the team significant leverage in demanding a deal less than normal for the sixth overall selection in the draft, especially since many already felt players were being overpaid. The local fan base would have blasted the team for selecting a dreadlock-wearing player with that history. But in Tennessee, their love of football is as important to them as perhaps anything else. Taking a chance on Pacman would prove to be acceptable, as long as he proved his worth on the football field. My job was to sell Pac as a difference maker on the playing field and chalk up his off-the-field issues as youthful indiscretions.

Steve Underwood was the senior vice president and general counsel for the Titans. He was owner Bud Adams's right-hand man on the team staff. Steve and I had remained cordial friends during my time in the league on the management side. I joked with him that I was his only black friend, and he fired back that he was my only white middle-aged lawyer friend from Tennessee.

It was customary to get college draft choices signed prior to the start of camp, but there was always the occasional first-round player, particularly at the very top of the draft, who often signed late, after practices began. (I had a history at Jacksonville of always getting my draft choices signed on time.) Protracted negotiations sour the player on the team's management, and they also sour fans on the player for not joining his teammates on time. Active players usually accepted contract negotiations as part of the business they had to endure and didn't begrudge another player for fighting for the best deal he could get, even if it meant his holding out into training camp. No player enjoys training camp. It's the hottest time of the year, and the team holds two grueling practices a day. There are ninety players fighting for fifty-three spots, the coaches are cracking the proverbial whip every moment of practice, and feelings run high. It is a necessary evil that all players and coaches accept as part of getting ready for the season.

If Pac was going to get a fair deal, the team would have to be forced into giving it. I had to keep Pac out of practices while I was negotiating his contract and prepared him for a potentially long holdout. After a while, watching your rookie teammate sit out can be aggravating to veteran players. I kept Pac in regular communication with his teammates so they would appreciate that he desperately wanted to be with them, but the business side was keeping him off the practice field.

Having been a general manager myself, to protect against other possible incidents, I would have laced the deal with conduct clauses and sprinkled out payments on the signing bonus over the length of the deal rather than up front. He'd have to earn the bulk of his money with good conduct. Now I had to figure out a way to defeat my own logic. The Titans needed Pac on the field. He would be their best cornerback as well as their punt return specialist. He was worth two roles to them, and that would be our leverage. I had to let the time get closer to the start of the season and thus the pressure to get him ready for the opener would be immense. Both parties would need to find a solution rather than to simply harden their positions.

In early to mid-July, many of the other first-round draft choices were signing their contracts. We would have been thrilled to sign a customary deal, but the Titans were not offering one. They proposed that Pacman agree to half the normal signing bonus and have the rest of the money be a back-end load into the base salaries of his contract. Under no circumstance would we agree to such a deal.

Signing bonus money is essentially the only "guaranteed" money that NFL players get. Unlike in the NBA and Major League Baseball, whose players get the bulk of their contracts fully guaranteed, football is completely different. Even though the injury factor is much greater in football, NFL players who suffer injuries can typically rely on only their signing bonus as protection. Their year-to-year salaries are normally not guaranteed, and if they are cut (because of either skill or injury), the team can avoid paying out the remaining years on their contracts. The signing bonus is critical to a player not only to protect against injury but also to put pressure on a team not to terminate the player on its roster after they have invested significant guaranteed money.

The media got wind of our demands for a normal contract structure, and several articles were written in the local newspapers supporting the team's position. How could they pay a big bonus to a guy who had already proved himself to be a potential risk? I argued that Pac had made poor decisions, but it was his overall talents that the team selected. As the first defensive player taken in that year's draft, he was entitled to the salary commensurate with that selection. If the Titans felt otherwise, I argued, they could have selected another player because they were fully cognizant of Pacman's poor conduct prior to selecting him, and they chose him regardless of his tarnished image. The Titans knew exactly what they were getting. They couldn't fairly ask for a discount after the fact.

I was gaining some modest support in the community

for looking past Pacman's past issues and focusing on his talents when on July 14 I got an unexpected call at 2:00 a.m. from Titans head coach Jeff Fisher. "Mike, I just got a call that Pac was at a nightclub here in Nashville and got into a fight, destroyed some property, and is in jail."

I lay motionless in bed, trying to take in all that he'd said while still waking up. "Oh, shit," I said to Jeff. "Is the media already aware?"

"Not yet, but you need to get somebody over there to bail him out quickly," Coach Fisher advised.

"Absolutely, Coach, I am on it. I'll be on the first flight to Nashville tomorrow." I hung up the receiver and called the local attorney in Nashville who handles player issues. Every NFL team has a "team criminal attorney" who often quietly handles the myriad of legal issues that pro players might get into. They handle everything from drug arrests and domestic abuse to assault and gun violence.

In a matter of a few hours, Pac was released on bond and back at his house. I phoned Coach Fisher to let him know, but Fisher was already at Pac's home when I called him. I was impressed that Jeff took the time to get out of bed in the middle of the night and personally deal with the issue. He certainly wasn't pleased with what happened, but he was there to support Pac, even if it was with tough love. I couldn't imagine many NFL head coaches making the same effort and investment in their players. Jeff was a special man. He wasn't just protecting his investment; he was concerned for Pacman.

I spoke to Pac on the phone, and he explained in detail

everything that had happened. Most people would be defensive, claiming they had done nothing wrong. Pac was not that way. If he was at fault, he would immediately fess up, as if his misbehavior were partially irrational, out of his control. That was a very appealing aspect of his personality. Pac had a temper. He grew up in a world most people could never imagine. Against all odds he made it all the way to be a first-round draft choice in the NFL, but he carried a lot of scar tissue and emotional baggage. Uncontrolled acts of violence were by-products of his upbringing, and without prolonged therapy and counseling, they would continue. Certainly such unacceptable behavior would not vanish overnight just because he was now an NFL player.

Before sunrise, blogger and online headlines brutally chastised the Titans for taking this "thug," a label that carried significant racial overtones.

The prospects of getting even a decent subpar deal seemed remote. Two weeks before the start of training camp, Pac had perfected the art of bad timing. Some felt the Titans shouldn't give any guaranteed money. I reminded the negotiators that Pac was a twenty-one-year-old kid who at eight years old watched as his father was shot right in front of him. His mom was involved in drugs, and his caretaker grandmother had died while he was in college. Now he was a first-round draft choice in the NFL without an established support group around him. I said I was slowly working to build that support system for him, honestly believed he was worth the effort, and was willing to do whatever it took to get him to a better place in his life.

The Titans agreed to let some time pass and evaluate the fallout in the community from Pac's arrest before continuing negotiations.

Pac was somewhat remorseful about getting arrested but stubbornly defiant about defending himself in the altercation. Pac said he was never looking for trouble; it just always seemed to find him. I suggested not going to bars in town, but he was not willing to do that. Pac had a small entourage of two close friends who lived with him, and I charged them both to be his protectors. "Don't let him get into any more fights, and if necessary, you'll have to intervene. Under no circumstances, though, can he get arrested again," I admonished them.

As training camp began in late July, there was little effort by the team to even sign Pac. I spent a lot of time with Pac during the first two weeks of the holdout. I worried that his tough outer shell would crack, but he seemed hardly worried that his entire career was hanging in the balance. He wasn't naive, just never one to panic. He was mentally prepared for whatever the outcome.

Pac told me when he was a kid, he was out late one night, and when he got home to his house in Atlanta, the door was locked. No one was home. He climbed into the Goodwill box and wrapped himself up in the donated clothes until morning. He often found himself in such abandonment situations. A child who has had to survive those extreme circumstances would hardly panic about a contract holdout.

As the media blitz continued to pile up on Pac, I decided to hold a televised press conference in Nashville on WKRN, the major sports station. I wanted the public to see that Pac was represented by an experienced, high-profile sports attorney who would provide good advice during this process. I said Pac was heartbroken that he was not on the practice field with his teammates, embarrassed about his conduct, and working hard to win back the trust of his coaches, teammates, and ultimately the fans. I thanked the organization for being patient with Pac and not rushing to judgment. I promised to be reasonable in my contract demands and said we only wanted a fair deal. I had hoped to assuage the anger of the fans and convince them not to give up on him.

Social media showed fans saying "Give him a chance," reasoning that Pacman was a kid from a tough background learning to adjust to the spotlight of the NFL. It moved the needle a tiny bit in our favor, but the mountain we had to climb to get a fair deal seemed clearly insurmountable. And whether Pac could stay out of trouble was an overriding worry in my mind.

Pacman was on the Athletic Academic Honor Roll at West Virginia University. That intelligence was combined with an incredible street savvy. He was perhaps the most honest player I've ever met. He never lied to me. He also lived completely without fear. Though he was incredibly small by NFL standards, he would not back down against any player on the field, regardless of size.

We once went to a private party in Miami hosted by Jay Z. Pac decided to sit in an area reserved solely for Jay Z's entourage, and Jay Z's personal bodyguard, who stood six foot seven inches tall and easily weighed more than three hundred pounds, asked Pac to move. As the bodyguard hovered over Pacman with a menacing look, Pac stood and said, "I'm gonna move, but you need to get out of my face right now."

I waited for the brawl, almost certain I would be speaking to Pac in his hospital bed. Instead, the menacing bodyguard briefly stared at Pac as if to size him up, then turned and walked away.

Pac's behavior reminded me of an incident at one of our Snoop Youth Football League games in Compton. Two teams of ten-year-olds were playing, and a couple of the little boys got into a very brief pushing contest after the whistle. The refs separated the boys and motioned them back to their respective teams. Some other little boys laughed at this admonishment. The boy who got pushed initially refused to go back to his huddle. The ref, a hulking black man in his mid-thirties, warned the boy that failure to comply would mean ejection from the game.

The young boy assessed the situation, then raised his fists in a fighting posture. The confused referee demanded to know what the boy was doing. The boy explained that he had lost face in front of the ref and now he would have to fight him to save his honor. Annoyed by the whole encounter, the ref picked the boy up by the back of his jersey and carried him, legs swinging in the air, over to the sideline and told him to cool down.

I watched, amazed and sad that this little boy felt such overwhelming pressure to save face in front of his teammates that he was willing to fight a grown adult man who would easily dominate him. It wasn't the outcome of the fight that mattered to this little boy. Protecting his honor in front of the other boys meant everything to him, regardless of the consequences. Pac was like that ten-year-old boy.

Our holdout continued into the start of the preseason games. On August 12 the Titans lost in overtime to the Tampa Bay Buccaneers, 20–17. Preseason games of course don't count, but the void of not having Pac on the roster was clear. The Titans' secondary needed a dominant cover cornerback, meaning someone skilled enough to line up against the opposing team's best wide receiver and cover him one-on-one. The club also needed Pac's skills as both their punt returner and kickoff returner on special teams. Bottom line, they needed Pac. Our only chance of getting a fair deal was to create necessity. If the Titans believed Pac was essential to their success on the field, they would find a way to overlook his off-the-field issues. So would the fans.

The second preseason game was special to Pac because it was against the Atlanta Falcons in the dome. Pac would be able to play his first professional game in front of his family and friends in his hometown. The Titans knew how important that would be to Pac, and so they sweetened their offer but kept many draconian clauses, especially regarding his signing bonus. It was still less than a normal deal for the sixth overall pick in the draft. The total money was close, but too many conditions were attached. I wanted a better deal. Pac never put pressure on me to get a better deal. He took responsibility for his conduct being the reason for the lower deal and didn't complain. I personally wanted to get him a better deal because I am competitive and also to ensure that he left the NFL with lifetime financial security if this was, in fact, the only deal he signed. Had I recommended the deal the Titans were offering just prior to the Atlanta game, I believe Pac would have signed.

I didn't. I told Pac the only way we would get the deal he wanted was if we missed the Atlanta game. If the team realized our resolve was strong enough to miss that game, they would know we were fully committed to a lengthy holdout. Coaches appreciate the necessity to get rookie players on the field early in the preseason. After the second preseason game, it is very difficult to get a player physically and mentally ready for the opening game (only three weeks later). The possibility of injury is much higher as well.

It was a risky strategy. The Titans could call our bluff and simply wait us out. History showed that after the third or final preseason game, the player typically suffered in the deal. The team would take the view that the player would not likely be ready for the start of the season in any event, so they had nothing to lose by shoving a crappy deal down his throat. It also sent a message to future draft picks about the consequences of a protracted holdout. We were playing a dangerous game, but I felt it was worth the risk.

We continued our holdout past the Atlanta game, which was played on August 19. The Titans won the game 24–21. Two days later, they offered us a deal we would have signed in early July. On August 21, Pac signed a five-year deal for $28 million, with $13.5 million guaranteed. The deal was an increase over the prior year's slot, and none of the excessive forfeiture conduct clauses were included. It was essentially a normally slotted deal for his position. It was a fair deal, but under the circumstances it was a touchdown for Pac. Never one to show a soft side, Pac looked up at me after slowly signing his contract, nodding his head, with no words spoken. It was one of the best compliments I've ever received.

On September 5, less than a week before the season opener, Pac got into a confrontation at a Nashville Sports Council Kickoff Luncheon. Later, West Virginia authorities filed a petition that he had failed to notify his probation officer of his second arrest in a timely manner, and thus his probation was extended ninety days. Shortly after his first season with the Titans, Pac was arrested in Fayetteville, Georgia, following an incident outside his home. Marijuana charges were ultimately dismissed, but he was charged with obstruction of justice. In August 2006, during training camp in his second season, Pac was arrested in Murfreesboro, Tennessee, for disorderly conduct and public intoxication. He was granted six months probation, conditional on his staying out of trouble. In October, Pac was arrested for misdemeanor assault after allegedly spitting in the face of a female college student at a Nashville nightclub. The Titans suspended him for one game.

Notwithstanding the string of arrests, Pac had a successful season on the field, including tying for an NFL-high three punt returns for touchdowns. He had four interceptions and was among their best players throughout the season.

Off the field, the season ended badly for Pac. In February 2007, during the NBA All-Star Game in Las Vegas, Pac and the rapper Nelly were allegedly inside a local strip club called Minxx, tossing dollar bills onto the stage—"making it rain." As the nude dancers began picking up the dollar bills, Pac and others got into a scuffle with the bouncers. Pac allegedly slammed one of the dancer's heads onto the stage. Hours later, one of the bouncers at the club was shot and suffered a paralyzing injury. Pac claimed he had nothing to do with the person who committed the shooting. Las Vegas police later charged Pac with felony coercion, misdemeanor battery, and a misdemeanor count of threat to life. He was promptly suspended for one year by Commissioner Roger Goodell under the league's personal conduct policy. I resigned as Pac's agent.

Shortly thereafter, I received a call from my childhood buddy Wayne Dobrutsky, whose family had treated me almost like their own son. He had become a fanatical University of Miami Hurricanes supporter, even though he never attended the school. I always found it odd that individuals could become ardent supporters of schools other than their alma maters, but I've discovered it is commonplace. Fans just adopt teams as their own even if they attended another school, especially if their university did not have a notable football program.

Wayne developed a friendship with a guy who was equally fanatical about Miami's college team, Nevin Shapiro. Nevin was a recognized booster; apparently, he paid a hefty fee to have the football team's locker room named after him. Wayne and Nevin wanted to come to Jacksonville to meet with me. I wasn't sure what Wayne wanted to discuss. My fear was that he wanted to join Axcess as a sports agent, perhaps along with his friend Nevin.

We met at a local restaurant in Jacksonville. Wayne, a small man of five-eight, had fought a losing battle for years with his receding hairline and had now opted to go bald. He lived in the Tampa area, and the sun had not been kind to his skin. When I saw my old friend, I worried that he was soon to be a melanoma candidate. Nevin, even more diminutive than Wayne, stood five-seven and weighed about 140 pounds. He was also Jewish and very sure of himself, but not cocky. He was respectful and deferential. I sensed he would follow instructions if I did agree to hire him and Wayne.

After Wayne reminisced, telling a lot of old Windsor High School stories, I asked what they wanted to discuss business-wise. Wayne started a long-winded introduction, but Nevin interrupted: "I have a very strong business background and have always wanted to expand into professional sports."

"And what type of role would you be looking for?" I expected the pitch for a job.

"Not much of a role," he countered. "I have my main business back in Miami. I just want to invest in your company and be a partner."

The response caught me off guard. I had originally raised capital to start the firm and hadn't considered a second raise of funds. "Well, what type of investment are you considering making?" I asked, not sure Nevin had capital to invest. He carried himself like someone who was not of significant means.

"I guess, depending upon the amount of equity, maybe $1 to $2 million."

I almost fell over backward. "You have that kind of money to invest?" My tone indicated I didn't appreciate a prank.

"Easily," Nevin responded self-assuredly.

Immediately a phrase I had frequently heard popped into my head: "Not all money is good." But the prospect of taking in $2 million overshadowed misgivings I might have otherwise had or should have had.

I asked Nevin how soon he might be able to effectuate an investment, and he said very quickly. If I was interested, he would have his lawyers contact me about the terms and specifics. He handed me the business card of a lawyer from the Miami-based law firm of Shook, Hardy & Bacon. He then stood up from the table, as if we had discussed something insignificant, and walked out.

The conversation was surreal. I trusted Wayne enough to know that he wouldn't be playing a practical joke on me. Still, where was this little man who looked so inconsequential coming up with $2 million?

Back at my office, I began searching the Internet for Nevin Shapiro and found little information other than his booster capacity at the University of Miami. I looked up the law firm he referenced; they were legitimate, top-notch. I had a hard time believing it was real. I called Nevin and said I would be interested in considering his investment but wanted to know what his expectations were.

"I just want to be a part of the business. It's yours to run. I just think I can help and it would be fun," he said rather nonchalantly.

"Okay, let's get to know each other a bit better," I responded. "How about I come down to Miami next week and we can spend a few days getting acquainted?"

"That would be awesome," he said.

That weekend I drove down to Miami and met with Nevin at a breakfast restaurant in Miami Beach, David's Café. Nevin explained that Miami's power brokers dined in this very understated restaurant. During the meal, he was overly boastful about how well connected he was and said he had access to VIP seating at University of Miami football and basketball games because of his booster status. He also claimed to have floor seats for the Miami Heat games. He was trying his hardest to impress me, and I was trying to confirm that he was real and had the money to invest. His puffery was inconsequential to me and hardly a thorough background check, but he said enough that I felt comfortable moving forward.

I contacted his lawyers at Shook, Hardy & Bacon, and several weeks later the investment was inked. Nevin purchased a 30 percent equity stake in my company for $1.5 million. He agreed to have no managerial or decision-making authority in the company.

We celebrated our new partnership in Miami at the steak restaurant Prime One Twelve. Nevin brought along his girlfriend, who was substantially taller and appeared to be a high-end fashion model. He had money. The steaks were said to be the best on the beach. Nevin ordered one of the most expensive bottles of red wine on the menu and covered the entire tab for the three of us, easily $650. As we left the restaurant Nevin said, "I think I have a player you might be interested in meeting."

"Who is that?"

"We'll talk tomorrow. Have a good night's sleep," he said, intentionally prolonging the suspense.

The next morning, we met for breakfast at David's Café. I was learning the way Nevin operated, his pattern and routine. I had started to look at the menu when Nevin blurted out: "Vince Wilfork is the player I was referring to. He's thinking about coming out this year, and he's a fucking stud!"

I had done very little recruiting at the University of Miami. Drew Rosenhaus, the well-known Jerry Maguire wannabe, lived in Miami and dominated the landscape representing South Florida athletes. Although there were no strict territorial rules regarding recruiting, Miami was Drew's backyard, and he didn't take kindly to competition. I asked Nevin if the player hadn't already linked up with Rosenhaus.

"Nah, he hates that Jew," Nevin responded.

That statement surprised me, since Nevin was Jewish himself. I figured it was like black people calling each other the N word.

"Okay, sure, I would be happy to meet him," I said, still

disbelieving Nevin had any real juice with Miami players. Knowing athletes as I did, I could imagine players using him to get free dinners at expensive restaurants, but ballers trusting him on a business level seemed far-fetched. I didn't want to burst Nevin's bubble by telling him that whatever players he knew were likely only using him. I knew I needed to stay as far away from his player contacts as possible. Again, I thought, *Not all money is good*, but I didn't know at the time what troubles lurked behind Nevin. I didn't know he was bad news. It was costing a lot of money to operate my sports agency, though, and I needed Nevin's money. One major hiccup in any of the sports divisions, and any losses would come directly out of my pocket. Having Nevin's money would provide a security blanket for my business and for me personally.

Letting him invest in Axcess would turn out to be a huge mistake that I would live to regret.

CHAPTER 12

Commish

I was fully immersed in my sports management business when, in the spring of 2006, just as I had forecast, the NFL announced that Paul Tagliabue was stepping down as commissioner. The league had hired the New York–based executive recruitment firm Korn Ferry to lead the search for his replacement. Hearing the news affirmed my decision to leave the league after flirting with the potential opportunity to position myself for consideration. Roger Goodell had invested twenty-five years in the league and was the all-American boy certain to be heir to the job. For a moment I wondered what would have been going through my mind now had I opted to uproot my family and move to New York in hopes of competing with Goodell for the job. I had made the right decision. The sports agent / marketing business wasn't easy, but we were successful, I called my own shots, and, most important, I could spend time with my family and participate in the lives of my children growing up. That would have been impossible had I been in the queue at the NFL. I had no regrets. I was a much better husband and father, and that was reward enough.

Then in June, I received a call from an executive at Korn Ferry. Unexpected! He told me three hundred candidates had been considered for the commissioner's position; they had whittled that number down to 185 candidates, and a final list of eleven had been compiled. I was one of the eleven candidates. They wanted to interview me in Detroit the following week.

I had never submitted my name for consideration. It seemed implausible to me that I could be seriously considered for the NFL top job because I was a sports agent, essentially a representative of the NFL Players Association. I routinely negotiated "against" the NFL member teams. My youthful dreams were not only rekindled, but whooshed aflame when I heard I had made that final cut list, and I considered myself a strong contender for the job. Yes, it was only an interview and might well have been one of those Rooney Rule–type interviews, but I was thrilled and excited nevertheless.

I learned that an eight-man executive team of NFL owners was overseeing the Korn Ferry search. Dan Rooney was chairing the committee along with members Jerry Jones (Dallas Cowboys); Mike McCaskey (Chicago Bears); Jerry Richardson (Carolina Panthers); Robert Kraft (New England Patriots); Clark Hunt (Kansas City Chiefs); Woody Johnson (New York Jets); and Al Davis (Oakland Raiders).

While I knew all the owners on the search committee

reasonably well, Roger had a far better relationship than I did with each one of them. Rooney was an old-guard owner, and I had little hope he would bypass Roger for the job, for all the same reasons I had chosen not to pursue a position in the league office back in 2001. Still, I had a modicum of hope that I would be selected. This had been my lifelong dream. I recognized its improbability but rationalized I could be a long shot. I could not bring myself to fully accept the inevitable. I flew to Detroit to meet with the Korn Ferry executive.

He was a tall black man with a wisp of gray hair. He was probably in his midfifties, professionally groomed, and had a deep voice. I interpreted almost immediately from his body language that he was in my corner, although he never let on as much. Years of working with sketchy player agents had taught me how to read the unspoken word. We discussed how I would manage the league as commissioner. I stressed having a greater connection with the players and finding long-term solutions to collective bargaining with the union. There was enough money for both sides, and continual work stoppages were simply bad for business. I stressed that unlike any other candidate, I had worked on both sides of the table as a team executive and a player agent, which earned me a unique understanding of all perspectives on the relevant issues. The brother took down periodic notes that coincided exactly with the points I wanted him to emphasize. I was confident he would recommend me—and not just because we were both black.

This was actually the first time I'd ever heard myself

speak passionately about why I wanted to be commissioner. The interview was therapeutic and cathartic. Even if I didn't get the job, I felt I had given it my best shot, and I could be comfortable with the outcome. I was told that they would reduce the group of eleven to five candidates, who would meet in Chicago in August for a final decision. I tried to get more information, but the recruiter remained professional. I appreciated his candor and thanked him for his time.

I never told Kim much about the interview, only that it had taken place. I didn't want her to know that the old dream had been rekindled, that I still very much longed for the position. I was happy as a sports attorney; I was around to be the husband and father I had promised to be. But I knew in my heart that if the chance arose to become commissioner, I would take it. Kim would support me in that role without question.

That I still longed for the position gave me some consternation. I hadn't fully let it go, as I thought I had.

A few weeks later I got a call from the executive at Korn Ferry. I hadn't made the final cut to five. He said I should be impressed that I'd made it to the final group of eleven, as some high-profile national figures didn't make it nearly as far. I believed he was honest with me and not just letting me down easily. He also said "off the record" that he had recommended I be selected as one of the final five. I thanked him for the call and his support.

I was disappointed. It didn't matter that the likelihood of my becoming commissioner of the NFL was perhaps wholly unrealistic from the day I'd first dreamed of it as a young child. It was my dream, and mine alone to believe in for as long as I wanted. But reflecting on the call helped me come back to my senses and realize that chapter in my life was over. It was time to move on. At least now I could once and for all stop believing.

A couple of days later I got a call from Amy Trask, CEO of the Oakland Raiders. I thought very highly of Amy; she and I had a long-standing friendship and often shared personal stories and anecdotes. I respected her tenacity in doing her job so well and, of course, also that she was the only woman in the league with that authority.

As much as I focused on the plight of African Americans in the league, I rarely took on the cause of the scarcity of women, of which Amy was a rare exception. Men believed football was a sport for men and overlooked women, even for positions that required absolutely no football knowledge, although Commissioner Tagliabue made a few significant female hires during his term. Most notable was Sara Levinson, who was president of NFL Properties, the NFL's marketing and licensing arm, from 1994 to 2000. The myopic view was to allow women to work only on the periphery of the game, and often, despite exceptional qualifications, women hired were reduced to roles that had fanciful titles but amounted to window-dressing.

I was quite familiar with what window-dressing looked like within the league. Today is different and indicative of progress. Several women work on NFL coaching staffs, many top senior female executives serve in the league and team front offices, and at the time of this writing, there is a female game official—whom I'm proud to say was first hired in the UFL under my leadership! But in 2006, when the search for a new commissioner was under way, the viewpoint that women could manage teams was simply not taken seriously. That's what made Amy's brash, in-your-face style so cool.

Although Al Davis was thought by other NFL owners to be a bit of a rebel, I figured he was ahead of the game, a true innovator for having put someone like Amy in charge. It was obvious to me that Amy was among the smartest team presidents in the league. Al had the courage to hire the most qualified person for the job without regard to race or gender. He did the same when he chose Art Shell, a former black player on his team, to be the Raiders head coach. Al really wasn't just a rebel; he was a visionary, too.

Amy called to say sorry that I hadn't made it to the final cut in the commissioner search. "Gosh, Amy, I didn't know that was common knowledge, but I guess everything gets out," I said.

"No, I don't think it's public knowledge," she said. "A little birdie filled me in." I was confused, and my momentary silence must have convinced her of as much.

"Al told me," she continued. "He was the one on the committee supporting your candidacy for commissioner. You were his top choice." I paused to reflect on what she'd said. I had barely known Al Davis. Our conversations were only in passing at typical league-related meetings and events. How could I have been his top choice? I wondered.

"I just wanted you to know Al thought very highly of

you. I also would have loved to see you become commissioner," she said.

"Thanks so much, Amy," I responded. "I can't tell you how much that means to me. Please also thank Mr. Davis for his support."

A month later, in early August, the owners met with the final five candidates at the Renaissance Chicago North Shore Hotel. Fred Nance, a Cleveland attorney with Squire, Sanders, and Dempsey, was one of the final candidates. Nance, a black man, worked on some NFL cases and was general counsel to the Cleveland Browns at one point. He was an experienced litigator and practitioner, but he hardly had my level of background and experience. It seemed to me that he had served as the token black in the final cut. I would have been utilized in the same manner. There would be no black NFL commissioner. I should not have let boyhood dreams and the lure of the position cloud my judgment. This finally closed one long chapter of my life.

The two leading candidates were Goodell and Gregg Levy. Levy was with the same law firm Tagliabue had originally worked with (Covington & Burling). He was the NFL's top outside counsel, though he lacked the charisma that Goodell possessed. Levy was by all accounts best suited to remain as the league's top attorney, and after five owner ballots, Goodell was selected as commissioner on August 8. He was only the third commissioner in the forty-eight-year history of the NFL, after the legendary Pete Rozelle and now Paul Tagliabue.

CHAPTER 13

The UFL

At age forty-seven I began taking flying lessons on the weekends. It kept my mind engaged, and I needed that constant stimulation. My instructor, Ernie Strange, a stickler on every minute detail of flight training, was a designated flight examiner who typically gave check rides only to students earning certifications in different stages of flight training. On rare occasions, he gave individual flight lessons. I was fortunate enough to be one of those rare students.

Every lesson with Ernie seemed geared toward what to do in an emergency. He wanted me to have an arsenal of every remedy at my disposal in the unlikely situation of a flight emergency. I anticipated flight training would be exploring new horizons, experiencing life at twenty thousand feet. Instead, with Ernie, it was engine failure, turbulence, icing, limited visibility, and bad weather conditions. Even on perfectly clear days, Ernie would suddenly reduce my engine power to idle and ask, "Where would you land right now?" In a single-engine training plane, you always had to consider where to land a plane without power. You would have five to seven minutes to safely get the plane on a hard surface.

The first time we practiced night flying, Ernie chose a small general aviation airport north of Fernandina Beach Airport, our home base; it was right off the Atlantic Ocean. Runway lights at night were operated by pilot assistance: the radio microphone button clicked seven consecutive times would activate the runway lights to full illumination; five clicks brought medium illumination. At a non-towered airport, incoming and outgoing traffic was managed by pilot-to-pilot "call out" communication of location and intentions.

As we approached the airport, the runway lights had just timed off. I was about to click the radio communication button on the steering yoke when Ernie shouted: "No lights!" I lined up the plane over the runway and began my final descent. I could barely see the runway. I asked Ernie, "When should I turn the lights on?"

Ernie stared straight ahead and said, "Just find the runway."

How did he expect me to find the runway in the complete dark? Frightened, I steered to what I assumed was a position over the landing spot and gently let the wheels down. Ugh! We were still flying. I pressed down a bit more, and the main wheels hit hard on the runway and we briefly bounced back up in the air.

"It's supposed to be a landing, not a carnival ride," Ernie muttered.

I wanted to say, "What the fuck did you expect with no lights?" but I wisely chose to remain silent.

We took off again and circled the pattern for another all-dark landing. This time we bumped again but not so abruptly.

"Again," Ernie commanded.

The fourth time, the landing was fairly smooth, to my surprise and delight.

"Now turn the lights on medium," Ernie instructed me.

I hit the microphone button five times, and the runway lights came on. It was so amazingly bright that I landed comfortably, even picking out the exact spot Ernie indicated to touch down.

"Now full lights," he said. I clicked seven times and the runway looked like a Christmas tree. It was almost too bright, but incredibly easy to locate and maneuver.

"Wow, it's amazing how bright that is," I said to Ernie.

We flew back to our home base and landed. As I was going through the engine shutdown procedures, I asked Ernie why he had instructed me to land in the complete dark. There had been a slight chance I could have crashed the plane.

Ernie explained that first, he wanted me to feel totally in control. Second, he said that if the plane lost its electrical functions, I would not have the ability to activate the runway lights or use any of my landing lights. In an actual emergency, I *would be* landing in the dark. Flying instilled in me a lesson I would soon need: to always be prepared for an emergency.

I passed my private pilot training for both single- and multiengine planes. Ernie continued with my training so I could get my instrument rating, which allowed me to fly in poor weather and into the clouds. I felt confident as a pilot and fell in love with flying. Ernie recommended I go further, and I did attain my commercial pilot's license. My local airport rented planes on an hourly basis, and I regularly began flying to destinations within an eight-hundred-mile radius.

A few years later I purchased my very own Piper Malibu Matrix single-engine plane. It was brand-new, serial number 59, a high-performance plane with a ceiling of twenty-five thousand feet. The plane had six seats and air steps, was certified to fly into icing conditions, and had all the most recent state-of-the-art glass avionics. I registered the tail number as N84MH; that stood for the year I graduated from college and my first and last name initials. In flight lingo, it was referred to as November 84 Mike Hotel. Almost everywhere I traveled, I flew myself.

At the start of the 2007 football recruiting season, I received a call from an old colleague, Bill Daugherty. He would sometimes call to bounce ideas off me, and I assumed this was just a call to check in. Bill was a Harvard Business School graduate and previously the senior vice president of business development for the NBA. He was a marketing guy, credited with creating the first NBA Store—located in the heart of Manhattan. Bill and I had crossed paths briefly in the early 1990s during the NFL World League start-up days. He was hired as a marketing consultant to the league, and we worked on several projects together. We were both somewhat trailblazers in our respective industries, and I considered him a friend.

It had been a while since we last spoke, so I was eager to catch up on his personal life. Bill explained that he had recently left the NBA and was working for a start-up— the United Football League (UFL)—that contemplated playing in the fall against college football and the NFL. Its two principal investors were Bill Hambrecht and Tim Armstrong. I was not familiar with either gentleman. I told Daugherty it was an incredible long shot to launch a new professional football league in competition with the NFL. There could be no viable competition to the NFL, so its existence would ultimately depend upon its ability to coexist with the NFL. He listened and then continued; he and another colleague from the NBA were charged with launching the league, and while they understood the sports industry as a whole, they needed someone with real NFL experience to consult with.

"Well, what can I do for you, Bill?" I asked. Axcess Sports had a consulting division, but we hadn't pursued much corporate business. This would be a great project for us. My experience with the World League and starting up the Jacksonville Jaguars could be of great value to this new league. I agreed to a monthly consulting arrangement and met with Bill in New York a few weeks later.

Bill shared the entire blueprint for the new league, along

with possible cities and venues for teams. What they needed was someone with real NFL experience speaking on their behalf. The coaches with NFL pedigree didn't have a personal relationship with him, which stalled his ability to have legitimate conversations. They needed me to sell the concept of their league to NFL coaches, players, potential new franchise cities, investors, and the media—clearly a big project.

I had little expectation that they would actually launch the league. All prior attempts to launch spring professional leagues had failed. The most memorable to me was the United States Football League (USFL), which featured high-priced players wooed from the NFL to compete with the NFL. While in law school, I had paid attention as the USFL featured celebrity owners like Donald Trump, who operated the New Jersey Generals franchise. After three fairly successful spring seasons (1983–1985), Trump encouraged the USFL owners to move to the fall season and, in turn, filed an antitrust lawsuit against the NFL. Surprisingly, the USFL prevailed in federal court, which ruled that the NFL had violated the antitrust monopoly laws. The USFL's victory was bittersweet, however, as the court awarded only $1 in damages, which under antitrust laws was trebled to $3. The USFL closed its doors after the litigation and was estimated to have lost more than $160 million.

If the USFL couldn't carve out a niche from the NFL, I saw very little opportunity for the UFL to survive. I was intrigued with the prospects of launching a new league; I just didn't agree with their strategy. Bill suggested I meet with Bill Hambrecht and explain my concerns.

Hambrecht had played tight end on the varsity football team at Princeton, where he graduated in 1957. He was a Wall Street investment banker, and his company Hambrecht & Quist was credited with creating the Dutch auction initial public offering (IPO) strategy, which bypassed traditional bank structures and allowed the public to directly participate in an open IPO market. Major companies began employing Hambrecht's concept, including Google in 2004. Hambrecht ultimately sold his firm to Chase Manhattan Bank for $1.35 billion. Hambrecht was also active in political fund-raising. A Democrat residing in San Francisco, he was a strong financial contributor to Congresswoman Nancy Pelosi. Daugherty explained that Hambrecht had a home on Martha's Vineyard and asked if I would be willing to meet with him there.

Not letting on that Kim and I also owned a home on the Vineyard, I said, "Sure, Bill."

I met Bill Hambrecht in early September at his home in West Tisbury on Martha's Vineyard. My family typically summered at our Vineyard home in Oak Bluffs, one of the five towns on Martha's Vineyard. Oak Bluffs is heavily populated with affluent black people. Because of the kids' school schedule, we normally arrived in early June and returned home at the beginning of August. Locals said September was the best month to be on the island, but although we had purchased our home ten years earlier, we hadn't spent one September day there. It was surprising how quiet the Vineyard seemed when I arrived. The weather was absolutely beautiful, with the temperature in the midseventies, abundant sunshine, and a soft ocean breeze.

Bill was a tall and lean man, well into his seventies. He had a quaint home with a spacious entry and an expansive backyard connected to a full dock and a classic all-wood boat. I was first greeted by Lulu, their black terrier dog. Sally Hambrecht introduced herself as Bill's wife and led me into their comfortably furnished living room. Bill wore khaki pants, a buttoned-down Vineyard Vines long-sleeve shirt, and docksiders—dress de rigueur for the Vineyard. Sally offered ice-cold lemonade and crackers for us to nibble on.

Bill seemed comfortably at ease and made the initial small talk, though I could sense he was eager to get down to business. "I think you have some great opportunities with a fall league," I began.

"Great," he chimed in with an approving look. "You like the concept of taking over the coaches and players from NFL Europe [which had recently disbanded] and reformatting it into the UFL?" he asked almost rhetorically.

"No, actually I don't think that is a very good idea," I said.

"What do you mean?" he asked, surprised and perhaps a bit confused.

"NFL Europe was not intended to develop talent. It paid lip service to that. The types of players and coaches it attracted, in my opinion, are not at NFL standards. They are a notch below. In my view, you need an exceptional product on the field if you want to have any chance of drawing an audience. The sports fan is already accustomed to high-quality football with college and the NFL. To have any traction, you need a product that is actually better than college and comparable to the NFL. The talent from NFL Europe simply won't cut it."

Bill looked at me pensively and pressed for more explanation.

"We need players who already played on NFL rosters but were released within their first three years. Some got injured, and others were replaced by veterans. But they all have the talent to play in the NFL. Those are the types of players we need," I said, catching myself off guard as I shifted from describing the UFL as *his* league to *our* league. "The same is true for the head coaches. We need top-rated former NFL head coaches who are currently sitting out. They might not be a team's first choice, but they have experience and could manage an NFL team right now. Those are the types of coaches we need, not inexperienced rookie coaches from NFL Europe. This will give familiarity and credibility to the fans. Players who are on the cusp of NFL rosters will also recognize these coaches as individuals who can best position them to resume their NFL careers. That perception is critical to recruiting the best talent." I was a consultant and free to speak my mind, even if Bill felt I'd dismissed all his plans for the UFL.

He listened and moved closer to me. "Well, it sounds like you have a much more viable plan for the UFL than we did." Hambrecht had been a minority owner in one of the USFL teams and had a good understanding of pro sports leagues. "Would you consider running it for us?"

He had already hired Bill Daugherty to serve as point man. "In what capacity?" I asked.

"What position gives you the authority to launch this league and succeed?"

"Commissioner, I guess."

Bill stood up and extended his hand to me. "How would you like to be our commissioner?"

I wanted the job the moment he offered it. Axcess was doing well, but we would continue to need additional capital to grow. Our staff and payroll were expanding, and that was always a cause for concern. I hadn't yet discussed the compensation, but I knew it would be a game changer in terms of what I had previously earned. The UFL wasn't on par with the NFL, but it was a professional football league with substantial resources. It would likely attract NFL-caliber players and broadcast over a national network.

Hambrecht offered me a lucrative three-year deal for $3 million per year with one three-year extension that he personally guaranteed. I also received a 50 percent equity stake in the league after buying out Tim Armstrong's initial investment. In total the compensation, which also included a $350,000 membership to the private Vineyard Golf Club on Martha's Vineyard, was worth more than $12 million. Part of me took it for the money and the other part for the challenge. I realized this was no substitute for missing out on the NFL commissioner job. It was another opportunity to test myself on a big stage. A new challenge and an opportunity to create and lead another organization.

I wasn't prepared when I left for Martha's Vineyard

to return with the possibility of having to dismantle my company. I flew myself back to Jacksonville, and along the way I realized that I would have to turn over the day-to-day responsibilities I had as president of Axcess Sports to someone else in the company. I would also likely have to divest any interest I had in the company during the period of time that I served as commissioner of the UFL. I had about twenty people working for me, and I needed to make some preparations for them. Once the news got out about my role at the UFL, there would be panic within the company. Moreover, many clients expected me to continue as their agent, and that would not be possible. The UFL commissioner job was my last chance at living an important dream. Axcess would have to be placed on the back burner.

I met with my senior leadership and informed them of my decision to accept Hambrecht's offer. I told them I would be installing a new person as president during my absence to prevent issues with elevating one of the existing vice presidents over the others. I promised that everything would stay the same from a budgetary standpoint for at least one year and then I would reevaluate. There was no guarantee that the UFL would play past one season, so it seemed like a fair compromise.

The head of my golf division immediately began the process of moving to another agency. Same for the head of the baseball division. I quickly learned that absentee ownership of a sports management company simply was not an option. By the end of the month, about half the company had bolted to greener pastures, taking clients with them.

I would have likely done the same if I were in their shoes. Axcess Sports was now a shell of its former self, with only half its client list remaining. Fortunately, the football guys stayed on, probably betting the UFL would crash and burn in short order.

On September 17, I was announced as the first commissioner of the United Football League. Hambrecht formed an ownership group that in addition to Tim Armstrong consisted of Bill Mayer, the former president of First Boston; the dean of the University of Maryland Business School, Paul Pelosi, spouse of congressional leader Nancy Pelosi; and Mark Cuban, billionaire owner of the NBA Dallas Mavericks and self-proclaimed maverick himself. His style was brash and often offensive, but he was brilliant and had a keen disruptive mind. If our league was going to challenge the NFL in any way, having Mark Cuban on board was a necessary evil. We had other smaller investors, but these were the main players. The story made national news, and suddenly I was referred to as Commissioner Huyghue. We hadn't signed one coach, player, stadium lease, or television deal, but I held the title of commissioner.

Shortly after accepting the UFL position, I met with Roger Goodell to assure him that our league was intended to be complementary to and not competitive with the NFL. I wasn't sure that would remain completely true over time, but I saw no reason to take on the goliath NFL right from the start.

I recall sitting in the lobby of the NFL's Park Avenue offices in New York and hearing the receptionist say over the phone, "Commissioner Huyghue to see Commissioner Goodell. *Wow*, I thought to myself, *that sounded pretty cool.*

Minutes later I was standing in front of Goodell's office. He had just finished a meeting with the league's top attorney, Jeff Pash, who extended his hand and with a smile said, "Hello, Commissioner" as he walked by.

I said, "Hello, Jeff."

Goodell then walked toward me and offered his customary bear hug. "Michael, how are you? Please come in."

"Nice to see you, Roger," I said as I walked in, noting protocol was for commissioners not to refer to each other as "Commissioner."

I glanced at the Wilson football on the shelf in his office that bore his signature on the lower right: "Roger Goodell—Commissioner." I imagined a UFL ball bearing my name. A few months later it arrived, the identical Wilson NFL football, only with the UFL logo and on the lower right, "Michael Huyghue—Commissioner." Very cool.

Daugherty had told me he initially made calls to Marty Schottenheimer, the legendary NFL former head coach. Marty was reluctant to even discuss the matter with Daugherty for fear that the UFL would be perceived as a threat (albeit minor) to the NFL. Daugherty told me no one wanted their name mentioned as potentially being part of our league. I knew enough former NFL head coaches that I did not believe that would be an issue.

I reached out first to Jim Fassel, the former New York Giants head coach. In 1997 Fassel was selected as NFL Coach of the Year. In 2000, at the age of fifty-one, he guaranteed that his club would make the play-offs. Guarantees of any nature in professional sports are verboten. Most famously, celebrity quarterback Joe Namath guaranteed that the New York Jets would beat the heavily favored Baltimore Colts the evening before the Super Bowl in 1969. The Jets ultimately backed up Namath's brash prediction with a 16–7 victory, but Namath faced much criticism for his cocky attitude.

Coaches always warned players against making public statements about the outcome of games for fear of motivating the opponent or facing the ridicule from the media if the guarantee didn't bear true. Fassel was wholly aware of the ramifications of his bold prediction, but he felt it necessary to put his own squad on the line. As luck would have it, the Giants backed up Fassel's guarantee and made the play-offs in 2000. He had a very successful track record as a head coach, which is even more difficult to accomplish in a big market like New York. Locking him in as a head coach in our league would surely add credibility. After leaving the Giants, Jim worked as an offensive coordinator with the Baltimore Ravens through the 2006 season. I heard through the grapevine that he was itching to get back into coaching.

I met with Jim in October, just a few weeks after I had been hired as UFL commissioner. I explained my vision for the league, signing players who had previously made NFL rosters to bolster the on-the-field product. Jim agreed that there were many NFL-caliber players who were on the sidelines waiting for an opportunity to get back on a roster.

Fassel liked everything about the league. He knew I was an experienced football guy and that there wouldn't be any "investor" types meddling with how we ran the league. The head coaches would form the competition committee and essentially make the rules we would play by.

I explained that we would pay a competitive wage on par with what the NFL paid its practice squad players (which at the time was about $4,000 per week). It wasn't an NFL minimum salary, but it would certainly be attractive to a quality player who was otherwise waiting for another player to get injured before he was called up to an NFL roster. More important, we would be providing these players with an opportunity to demonstrate their talents in a fully competitive game environment. All thirty-two NFL teams would get copies of the game film. That alone, I felt, was reason enough for the players to participate.

It was an ideal situation for a head coach who would also serve as his own general manager. The salaries initially were slated at $750,000 for the head coach/GM. I knew I could essentially go after anyone who was in contention for a head coach or general manager position in the NFL but lost out to someone else. We would be the next-best alternative for that coach. In January 2009 I signed Jim Fassel as our first head coach and assigned him to coach the Las Vegas Locomotives. Bill Hambrecht would be the owner of that team.

Next, I contacted Larry Upson, who had recently been the number two man at the NFL for officials. Larry had served a number of years on the field as an NFL game official and now was second in command at the league office. Many thought he would get the head officials job, but Commissioner Goodell selected someone else. That created an opening for me. Larry and I were friends from years back and respected each other. Larry was African American, and it would have been a progressive move for the NFL to have hired him, but they didn't. I told Larry he would have full authority to develop the officiating program and handpick his officials. He was sold. In February, he came on board as our head of officials, pro football's first African American head of officials. Progress.

After that, I contacted Denny Green. Coach Green and I had become friends many years before, during my time in the NFL. Denny had experience as a college head coach both at Northwestern and at Stanford University. He was also the head coach of the Minnesota Vikings from 1992 through 2001, making the play-offs in the first eight of his ten seasons there. Additionally, he'd been the head coach of the Arizona Cardinals, where he was perhaps most famous for a postgame meltdown after losing to the Chicago Bears in 2006. Denny was a highly respected coach and became our first African American coaching hire. Almost immediately, Denny shared my enthusiasm for the league and readily accepted my offer to coach the California Redwoods. Paul Pelosi was slated as the owner of that team.

Following those two hires, I reached out to Jim Haslett. Jim was a former second-round draft choice of the Buffalo Bills back in 1979, where as a linebacker he was selected as NFL Defensive Rookie of the Year. Haslett was named head coach of the New Orleans Saints in 2000 and led the team to their first play-off victory in franchise history. He was also named NFL Coach of the Year that season. In 2008 Haslett was made interim head coach of the St. Louis Rams, though he was not retained at the conclusion of that season. He had just finished his role as head coach of the Rams and was willing to consider a job as head coach of a UFL team. This would be a major coup for our league and add even greater credibility. Prior start-up professional leagues, even NFL Europe, had not been able to attract this caliber of head coach. It would send a strong message to players that we were serious about the brand of football we expected to play. Haslett said yes, and he was named head coach of the Florida Tuskers.

With four teams established for our first season, I wanted the final coach to be African American. It was important to me that our league example diversity for the NFL, in which almost four of every five players is black. It wasn't for show, but rather to prove that many qualified black coaches and front-office personnel, if given the opportunity, would excel. The UFL would stand out in stark contrast to the lack of such diversity in the NFL. The UFL would be different, I promised myself. I began speaking to large numbers of black head coaching candidates.

I spoke with Herm Edwards, the former New York Jets and Kansas City Chiefs head coach, but he was currently working as a broadcaster with ESPN and didn't want to leave. I phoned Leslie Frazier, who was the defensive coordinator of the Minnesota Vikings and on almost everyone's list as a potential NFL head coach. Leslie didn't want to lose his spot in line for an NFL job and declined. I pursued several other top candidates and they all turned me down. Black coordinators were unwilling to gamble on a start-up league. White coaches I interviewed had the comfort of the belief that if things didn't work out, they could go back to the NFL. The vast majority of the top black assistant coaches didn't feel they had that luxury, and so they declined to take the risk. I was disappointed, but I understood that for a black assistant coach there was no safety net. If they branched out of the queue to join our league, they might never get back into the NFL. Black coaches didn't have the same mentors and protectors to scoop them back in should things go sideways for the UFL.

I believe that to succeed in any predominantly white career environment, black people need to take chances and risks. There were no promises that by staying in line, those coaches were ever going to get their shot at being head coach. From my perch in the NFL, I've seen that being a "safe choice" is often as risky as being a renegade. My philosophy was to control my own destiny by betting on my own success and not waiting to be anointed for a job opportunity. It is not the right strategy for everyone, but I believe it is for those whose aspirations are to hold top positions and to have a damn interesting time along the way.

Finally, I contacted Ted Cottrell, considered an innovator of the 3–4 defense and wildly popular in his defensive coordinator roles with the Buffalo Bills and the New York Jets. He was highly respected and, while he had interviewed for several NFL head coaching jobs, was routinely passed over. I sensed something kept him from earning a head job in the NFL and could tell from my interview with him that he was not as detail-oriented as other coaches. Still, I felt confident that as a defensive guru he would get his players to play strong defense, which in a start-up league means a chance to win.

I was pleasantly surprised when Ted accepted the position because I had been turned down by so many other black assistant coaches. Perhaps Ted, having failed to land an NFL head job, had put that goal behind him and was eager to move on. Whatever Ted's reason, I wanted a black coach and he seemed uniquely qualified for the task. I selected him to run the New York UFL team, which was nicknamed the Sentinels.

Unfortunately, I was wrong. Ted wasn't ready to be a head coach, and his team went winless in the first season. Like many defensive coordinators who are first-time coaches in the NFL, he had no offensive experience, no two-minute offense know-how, no end-of-game decision-making skill, and often struggled to put all the pieces together. I let him go after the first winless season.

The UFL's first-season games in 2009 were all broadcast nationally on Versus, a Comcast-owned cable station that eventually became branded as NBC Sports Network and HD Net, which was owned by Mark Cuban.

The financial markets collapse of 2008 played a significant role in our inability to finance more teams. Individuals interested in buying a start-up pro football team were scarce because high-income investors who typically would have jumped at the opportunity to own one of these teams could not. Fortunately, Hambrecht was a fervent believer in the league. He was committed to seeing the league through, even if he had to personally fund the entire operation.

Bill told me a story once of how he got into the wine business after he sold his investment company. I guess rich white guys who become billionaires purchase vineyards. Hambrecht had a few modestly successful vineyards in the Sonoma County Russian River Valley area of Northern California. He made a great Chardonnay and Pinot Noir. One such brand, Belvedere, was a very popular wine for Hambrecht. He owned the licensing rights, and somehow the parent company apparently violated the trademark rights, resulting in a lawsuit. According to Hambrecht, his wine company was awarded $87 million for breach of the licensing rights they held to the Belvedere name, which subsequently became a popular vodka label.

Bill said he was essentially launching the UFL on the windfall proceeds from the Belvedere lawsuit. How fitting that our league was being financed on the heels of a trademark infringement case for a brand of vodka. It reminded me of how the Pittsburgh Steelers franchise was allegedly acquired by the winnings of founder Art Rooney, who was an accomplished gambler on horse racing. Back in 1933, it cost Art Rooney $2,500 to acquire the franchise, which at the time was called the Pirates. Maybe Hambrecht's Belvedere winnings would be a good omen for our league as well.

The UFL gained widespread notoriety with the cadre of

top NFL coaches we hired as well as the few recognizable players we signed. Each NFL team had a roster of fifty-three players. Because the NFL operated under a salary cap, teams were limited on the amount they could spend annually on all fifty-three players. On average, the top ten players on each roster were paid about 55 percent of the overall salary cap. Even though I left the Jaguars with a bloated salary cap in 2001, I still had a firm grasp on the NFL system. I knew the vulnerabilities in their cap that would cause some of their players to be enticed to play in our league. And I also knew that because league rules prevented any team from operating over the cap, several teams would be forced to restructure as many deals as they could to remain safely under the cap. That meant some players whom teams would prefer to keep would nevertheless have to be sacrificed and released. Those were our target players: salary cap casualties. *We can beat them at their own system,* I thought.

In 2009 the NFL salary cap for each team was approximately $123 million. Interestingly, the amount of money each team received from the league-wide television agreements was essentially the same amount they spent on the overall salary cap. The top twenty-five players on each roster were paid on average about 80 percent of the overall salary cap. That meant the twenty-sixth through fifty-third players were paid only 20 percent of the overall cap. The vast majority of those players (who were essentially the backup players) were paid the minimum salary for their years of service in the league.

Each year about seven drafted college players were added to the roster, and their salaries, while part of the overall salary cap, were carved out in what was called a "rookie pool." And each year about fifteen of the overall fifty-three players were replaced by attrition at the end of the season, because of injuries, lack of talent, or because the club simply found a better player. Those fifteen players on the thirty-two NFL rosters amounted to about five hundred experienced NFL players who were often left without a job. They would typically wait until an active player was injured at some point during the next season and then sign with a new team or even perhaps their old club. They were the players who made up what was informally referred to as the NFL-ready list.

My strategy was to fill our team rosters with these out-of-work NFL-ready-list players. These were players who had already made an NFL roster and, in many cases, had gotten some significant playing time. Since the league could pay these players only the minimum salary, they were considered fungible. If NFL rosters were increased, the clubs would sign these players first. Our league would provide a proving ground for these players to earn their way back onto an NFL roster. They could not command a high salary because they currently had no alternative. They were NFL-caliber players, so going to the lesser Canadian Football League was not a realistic option for them.

Having experienced NFL head coaches would give these players confidence that they would run NFL-style offenses and defenses that the current NFL scouts and coaches could easily evaluate. Because our season was only eight weeks long, the players could rejoin NFL rosters midway through the season and be in great football shape. This would be more attractive to an NFL club than signing the usual ready-list player who had been sitting on a couch those eight weeks.

While these players typically did not have names recognizable to the public, they were legitimate NFL players, and their performance on the field would be representative of an NFL-caliber game. Other than the USFL, which had sought to sign several marquee NFL players to its rosters, our league would have the best product of any other prior start-up professional football league. We would be attractive to the NFL, essentially developing talent for them. The players we developed would not be long shots, hoping one day to wear an NFL shield on their uniforms, but players who already had real NFL experience and were eager for that second chance. Some called us a development league, but I referred to us as a second-chance league.

This meant, from an investment standpoint, the NFL might someday want to own our league. We already had the bulk of their ready-list players. We also had coaches, personnel directors, and officials with long histories in the NFL. We were an authentic NFL product. We even formed a competition committee and piggybacked off the new innovations the NFL was hesitant to try in their own game. We put all those rule changes into our game, serving as a think tank for rule changes and game innovations for the NFL. We even hired the first female official, Sarah Thomas, whom the NFL later hired as their first. We were NFL-lite.

I stayed in regular contact with Jeff Pash (NFL general

counsel) and Roger Goodell. I wanted them to know that despite some competitive aspects, we wanted the UFL to coexist with the NFL. Throughout the first season, I continued to engage the NFL brass with the hope that they would ultimately purchase the league. That was truly our endgame. We spent a good chunk of Hambrecht's Belvedere money in the first season. I knew our money wouldn't last long. Owning 50 percent of the league gave me an incredible incentive to consummate a sale. In our initial discussions with the NFL regarding a sale, we had in mind that a realistic number would be about $60 million—less than a $2 million contribution from each of their teams. Hambrecht had already sunk more than that into the first season of our league, and he wanted more. So, no deal.

The NFL was facing a potential lockout for the 2011 season, and we knew if we could survive our first two seasons, 2009 and 2010, then the value of our league could increase substantially in 2011. The lockout was expected to last well into the season; we could be the only brand of pro football being played; star players from NFL rosters might choose to play in our league during the lockout; we could have the opportunity to select among the networks for broadcast rights to fill in during the NFL blackout. We would be cash-strapped at the conclusion of the second season, and the NFL lockout was truly our only endgame. It was the only viable strategy we had to succeed.

The first season's championship game featured the Florida Tuskers, who were coached by Jim Haslett, against the Las Vegas Locomotives, who were coached by Jim Fassel.

Haslett's team had gone undefeated and featured a high-powered offense engineered by offensive coordinator Jay Gruden (brother of former NFL head coach Jon Gruden). Haslett was named UFL Coach of the Year in that first season. The game was played on November 27, 2009, at Sam Boyd Stadium in Las Vegas, which is the home stadium for the Fighting Rebels of the University of Nevada, Las Vegas. The Locomotives edged out the Tuskers 20–17 on a 33-yard field goal in overtime. Thirteen thousand fans were in attendance, which is a fraction of the seventy thousand fans who attend major college or professional games. Still, for a start-up league, anything close to twenty thousand fans would be considered wildly successful.

In the second season, I replaced Ted Cottrell with Chris Palmer. Coach Palmer had worked with me in Jacksonville as offensive coordinator of the Jaguars. Palmer had been a college head coach at Boston University, was the former head coach of the Cleveland Browns during the 1999 and 2000 seasons, and in 2007 rejoined Tom Coughlin's staff with the New York Giants as quarterbacks coach. He considered retirement in 2010 and instead agreed to come on board as coach of the New York Sentinels franchise, which we relocated to my hometown of Hartford, Connecticut, and renamed the Hartford Colonials. Palmer was another experienced NFL coach and was widely recognized for his ability to tutor quarterbacks. He successfully guided Mark Brunell with the Jaguars to three Pro Bowl selections. He was able to recruit Josh McCown, a former third-round draft choice of the NFL Arizona Cardinals, to the Colonials.

After the first season, some fifty players from the UFL joined NFL rosters, which far exceeded the success of the NFL's sponsored World League or NFL Europe as developmental teams. In fact, several of those players from even as far back as 2010 are on NFL rosters today, including Josh McCown, who is currently a quarterback with the New York Jets.

It was also routinely acknowledged by our fan base and the media that we had an excellent football product. Our product on the field was much better than any of the prior non-NFL leagues. Haslett had just coached the St. Louis Rams the preceding season, and while his UFL squad was not as competitive as the Rams, it could have competed successfully against the bottom teams in the NFL.

After his first season, Coach Haslett was hired by Coach Mike Shanahan to become defensive coordinator of the Washington Redskins. Our policy was to let both players and coaches use the UFL as a springboard back to the NFL. The fact that so many players and now coaches were matriculating back to the NFL gave further credibility to the overall makeup of our league. It was working. Still, money was tight. The costs to field the teams and players' and coaches' salaries were choking us without a rights fee payment from the networks.

We were able to secure national television deals, and even a regional sports network deal in Hartford with NESN (New England Sports Network), but none that paid rights fees. The networks paid all of their own production costs to produce the games (anywhere from $75,000 to $100,000 per game) but paid nothing to us in additional rights fees. In contrast, the NFL was raking in $2 billion annually in rights fee payments, more than 75 percent of their total revenues. No pro sports league was sustainable without a television partner paying substantial broadcast rights fees. At best, we could survive one additional year on the backs of our owners, who in two seasons had already fronted more than $120 million.

Because of the strong interest NFL clubs had in UFL players, I changed the structure in the second year. Instead of allowing the players to go freely back to the NFL teams, I invoked a transfer fee of $150,000 that the NFL teams would have to pay. The money covered the investment we'd made in developing our players. It didn't seem fair to me that the NFL, with all its wealth, should be the beneficiary of the costs and hard work we put into developing these players and then reap the full benefit scot-free. Mark Cuban applauded my plan, calling it "brilliant," and even suggested raising the fee to $250,000 per player.

The NFL owners did not have a similar reaction. They pushed back against paying any fees for players they considered their own. The UFL was hemorrhaging cash and needed other sources of income. There was a clear value to the players we had further developed, and I firmly believed it was worth fighting for.

At first the NFL teams stood steadfast against the payment, which created the first big controversy in our league. Many in the media heavily criticized me for the decision, but I had long since lost any concern about the media. In the sports business, one day you were a genius, the next an idiot. You learned to make decisions governed by your own principles and not measured by the media's approval. Chips fell where they may. But when several prominent players voiced their displeasure publicly, I decided to lower the fee to $50,000. The Minnesota Vikings were the first team to accept. I was not sure whether they made the player pay the fee or not, but it broke the impasse.

Fewer of our players moved to the NFL in the second year, and the transfer fee, for all the headaches it was causing, was not going to generate enough revenue. It also pitted me directly against the NFL owners, and the NFL shut down the discussions we were having regarding a sale. Ultimately, the negotiations were killed by the NFL in-house lawyers drafting a potential sales agreement. The deal was so one-sided we could never come to mutually acceptable terms. The NFL does only deals that give *them* control. Our owners were not willing to simply turn the UFL over to the NFL owners.

We still had one viable strategy left, though: if the 2011 NFL season was even partially canceled because of the impending collective bargaining agreement expiration and lockout by the owners, there was a chance a network would be willing to pay rights fees to broadcast our games. It wasn't a great bet, but it was the only one I felt we had left.

Hambrecht lacked confidence in a protracted NFL lockout in 2011. He believed an open market interest existed in taking the teams public. As the IPO king, he believed fans in large numbers would invest small amounts of money to "own" the UFL teams. Similar models were occurring with soccer in Europe, but there was very little traction here in the States. Both strategies, however, were Hail Mary passes and huge gambles.

I hired Jay Gruden, who had been Coach Jim Haslett's offensive coordinator, to become head coach of the Florida Tuskers. I went into the interview with Jay fully expecting not to offer him the job. He is the lesser-known brother of former *Monday Night Football* analyst and now Las Vegas Raiders head coach Jon Gruden. Notwithstanding the strong recommendations he was getting from people I respected within the NFL, including his brother, I wasn't convinced. I owed him a perfunctory interview and opted to meet with him in a very casual burger restaurant in Orlando. (I had given up eating beef in 2008, so I wouldn't be eating during the interview.)

Jay fully impressed me. His demeanor demonstrated great command of the intricacies of coaching and that he was, at heart, also an excellent teacher. That resonates well with players. I was surprisingly sold. I offered him the job right there in the restaurant, and he accepted.

Attendance picked up modestly in our second season but not enough to move the needle financially. Large numbers of complimentary tickets to each game were given out, and we were forced to price our games closer to those of minor-league baseball.

We also added a team in Omaha and hired Joe Moglia, the former CEO of TD Ameritrade, as head coach. The hiring of Moglia was a huge story because he was a current Fortune 500 CEO who also coached football. At the time, he was working as a special assistant to the head coach of the University of Nebraska football team and had been a college defensive coordinator prior to starting his business career. Joe helped with the strategic planning of the league, recognizing that the model simply was not sustainable without television revenues. Joe helped us put spending restrictions in place that allowed us to get to the third season.

True to form, the NFL locked their players out after their collective bargaining agreement with the NFL Players Association expired on March 12, 2011. The players were arguing over free agency, the salary cap, rookie compensation, minimum salaries, and use of the franchise tag (which was a financial restriction available to each NFL club to unilaterally impose on one "franchise" or star player on its roster who would otherwise be entitled to free agency).

DeMaurice Smith, the recently hired head of the NFLPA, had previously made overtures that the union was in the fight for the long haul with the owners. Smith was a very polished black attorney, a trial lawyer and litigator from a high-profile law firm in Washington, DC (Patton Boggs). Smith publicly gave strong indications that the lockout would last well into the season, but the players unexpectedly came to a full agreement with the owners on July 25, well before the start of the season.

That was the final straw for the UFL. Our success financially hinged on our ability to attract networks that were willing to pay rights fees. Without a canceled or partially canceled NFL season, no network was willing to pay to broadcast our games. Revenues were not sufficient to support the substantial league and individual team costs for a full season; however, against my strong recommendation to the contrary, the UFL owners opted to go forward with the 2011 season. I pleaded with them to suspend operations and attempt to reach an agreement with the NFL. Foolishly, they were still "all in." Hambrecht argued that he would ultimately cover any financial shortfalls. We were already $150 million in the hole at this point, and the old adage about throwing good money after bad glared in our faces.

We hobbled into the third season, only to have to cut the season short after four games. We could no longer afford our players' salaries, and our outstanding debt was becoming unmanageable. We finished the season midstream with a "Championship Game" played on October 21 between Virginia (which was now coached by former NFL head coach Marty Schottenheimer) and Las Vegas. Chris Palmer was hired away to become offensive coordinator of the Tennessee Titans, and Gruden left for the same position with the Cincinnati Bengals prior to the start of our third season.

The media began predicting our demise. I didn't want to admit it to myself, but I knew they were spot-on.

CHAPTER 14

Not All Money Is Good

We needed to shut down operations of the UFL. I flew to San Francisco to meet with Bill Hambrecht, at his primary residence, to discuss the future of the league. Bill was the original architect of the league, and if he agreed with me, I was confident the other owners would follow suit. But Bill was too committed to the league to pull the plug. I pleaded with him to suspend operations and look for additional investors to run on all cylinders, rather than continue the hand-to-mouth strategy our mounting losses precipitated. He rose from his seat and said, "Michael, let's press on."

I understood then that my time would soon be over as commissioner of the league. Bill didn't seem to want to accept it, but I knew the UFL was done. We didn't have the financial resources to continue. As brilliant as Bill was in business, he could not accept that moving forward was "throwing good money after bad," as they say in his finance world.

While the impending demise of the UFL was

disappointing, it was also bittersweet. I had accomplished that childhood goal of becoming a commissioner. My career was littered with "first black" position labels, which meant nothing to me, but this had been a chance to measure myself as the head of a league. My scorecard? Honestly, some good, some not so good. But I was at the steering wheel, just like in my Piper Malibu airplane. The UFL was rare air. Although the league was destined to face more losses and to hear "I told you so" plenty of times from the media and the pundits, I was proud, even in failure.

To make matters worse than the inevitable UFL shutdown, Nevin Shapiro, the investor in my sports management company, was convicted in 2010 of participating in a $930 million Ponzi scheme. He pled guilty to one count of securities fraud and one count of money laundering. I was shocked by the revelation of his criminal activity. I sensed he was a shady guy, but I would never have guessed he had the capacity to orchestrate massive criminal fraud. His arrest was completely unrelated to his investment in my company, and fortunately I was never required to forfeit any of his money. Initially, it was just a matter of Nevin committing a massive crime that caught everyone by surprise.

Later, though, from his jailhouse cell, Shapiro gave more than one hundred hours of interviews to a reporter from Yahoo! Sports that included salacious claims that he gave illegal benefits to players at the University of Miami, paid for prostitutes for players, and that I was complicit in his activities while he was an investor in Axcess Sports some eight years prior. I was no longer working at Axcess, and we were no longer representing professional football players. I'd hired a new president who focused on marketing and sponsorship deals and discontinued any athlete management functions. Axcess was operational but essentially dissolving slowly. For Shapiro, a convicted felon serving a long-term sentence, to implicate a sitting commissioner of a professional sports league was blockbuster news. My name was splashed across every television screen that reported the story. The potential scandal broke just as we were wrapping up our third UFL season.

My staff immediately recommended we hire a high-profile media consultant to deal with the onslaught of negative publicity the league was facing. It wasn't the league facing the bad publicity, however; it was me personally. I had been in the media hot seat as a general manager many times before, but this time I was falsely accused of something that could forever damage my reputation. I had done nothing wrong and dismissed hiring a media consultant.

"I am going to rely on the truth to see this through," I said.

My chief operating officer, Bill Peterson, rebutted my position, telling me, "It's never about the truth, Commissioner; only the perception of the truth matters." He was right, and I knew it. But I felt that no matter how much I protested my innocence and spun it via a media consultant, the presumption would be that the story was at least in part true. So I stood firmly on the principle that the story was false and would blow over; and, with time, I would be vindicated. I realized that at a minimum, I would be severely tarnished by the bad publicity alone. I just wasn't certain how much damage I would incur in the process.

Hambrecht immediately sent out a press release supporting me as UFL commissioner. Fortunately, only a small number of people on social media were calling for my resignation, but those who did said the harshest things: "The UFL is in the tanks and its Commissioner is caught up in a Ponzi scheme web. Enough already—fire the moron." Some even attached racist name-calling to their demands for my termination. It was rough.

Kim stayed stoic, hoping to not reveal her fear, but I knew she was scared that I might be investigated or even arrested. She worried about how our kids would handle seeing their dad's name smeared so viciously in public. I was scared, too, because I understood how stories like this could go viral and their outcomes become wholly unpredictable. I never withered but maintained my composure and just kept doing my job.

Most did not believe Shapiro. It helped that my company represented dozens of high-profile college football players and signed only two of those players from the University of Miami. Had there truly been a massive illegal pay scheme to induce players to sign with my sports agency, as Shapiro falsely alleged, we certainly would have signed more than two players. Gene Frenette, a local sports beat writer in Jacksonville, penned that information in a story. It helped resuscitate my innocence and removed some of the criticism from me personally.

Eventually, the story moved squarely to the University

of Miami. After a lengthy and partially botched investigation by the NCAA, Shapiro's claims were proved to be mostly false. None of Shapiro's allegations against me personally were ever proved. It was a massive hiccup but not a fatal blow to my career. The damage of being linked to him was alone a heavy price to pay. Remember, "Not all money is good."

As my focus shifted back to the UFL, I again recommended to Hambrecht that we suspend operations. It was the only financially viable course of action for the league. Hambrecht had already personally invested more than $100 million in the league, and he couldn't let go. It looked to me like a poker player chasing losses after an all-in bet. I decided at the end of that year to call it quits and tendered my resignation on January 31, 2012. I still had more than $6 million in salary coming to me, and while my equity stake looked inconsequential at that point, I still owned 50 percent of the league. I would be fine financially.

My departure from the UFL was ultimately the final deathblow to the league. Hambrecht believed he could pull off another season, and rather than hire a new commissioner, he and the few remaining owners opted to run the league themselves. They were able to cull together four teams and kick off the fourth season, even getting CBS Sports Network to broadcast the games, albeit without rights fee payments. After four short weeks and dramatically reduced attendance, the league abruptly ceased operations.

More than 150 UFL players joined NFL rosters over those three UFL seasons, and many went on to become starters. Several remain on rosters today, including Josh McCown. In 2014, Jay Gruden was hired as the head coach of the Washington Redskins. He hired Jim Haslett as his defensive coordinator and Sean McVay as his offensive coordinator, all from his UFL staff. McVay would go on to be hired as the youngest head coach in NFL history with the recently relocated Los Angeles Rams. This all proves that the product on the UFL field was exceptional.

The first female official we hired was selected by the NFL to be their first female official; and several game innovations tested in the UFL were adopted by the NFL.

It was a good brand of football. I am proud of what we accomplished. I learned many great lessons from the UFL experience. Perhaps most of all, I learned to be careful what you wish for. From an early age, I had set my sights on becoming the NFL's commissioner. Having had my own run at being a "commish," I realized that what one attains in life isn't as promising as make-believe.

No regrets, just tough outcomes. I still keep the Wilson UFL-logo football inscribed with my name on my desk. It reminds me that life teaches tough lessons. I am stronger now and, I hope, a bit wiser. I traveled a road few in the world of football had the opportunity to experience.

As I reflected upon my thirty-year career, I decided that I wanted to write a book that would chronicle my experiences as one of the first black senior executives in the all-white inner sanctum of the NFL. I wrote it with no intention that I serve as a blueprint for others to emulate. It is intended to provoke discussion and perhaps shed light on the aspects of structural and institutional racism that operate not only within the NFL but in society at large. I recognize that in many instances I received opportunities and advancement within the league solely "because" I was black. But that narrow and limited opportunity was not extended to many other African Americans.

A hefty price must often be paid by people of color in positions of authority—a sacrifice of your own culture to assimilate into mainstream culture. It is a tricky dance, one I sometimes tripped, stumbled, and fell doing. I have had to pick myself up. I always felt I was dancing without a partner, because no mentors were available to teach me the steps. I never felt settled in any position. I was always operating under a microscope, always competing, always trying to be twice as good as my white counterparts.

I hope this book sparks conversations about race, beginning in the world of sports, but in every sphere. I hope black people who work in predominantly white environments will dog-ear pages, and underline and highlight their "aha!" places in my story. I trust that I have clarified and outlined challenges and obstacles that are often misunderstood by whites.

And before we call for the termination of the next black NFL player who takes a knee in protest of important social injustice issues, I pray this book will help us all pause for a moment to acknowledge that racism is prevalent in our society and affirm these brave athletes as the freedom marchers of yesterday.

May we all play together and find common ground.

Acknowledgments

It has been an incredible joy and a privilege to write this book. I am so very thankful to the hundreds of NFL players, coaches, scouts, administrators, and owners I have worked with over these many years who among other things have strengthened my love for the game of football.

Thanks to my fabulous editor, Adrienne Ingrum, who helped me share my story about the impact of race in my thirty-year NFL career and ultimately in society at large. Thanks also to Grace Tweedy Johnson at Center Street for guiding me through the first-time process of publishing a book; to Carolyn Kurek, who managed production; and to Laini Brown, my publicist. Thanks also to my wife, Kimberly, for patiently waiting until the manuscript was finished before she read it, so as not to chill my voice. To my eldest daughter, Kristen, for offering to serve as my business partner. To my daughter Kathryn for her fruit-not-far-from-the-tree sense of humor about the first draft of my book. And to my son, Tyler, who throughout this process became emboldened in his own self-awareness and racial conscientiousness.

And finally, to my mom and dad, who gave me the gumption to believe I could one day become commissioner of the NFL.

Appendix

Why the NFL Systematically Excludes Blacks from the Coaching Ranks

Football teams are made up of eleven players on offense and eleven players on defense. On the offensive side of the ball, five of the eleven players are offensive linemen, whose job is, among other things, to form the foundation at the line of scrimmage to protect the quarterback and provide blocking for the running game. They are among the biggest and strongest players on the offense, averaging over three hundred pounds each. The offensive linemen within the NFL have historically been predominantly white players. They are generally considered the more intelligent players on the team. The lineman's position is considered a thinking position in that the lineman makes frequent adjustments prior to the snap of the ball in reaction to the strategic formations and attacks orchestrated by the defense. Linemen typically achieve the highest scores in intelligence tests (Wonderlic) administered to all incoming NFL rookie players.

The other six positions on the offense are considered "skill" positions and consist of three wide receivers (whose job it is to catch passes from the quarterback); a tight end (who is a hybrid offensive lineman and wide receiver in that he is asked to carry out both functions); a running back (whose job is to gain as much yardage as he can carrying the football); and the quarterback (the team captain who touches the ball on every offensive play, either handing off to a running back or passing to a receiver).

Only the quarterback position is considered a thinking position among the skill players. The quarterback's job is to make adjustments to the plays prior to the snap of the ball based upon the changing alignments of the defense. He also has to instantly locate a weakness in the defensive pass coverage through his peripheral vision to determine which receiver to throw the football to. He must also have full knowledge of what every other offensive player is required to do on every offensive play.

On the defensive side of the ball, there are typically four defensive linemen who are similar in size and strength to the offensive linemen. The defensive line, though, is not considered a thinking position. These players, often black, are more athletic than their offensive counterparts, relying primarily on their physical rather than mental skills. The four linebackers are responsible for stopping the running game and the short-range passing attack. The linebacker located closest to the middle of the defense is typically referred to as the middle or "Mike" linebacker. The Mike linebacker position alone is considered a thinking position because the player is required to recognize and communicate the defensive alignment adjustments for the entire defensive unit. The last three defensive players are called defensive backs and are located in what is referred to as the secondary. Their job is primarily to defend against the pass attack from the offensive wide receivers. They are typically more physical than wide receivers, as they also play a role in stopping the running game. The defensive back position is not considered a thinking position. It is instead considered a reaction skill position.

Quite naturally, all the positions on the offense and defense require some degree of thinking to compete effectively. There are gradations, however, that prioritize the cerebral aspects of the game in contrast to the overall athletic skill requirements.

Black assistant coaches in the NFL are far and away more likely to be hired to coach the skill positions rather than the thinking positions. The statistics are overwhelming in how few black assistants coach the offensive line, quarterbacks, and middle linebackers. Although white head coaches are able to add diversity to their coaching staffs by adding black assistant coaches, they rarely give them the opportunity to coach any of the thinking positions (typically where there are more white players associated with those positions).

The vast majority of first-time head coaches in the NFL have advanced from the position of either offensive or defensive coordinator. The logic is that having the responsibility for managing one side of the game (offense or defense) best prepares someone to assume the overall head coaching responsibilities. Each year, the highly anticipated new candidates for head coaching positions almost all have coordinator or prior head coach experience.

In selecting prospects for the coordinator position, history has shown that the assistant coaches at the "thinking positions" are much more likely to be hired as head coaches. On the offensive side of the ball, most coordinators are either former offensive line coaches or quarterback coaches. The standard logic is that an individual who coaches the offensive line must fully understand run blocking and pass protection from all vantage points of defensive preparation. Every offensive play is predicated on whether or not the ball carrier or quarterback can be adequately protected against the defensive coverage. Similarly, quarterback coaches are required to demonstrate full command of the entire offense in order to be able to adequately coach that position. They are typically in charge of the offensive play calling as well.

The same is not true for the skill position assistant coaches. The receivers coach, for instance, does not necessarily have to fully understand the offensive line blocking schemes. Nor does he need to know what specific requirements the quarterback or running back has on each and every play. Instead, he simply has to comprehend the defensive backs' pass coverage and how the receivers need to run their pass routes. The same is true for the running backs coach. His knowledge can be even more limited, to the role of the running back alone.

On the defensive side of the ball, only the linebackers

coach has to command full knowledge of the defensive linemen's responsibilities (those players in front of the linebackers) as well as the defensive backs' responsibilities (those players positioned behind the linebackers). The middle linebacker typically makes "calls" or verbal adjustments during the course of a play, signaling to his teammates what specific coverage they will use to defend on that particular play.

The predominantly white head coaches in the NFL have sought to maintain diverse coaching staffs. In many cases a coaching staff in the NFL consists of fifteen to twenty assistant coaches. The problem, though, is that black assistant coaches are in alarming numbers relegated to coaching the nonthinking positions on their staffs. In 2002 there was only one black offensive coordinator of the thirty-two total offensive coordinators in the league. That speaks volumes as to why almost every black assistant coach that is promoted to coordinator comes from the defensive side of the ball.

Of the dozen or so noninterim black head coaches hired by NFL teams between 1990 and 2010, ten of them came from the defensive side of the ball (Denny Green, Tony Dungy, Herm Edwards, Marv Lewis, Ray Rhodes, Romeo Crennel, Lovie Smith, Mike Tomlin, Mike Singletary, and Raheem Morris); and only two (Art Shell and Jim Caldwell) came from the offensive side. This wide disparity of promoting mostly black assistant coaches who have backgrounds in defense means the pipeline for black offensive assistant coaches to gain promotion pales significantly in comparison to that of their white counterparts.

Index

About the Author

One of many speaking engagements on the subject of diversity in sports, here at the University of Florida in Gainesville.

MICHAEL HUYGHUE (pronounced "hewg") is widely regarded as one of the most prominent figures in the professional sports industry; his career has spanned more than thirty years. Twice named to the *SportsBusiness Journal*'s 40 Under 40 Top Sports Executives, he has been a pioneer in the industry, paving the way for many other African Americans.

Mr. Huyghue is currently president of his own boutique sports management and consulting agency headquartered in Jacksonville, Florida.

Most recently, Mr. Huyghue served as commissioner of the United Football League, which was composed primarily of young National Football League players and former NFL head coaches. Mr. Huyghue founded and directed the UFL, raising more than $200 million in seed money. The UFL operated for four nationally televised seasons, competing directly against the NFL. The UFL saw limited viewership, but more than 150 of its players and dozens of its coaches found full-time starting positions within the NFL, including the current head coaches of the Washington Redskins and the Los Angeles Rams.

In 2001 Mr. Huyghue launched his own highly successful sports and entertainment agency, Axcess Sports and Entertainment, which represented professional athletes, Olympic athletes, and entertainers across all team and professional sports. Mr. Huyghue has partnered with or represented many prominent celebrities and athletes, including Magic Johnson, Oscar De La Hoya, Snoop Dogg, Billy Butler, Fred Funk, Vince Wilfork, and other NFL Pro Bowl and Heisman Trophy winners.

In 1994 Mr. Huyghue was selected to run football operations for the NFL start-up Jacksonville Jaguars. Under the leadership of Mr. Huyghue and then head coach Tom Coughlin, the Jaguars collected more wins in their first five seasons than any other new franchise in the history of the NFL, including a remarkable two-time AFC Championship Game appearance. Mr. Huyghue oversaw the signing of all players during his eight seasons with the Jaguars and had the fewest holdouts of any team in the league. In just their second season, the Jaguars saw nine first-time players selected to the Pro Bowl, more than any other team.

Prior to joining the Jaguars, Mr. Huyghue served briefly as the head of football operations as well as general counsel for the NFL Detroit Lions. Mr. Huyghue completely overhauled the culture of the team, and in just his second season the Lions won their first postseason play-off game, a feat they haven't repeated in the last thirty years.

Mr. Huyghue gained widespread prominence in 1991 as the youngest and one of the first black general managers in professional football with the NFL's World League of American Football (Birmingham Fire). Mr. Huyghue went on to hold the most senior position in the league, reporting directly to a committee of NFL owners. Mr. Huyghue led operations for the league, working overseas in Spain and Germany and becoming fluent in both languages.

Mr. Huyghue began his professional career as a legal assistant with the NFL Players Association under then executive director Gene Upshaw. Mr. Huyghue was hired away from the Players Association by the NFL Management Council in 1987 shortly after graduating from law school. As labor relations counsel, Mr. Huyghue organized efforts on behalf of the NFL to direct replacement football games during that year's players' work stoppage. Mr. Huyghue also served as league counsel for the NFL member clubs in injury and noninjury grievances, conducting more than two hundred arbitration hearings.

Under then NFL commissioner Paul Tagliabue, Mr. Huyghue was appointed to numerous high-ranking committees, including the Management Council Executive Committee, the College Advisory Committee, and was the senior member of the Committee on Minority Hiring. During his twelve-plus years spent working with the NFL and its member teams, Mr. Huyghue was among its highest-ranking African American employees.

A lawyer by training, Mr. Huyghue attended the University of Michigan Law School, earning his juris doctor degree in 1987. Mr. Huyghue was a standout four-sport athlete in high school in Windsor, Connecticut, and was selected for inclusion in its Hall of Fame. Mr. Huyghue was recruited in athletics by many colleges and universities and chose Cornell University, where he played varsity football and freshman baseball. Mr. Huyghue was elected to the board of trustees at Cornell and is listed among its distinguished alumni. Mr. Huyghue is currently an adjunct professor of law at Cornell University.

Mr. Huyghue is married to his law school classmate, Kimberly Wyche, has three children (Kristen, Kathryn, and Tyler), and resides in Ponte Vedra Beach, Florida. Mr. Huyghue is a board member of the Boys and Girls Clubs of Northeast Florida, among many other charitable organizations. He is an avid golfer and a commercial-rated pilot.

Photo Captions

The photos can be found on the front and back inside covers and are numbered there.

1. Windsor High baseball team huddled up prior to the start of the game. We went on to win the Connecticut State Championships in 1979. *Credit: Family Photo*

2. You could always easily pick me out of a youth sports picture growing up in Windsor. Here I was a member of my sixth-grade All-Star basketball team, which traveled to Maryland for a tournament. *Credit: Family Photo*

3. Promotional photo of me—the commish—and the UFL players, launching our inaugural season.
   Credit: UFL Photo Owned by Michael Huyghue

4. Addressing the media during one of our regularly scheduled press conferences. *Credit: UFL Photo*

5. Standing with my first boss at the NFL Management Council, Dennis Curran, while attending the commissioner's party held at Super Bowl XXII.
   Credit: Family Photo

6. With my childhood friend Jeff Bassell, who also went to Cornell University and played on the football team.
   Credit: Family Photo

7. Postgame in the locker room, I presented the game ball to head coach Jim Fassel and congratulated the Las Vegas Locomotives players on winning the inaugural UFL Championship.   *Credit: UFL Team Photo*

8. NFL Cowboys owner Jerry Jones, who first threatened to fire any of his players who disrespected the flag, kneeling arm in arm on the playing field with his team prior to the playing of the national anthem.
   Credit: AP Photo

9. Induction ceremony into the National Honor Society at Windsor High School. I would go on to be voted "Best Athlete" and "Student Most Likely to Succeed."
   Credit: Family Photo

10. Attending my high school graduation with my parents.
    Credit: Family Photo

11. My crew and me posing for a family picture: Kathryn, Kim, and Kristen; Tyler and me.   *Credit: Family Photo*

12. President Donald Trump walking with NFL Patriots owner Bob Kraft (left) and head coach Bill Belichick (middle) to a reception on the South Lawn at the White House to celebrate their Super Bowl Championship.

Almost twenty players were no-shows, including star quarterback Tom Brady. *Credit: AP Photo*

13. Former San Francisco 49ers quarterback Colin Kaepernick kneeling during the national anthem in an NFL game against the Seattle Seahawks. Kaepernick donated $1 million to organizations that work in oppressed communities, and Amnesty International gave him its top human rights award—Ambassador of Conscience—for his public opposition to racial injustice. Nelson Mandela was a previous award recipient.

Credit: AP Photo

14. Ripping a shot against Bishop Moore Catholic High School in a spring game held at their school in Orlando, Florida. I played third base and batted third.

Credit: Family Photo

15. I'm back left in the last row, seated with all of the administrators and counselors of Boys State in Connecticut.

Credit: CT Boys State Photo

16. Our first little bundle of joy, Kristen Nicole, already trying to be a Jaguars fan. *Credit: Family Photo*

17. My junior year at Cornell (circled) as a member of then head coach Bob Blackman's Big Red football team.

Credit: Cornell University Photo

18. Sitting front and center as a counselor at Connecticut Boys State. I was selected to attend Boys Nation in Washington, DC, the following year.

    Credit: CT Boys State Photo

19. With Snoop Dogg (center) and former Pittsburgh Steelers Pro Bowler Carnell Lake (right) talking football in my office.

    Credit: Axcess Sports Photo

20. On the field with Snoop in Detroit just prior to the start of the second annual Snoop Youth Football League Championship game at Ford Field in 2006.

    Credit: Axcess Sports Photo

21. Playing sports was a vehicle for me to fit in with the other kids. In high school I played football, baseball, basketball, and tennis. Years later I was the first black student inducted into my high school's Hall of Fame.

    Credit: Windsor High School Photo

22. Sporting a mustache for a photo in my football uniform outside the locker room at Cornell University.

    Credit: Family Photo

23. One of the most special days in my life, pondering the future with my soul mate, Kimberly, on our wedding day in 1993. *Credit: Family Photo*

24. Standing with my wife, Kim, and legendary golf pro Arnold Palmer at a promotional event managed by my

company, Axcess Sports, to attract new members at White Oak Conservation in Yulee, Florida, in 2003.

Credit: Family Photo

25. Infield warm-ups prior to a game in Windsor, throwing a red baseball that Coach Barry Chasen thought would intimidate the other team. It didn't.

Credit: Family Photo